THE SINCERE IDEAL

THE
SINCERE
IDEAL

Studies on Sincerity in Eighteenth-Century English Literature

LEON GUILHAMET

McGill–Queen's University Press

MONTREAL AND LONDON 1974

Design by Anthony Crouch
Printed in Canada by T. H. Best Printing Co. Ltd.

To my mother and father

ACKNOWLEDGEMENTS

Anyone who writes a book incurs more debts than he can reasonably acknowledge in a preface. It is with a deep sense of appreciation that I pay homage to those who have helped directly with this volume or contributed to it in other ways.

My most serious intellectual debt is to Walter Jackson Bate, whose prodigious scholarship has proved authoritative to specialists in the eighteenth century and in the Romantic period and indispensable to those who assess the transition between the two. Without his invaluable contributions this study could never have been undertaken.

For what I understand of the seventeenth century, William Haller, whose name is consociate with sound scholarship and brilliant insight, is most responsible. It was his remarkable volume, *The Rise of Puritanism*, that first fired my interest in intellectual history. And of course H. R. Trevor-Roper's grasp of major intellectual issues and his precise and graceful expression of that understanding have proved an example impossible of emulation.

My earliest studies in the eighteenth century were under the masterly tutelage of Arthur W. Hoffman, who has remained a good friend and patient counsellor. During the early development of this work, I enjoyed the benefit of conversation with Gerard Bowers and John C. Ulreich, Jr., who helped me to clarify basic issues and proceed on sounder principles. David Perkins, whose excellent study of Wordsworth provided a major impetus, read my manuscript at an early stage and offered many helpful comments.

Maynard Mack generously read a later version and offered his usual incisive and thoroughgoing commentary. Paul J. Korshin, in editing for earlier publication two of the essays that appear here in shortened form, offered good advice and encouragement. Along the difficult way to completion of this work I benefited greatly from the kind concern and sage counsel of Francis Fergusson, Daniel F. Howard, and the late Mark Van Doren.

Thomas E. Crooks, as Master of Dudley House at Harvard,

granted me unique hospitality and fellowship at a critical time. Lionel Jacques and his family have helped in too many ways to recount.

The Department of English at Harvard University awarded me a Charles Dexter Traveling Fellowship for the summer of 1967, during which time I was able to complete some important research in England. The bulk of work for this study, however, was conducted at the Harvard College and Yale University libraries.

My colleagues and students at Harvard, Yale, and The City College of The City University of New York have made available to me so much intelligence and shown such kindness that this book should be a good deal better than it is. Its deficiencies are all my own.

Grateful acknowledgement is made to the AMS Press of New York for permission to reprint parts of my essay "Imitation and Originality in the Poems of Thomas Gray," published in chapter 6 of *Proceedings of the Modern Language Association Neoclassicism Conferences, 1967–1968*, edited by Paul J. Korshin and published in 1970, and to Scolar Press Limited of Menston, Yorkshire, for permission to reprint parts of another essay, "From *Pamela* to *Grandison*: Richardson's Moral Revolution in the Novel," which appeared in *Studies in Change and Revolution: Aspects of English Intellectual History, 1640–1800*, edited by Paul J. Korshin and published in 1972, as an appendix to this volume.

Thanks are due to Theresa, Eric, and Mrs. Mary Jacques for help with the proofreading.

Contents

vi   ACKNOWLEDGEMENTS

x   A BIBLIOGRAPHICAL NOTE

1   INTRODUCTION

9   The Background of Sincerity

27   The Puritan Contribution and Milton

49   Dissent and Latitude to 1748

     Isaac Watts 49

     Benjamin Hoadly 60

69   The Prelapsarian World of the Deists

     Shaftesbury 72

     James Thomson 77

     Mark Akenside 101

     Henry Brooke 119

127   The Augustan Impulse to 1744

     Joseph Addison and Thomas Tickell 127

     "Retirement: A Divine Soliloquy" 133

     Alexander Pope 136

     Jonathan Richardson 151

     Aaron Hill 162

     Edward Young 171

189   Augustans and Others to 1800

     William Collins 189

     William Shenstone 202

     Thomas Gray 215

     Samuel Johnson 231

     The Scots 236

     William Cowper 243

259   Sincerity and Romanticism

     William Blake 259

     William Wordsworth 269

279   CONCLUSION

287   APPENDIX: The Novel of Sincerity

301   BIBLIOGRAPHY

303   INDEX

A BIBLIOGRAPHICAL NOTE

In the case of often-quoted primary sources, only a short reference has been given in the footnotes, and succeeding references are contained in the text. Full bibliographical information for these sources is presented at the rear of the volume.

Though I have used modern editions wherever possible, I have often had to resort to texts which are inadequate by scholarly standards. Since line numbers are not consistently provided in eighteenth-century editions of poetry, at times the best I have been able to do for the reader is provide him with a page number. In the case of relatively short poems, I have taken pains to give the title so that the reader may track down my references in any edition at his disposal.

Introduction

Shortly after 1750 in England the curious notion that poetry ought to be written with a personal sincerity began to afflict the common reader, poets, and even critics, on a relatively wide scale. The movement started and flourished without the help of Jean-Jacques Rousseau, for indeed the basis of this phenomenon had been laid long before the Swiss genius had appeared on the literary scene. Rousseau's own development of a standard of sincerity probably owed much to his reading in English authors, but in any case the subsequent reception of his work in England was seldom unqualified, usually reserved, and sometimes hostile.

England, never very hospitable to what she regarded as outside influences, had tried for a while a classical mode, derived in substantial part from France. But even while enjoying some major successes in this mode, the English mind was in the process of returning to more native moral and literary values. Such revision, of course, is never a true return to older values, although it may represent itself as such, for as each generation necessarily values the past for different reasons, if it does so at all, it recreates according to its own lights.

In the return to interest in Chaucer, Spenser, English ballads, and folk tales, the natural and the sincere were often specified as most valuable. Shakespeare and Milton were praised, not for their formal achievements in drama or epic, but for their spontaneity and originality. The impetus in England to what we have learned to call Romanticism came, not from Continental traditions, as classicism had done, but from the natural genius that grew on English soil alone.

This revised estimate of past English authors provided both an ideal for emulation and a severe burden to every English Romantic poet, as W. J. Bate has shown.[1] If a major thrust of the Romantic

1. W. J. Bate, *The Burden of the Past and the English Poet* (Cambridge: Harvard University Press, 1970).

revolt is the transference of "order from the objective universe to the
subjective mind," making order relative to individual experience,[2] it
is also involved in rendering the great English poetic past understandable and relevant to the individual, subjective mind.
But the social context of an author's relation to past authors, as
well as to men and women of his own time, was almost always kept
in mind. Even as the Romantic poet strove for a paradisiacal state of
perfect sincerity or oneness with the universe, he realized that movement toward self-suffering, untrammelled by social responsibility, was
essentially evil.[3] Thus sincerity provided for the Romantic a simul-
taneously spiritual and social ideal, a flight from the vain deceits of
the modern world and a bond with natural man.
Of the concept of sincerity and its importance to the development
of the English mind, surprisingly little has been written. The chief
reason for this slow emergence to scholarly attention has been the
uncritical acceptance in the nineteenth century of sincerity as a standard of literary criticism and the consequent repudiation of it by
influential scholars and critics in our own time. Among these con-
demnations none seems more definitive than René Wellek's:

As for "sincerity" in a poem: the term seems almost meaning-
less. A sincere expression of what? Of the supposed emotional
state out of which it came? Or of the state in which the poem
was written? Or a sincere expression of the poem, i.e. the lin-
guistic construct shaping in the author's mind as he writes?
Surely it will have to be the last: the poem is a sincere expression of the poem.[4]

2. Earl R. Wasserman, *The Subtler Language: Critical Readings of Neoclassic and
Romantic Poems* (Baltimore: The Johns Hopkins Press, 1959), p. 184.
3. M. H. Abrams, *Natural Supernaturalism: Tradition and Revolution in Romantic
Literature* (New York: Norton, 1971), p. 266.
4. René Wellek and Austin Warren, *Theory of Literature*, 2nd ed. (New York:
Harvest Books, 1956), p. 198. Some more recent monitory statements regarding
sincerity are Patricia Meyer Spacks, "In Search of Sincerity," *College English*, 29
(1967–68): 591–602; Herbert Read, "The Cult of Sincerity," *Hudson Review*, 21
(1968): 53–74, reprinted in Read's *The Cult of Sincerity* (New York: Horizon Press,
1969); and Donald Davie, "On Sincerity: From Wordsworth to Ginsberg," *Encounter* (Oct. 1968): 61–66. An extremely valuable defence of sincerity may be found
in I. A. Richards, *Practical Criticism* (1929; reprinted New York: Harvest Books,
n.d.), pp. 263–74.

But fruitless as attempts to deal with sincerity in the abstract have doubtless been, the concept remains an actual motivating force in the daily lives of nearly everyone reared in the Western tradition. To Henri Peyre's assertion that sincerity is a French virtue,[5] Lionel Trilling has answered that some distinctions need to be made along national lines:

> In French literature sincerity consists in telling the truth about oneself to oneself and to others; by truth is meant a recognition of such of one's own traits or actions as are morally or socially discreditable and, in conventional course, concealed. English sincerity does not demand this confrontation of what is base or shameful in oneself. The English ask of the sincere man that he communicate without deceiving or misleading. Beyond this what is required is only a single-minded commitment to whatever dutiful enterprise he may have in hand. Not to know oneself in the French fashion and make public what one knows, but to be oneself, in action, in deeds, what Matthew Arnold called "tasks"—this is what the English sincerity consists in.[6]

The generalization is a broad one, perhaps overly broad, and subject to criticism on that score. But if it is at all sound, it owes its credibility to the practised observation of the historian. The generalization is not dependent on the legitimacy of an abstract concept, but on the grasp of complex evidence, mainly textual, related to a particular place most specifically, and also implying a time or stage in the development of the Western mind. In short, the knowledge is historical.

David Perkins was the first to define sincerity in relation to a single great English poet, and he does this by reaching out beyond the limits of the abstract to the real sincerity as Wordsworth understood it:

> There is . . . only one sense in which it is even possibly appropriate to say that a poem must be sincere. It may be that in order to write well a poet must deeply feel the emotion he

5. *Literature and Sincerity* (New Haven: Yale University Press, 1963), p. 1.
6. *Sincerity and Authenticity* (Cambridge: Harvard University Press, 1972), p. 58.

expresses as he creates the poem, though he need not feel it ever before or after. This is what Wordsworth meant by sincerity, but not all that he meant; and if sincerity suggested nothing more, it would have little influence on poetry or criticism. For in this sense sincerity would be merely a sufficient power of sympathetic imagination. It would have nothing to do with personal honesty, and the whole sting and effect of the poetic ideal of sincerity proceed from the fact that it refers to moral qualities—veracity, earnestness, integrity.[7]

The advantages to such an approach are clear: the theoretical objections to sincerity are negated by Wordsworth's accepting it as a standard for his own art. The fact, the reality, substitutes itself for what Pope called the "high Priori Road." Sincerity as both critical and moral ideal becomes an object of the historian, whether or not it can be accounted for by speculative reasoning. Samuel Johnson's putative attack on Berkeley's system is perhaps a model for emulation here. Metaphysicians and historians have different epistemologies.[8]

This is a historical study, then, of the development of the ideal of sincerity in eighteenth-century England as it gradually became a literary standard. Authors are treated less for their intrinsic greatness than for their commitment to sincerity, and I should be less than candid were I not to admit that the results of such a procedure are often unconventional. For example, less attention will be paid to literary criticism than is usual in literary history of this kind, since sincerity is seldom expressed overtly as a critical principle. Indeed, it is safe to say that critical theory lags far behind literary practice in this regard. Though poems in the eighteenth century often come directly to terms with the complexities of sincerity, criticism barely begins to do likewise.

Sincerity in the eighteenth century and earlier is elusive in other

---

7. *Wordsworth and the Poetry of Sincerity* (Cambridge: Harvard University Press, 1964), p. 3.
8. G. R. Elton holds that history "is concerned with all those human sayings, thoughts, deeds and sufferings which occurred in the past and have left present deposit; and it deals with them from the point of view of happening, change, and the particular." *The Practice of History* (New York: Crowell, 1967), p. 12.

ways as well. Not at all a convenient "unit-idea," as Lovejoy would have understood it, sincerity is a broader, more complicated concept, involved as much with human psychology as with historical process. It is for this reason that I have chosen to study authors separately, for the most part, while attempting at the same time to keep before the reader the fact that an historical process is involved. Though each author is influenced by his milieu, he probably influences it as profoundly as it does him. In the complexity of this interaction, my final object is the sincere ideal as it is imaginatively conceived by each author.

The claims I make for sincerity here are not meant to be excessive. I neither pretend to a new discovery nor intend to suggest that sincerity is the chief *idée force* of the eighteenth century or any other age. Students of the eighteenth century and the Romantic period have long been aware that sincerity was a significant force before Wordsworth.[9] But as that awareness has not yet been given full scope, I hope to provide some documentation that will at least suggest the importance and complexity of the subject. On the other hand, I want assiduously to avoid reducing this major period of literary history to a single catch phrase. Underrated as sincerity may be, I do not wish to redress the balance by claiming more for that ideal than the evidence will fairly admit. Though most of the evidence I present here must necessarily be favourable to the claims I do make, I expect that the reader will be able to supply a just corrective. If sincerity should prove to be a passable road into a great period of literature, I shall be very far from insisting that it is the high road. There are major figures, such as Swift and Gay, to whom sincerity was a vague threat or a dull joke (though they were certainly affected by it). There is a veritable army of minor writers whose scribblings reflect little or nothing of the ideological transformation which sincerity and other attitudes were gradually effecting.

The derivation of "sincere" and "sincerity" is an uncomplicated matter. Sincere comes from the Latin *sincerus*—pure, unmixed, or unadulterated, and sincerity from the French *sincérité*.

9. See for example M. H. Abrams, *The Mirror and the Lamp: Romantic Theory and the Critical Tradition* (New York: Oxford University Press, 1953), pp. 317–20.

The Oxford English Dictionary defines sincere in four related ways: (1) not falsified or perverted in any way; (2) pure, unmixed; free from any foreign element or ingredient; (3) containing no element of dissimulation or deception; not feigned or pretended; real, true; (4) characterized by the absence of all dissimulation or pretence; honest, straightforward. Each of these English meanings was established as early as the sixteenth century.

Sincerity is given two chief definitions by the *OED*: (1) freedom from falsification, adulteration, or alloy; purity, correctness; (2) freedom from dissimulation or duplicity; honesty, straightforwardness. The first of these meanings was established in the seventeenth century and the second in the sixteenth century.

Though varying meanings of sincere and sincerity create some problems in the ensuing discussion, the primary difficulty is that the word sincere is not alone the criterion for the detection of sincerity. Words such as openness, ingenuousness, frankness, and artlessness were established English words in the sixteenth century. Candour, on the other hand, most often in the eighteenth century means "kindness," although notions of purity and innocence, associated with sincerity, can be assigned to it.[10]

By the phrase "the sincere ideal" I hope to express at once two somewhat different meanings of the word sincere. First, the utopian goal toward which many eighteenth-century authors strove was one of perfectly guileless behaviour. But some thinkers went beyond that and visualized the sincere state as an almost prelapsarian condition. So the second meaning of the sincere ideal is a state singularly uncorrupt. Observance of the standard of behaviour was to lead to a state of perfection sometimes identified with divine salvation itself.

The central theme of this study, then, is that a significant intellectual and moral movement in the eighteenth century was the quest for self-perfection and a perfect society, characterized significantly by the virtue of sincerity. Some authors took part in this nonviolent revolution quite consciously, while others did so only instinctively. Because the ideal was more secular in conception than the *Civitatis*

---

10. Susie I. Tucker, *Protean Shape: A Study in Eighteenth-Century Vocabulary and Usage* (London: The Athlone Press, 1967), pp. 212–14.

Dei of an earlier age, the old religious and moral schemes being inadequate, new solutions to the difficulties of man's psychological preparation for it had to be found. Sentimentalism, for example, is both one of these solutions and the result of the change which the human psyche underwent as new modes of thought and feeling evolved. Other solutions, reflected in key terms of the age, such as sympathy, simplicity, disinterestedness, and originality,[11] figure importantly. These methods, whether psychological, mythic, or formal, used by a number of representative authors to discover this social and moral ideal, are the subject of this essay.[12]

11. Bate, *The Burden of the Past*, p. 107. The best account of these terms remains W. J. Bate, *From Classic to Romantic: Premises of Taste in Eighteenth-Century England* (Cambridge: Harvard University Press, 1946).

12. I should make clear at the outset that I propose to study sincerity in its formal effects rather than as genetic fact. These formal effects are patterns of imagery and ideological positions, as well as a certain posture or "voice" of the poet which is the formal correlative or sign of genetic sincerity, whether or not genetic sincerity underlies it. Since the genetic fact, the existence of sincerity, must always remain in doubt, all of these signs and patterns may be considered conventions.

La sincérité est une ouverture de coeur. On la trouve en fort peu de gens et celle que l'on voit d'ordinaire n'est qu'une fine dissimulation pour attirer la confiance des autres.

La Rochefoucauld

1

The Background of Sincerity

Sincerity as an ideal of behaviour as we know it today is relatively new in Western thought. Though it can be traced in Greek antiquity, in Rome, and in the Middle Ages, it reached its first point of significance only after the Protestant Reformation.[1] Its apogee as a moral ideal comes during the Puritan movement of the seventeenth century.

Though sincerity enjoys only a somewhat ephemeral existence as a positive moral ideal in classical antiquity, it is there that the basis for much of its later development can be found. In the *Iliad*, Achilles expresses a downright distrust of guile:

> For as I detest the doorways of Death, I detest that man, who
> hides one thing in the depths of his heart, and speaks forth
> another.[2]

Though the upright, guileless behaviour of Hector provides an example of admirable action, the poem's general ethical stance on the matter of sincerity seems to be noncommittal. After all, Zeus himself is characterized by guile, and Hera, who accuses him, is no model of sincerity herself:

> Treacherous one, what god has been plotting counsels with you?
> Always it is dear to your heart in my absence to think of secret
> things and decide upon them. Never have you patience frankly
> to speak forth to me the thing that you purpose.[3]

1. For commentary on the history of sincerity see Peyre, *Literature and Sincerity*, pp. 13–78, and Trilling, *Sincerity and Authenticity*, pp. 1–25.
2. *The Iliad*, trans. Richmond Lattimore (Chicago: University of Chicago Press, 1951), p. 206, bk. 9, 312–13.
3. Ibid., p. 73, bk. 1, 540–43.

Ambiguity is created by the fact that though guile does not receive a positive assessment, Zeus is the father of the gods and his characteristic behaviour, which includes guile, is affirmed by the power he wields. Further, his deceptive nature is taken beyond ethical consideration by its comic treatment. In both the *Iliad* and the *Odyssey* guile is associated with the gods. Though Odysseus does not always seem ethically sound in the *Iliad*, most of his behaviour in the *Odyssey* is exemplary. Indeed, in Book XIII of the *Odyssey*, Athene specifically praises the craft of Odysseus and likens that quality to her own "wit and sharpness."[4]

The Athenian dramatists do not seem to take the problem of sincerity beyond a conventional aversion for guile, but one significant exception from Euripides' *The Suppliant Women* should be noted. A possible source for the later and more famous Horatian dictum on literary sincerity comes in a speech by Adrastus, king of Argos:

> The poet bringing songs into the world
> Should labour in joy. If this is not his mood,
> He cannot—being inwardly distressed—
> Give pleasure outwardly. That stands to reason.[5]

Horace's lines from *The Art of Poetry* may profitably be cited here: "si vis me flere, dolendum est / primum ipsi tibi" (if you would have me weep, you must first feel grief yourself).[6] Coming from Horace, this affective principle of art, which was to become a staple of sincerity and sympathy both, assumed the authority of a neoclassical rule.

The *locus classicus* for the philosophical delineation of sincerity is Plato's *Republic*. At the end of Book II Socrates and Adeimantus agree that the lying attributed to poets does not belong to the "god": "the god is altogether simple and true in deed and speech, and he doesn't himself change or deceive others by illusions, speeches, or

4. *The Odyssey*, trans. Richmond Lattimore (New York: Harper & Row, 1967), p. 206, bk. 13, 299.

5. *The Suppliant Women*, trans. Frank William Jones in *The Complete Greek Tragedies*, ed. David Grene and Richmond Lattimore (Chicago: University of Chicago Press, 1958), 4, ll. 180–83.

6. *The Art of Poetry*, ed. H. Rushton Fairclough (Cambridge: Harvard University Press, 1929), pp. 458–59, ll. 102–3.

the sending of signs either in waking or dreaming."[7] The "god" here is the prototype of the soul, which should be in a similar state— simple, calm, and undisturbed by inner division or turmoil.

This general view is applied to poetry by distinguishing between the voices which might be heard in a poem. Socrates holds that "everything that's said by tellers of tales or poets is a narrative (diēgēsis) of what has come to pass, what is, or what is going to be." Narrative is then divided into three categories: "narrative that is either simple or produced by imitation, or by both together" (p. 71).

Thus simple narrative in the speaker's own voice is preferred to imitation, since "it turns out that the man who speaks correctly speaks mostly in the same style and in one mode." Imitation on the other hand, involves "all modes and all rhythms," producing a man who "doesn't harmonize with our regime because there's no double man among us, nor a manifold one, since each man does one thing" (pp. 75–76).

Plato's man, like Plato's soul, is calm, philosophic, and directly opposed to Homer's Achilles, in Plato's view, the product of inner turmoil and a divided mind. Plato is interested in displacing the heroic ideal in favour of the philosophic contemplation of ideas as personified in Socrates.

Thus the poet as imitator is bound to copy existing ethical situations; the heroic ideal and other attitudes must remain, under such conditions, perpetually *in statu quo*. Heroic and tragic behaviour, involving division and turmoil of soul, is an improper expression of the ideal status of that soul. This ideal status is, of course, a clear relationship to truth, as the following passage from Book X will serve to show: "the imitative poet produces a bad regime in the soul of each private man by making phantoms that are very far removed from the truth and by gratifying the soul's foolish part, which doesn't distinguish big from little, but believes the same things are at one time big and at another little" (p. 289). In short, the object of each man should be to express the truth of his own humanity, that is, his nature. For Plato the obvious "insincerity" of poetic imitation is a contradiction of his ideal of sincerity.

7. Plato, *The Republic*, p. 61.

In pointing to the *Republic* as a *locus classicus* of sincerity, I am not arguing that the seventeenth and eighteenth centuries recognized it as such. The mystical and transcendent aspects of Plato's philosophy and especially of Neoplatonism do find their way into English Puritan thought, though largely through earlier Christian syntheses. Plato's influence on Shaftesbury, Akenside, and others of deist leanings is well known.[8] But the Platonic influence with regard to sincerity, if it exists at all, is indirect. Indeed Thomas Gray is the only major figure to recognize the implications of Plato's distinction between pure narrative and personation.[9]

But a combination of tendencies toward transcendence and rationalism, discernible in Platonism, provides the substance of the ideal of sincerity. Neoclassical, Horatian ideals of clarity, honesty,[10] and retirement approach the ideal of sincerity without encompassing its subjective qualities. On the other hand, the Puritan passion for transcendence and the pure spiritual state is often oblivious of the secular attitudes which contribute to sincerity, such as sentimentalism. The fundamentalist who believes in the absolute authority of the Bible may be a Puritan, but his dogmatic interpretations of scripture do not provide the ideological latitude necessary within the ideal of sincerity. Orthodox religious attitudes, whether held by the conservative nonjuror Thomas Ken or the reformer John Wesley, are usually sufficient in themselves and provide no impetus to the formation of a new ideal. The ideal of sincerity is neither Puritan nor neoclassical but a combination of the major tendencies of both. The

8. I do not claim that Shaftesbury was in every respect a deist, since he called himself a theist and attacked deism. But Peter Gay is probably correct when he writes that "Shaftesbury was a deist in fact, if not in name; he was anti-clerical in the deists' way, ridiculed supernatural tales in their way, maligned 'enthusiasts' in their way, and, above all, developed an ethical system that dispensed entirely with religious sanctions." *Deism* (Princeton: Van Nostrand, 1968), pp. 78–79.

9. For more extensive treatment of this aspect of Gray's work see my "Imitation and Originality in the Poems of Thomas Gray" in Paul J. Korshin, ed., *Proceedings of the Modern Language Association Neo-Classicism Conferences 1967–1968* (New York: AMS Press, 1970). My section on Gray in this volume is a shortened version of this essay.

10. See Rachel Trickett, *The Honest Muse: A Study in Augustan Verse* (Oxford: Clarendon Press, 1967). "Honesty" would seem to be the Augustan version of sincerity, the plainness inspiring the muse of satire. Its affinity with sincerity contributed to the development of the sincere ideal along classical lines.

forging of this compromise was begun largely after the restoration of Charles II, when it began to be apparent that England would not sanction domination by either Puritans or Cavaliers. The extremes of French neoclassicism and revolutionary Puritanism would be required to meet and combine on some middle ground. This complex process of transformation and gradual institutionalization results in what I call the sincere ideal.

Thus we shall find that those authors who hold high the sincere ideal are often involved in an unholy alliance of deists and liberal Protestants, many of whom have dissenter backgrounds. These are drawn to at least some aspects of Natural Religion, but more important, they share a common aversion for Roman Catholic tradition and dogma.[11]

The Platonic singleness of role is best exemplified in Roman poetry by Virgil's *Aeneid*. Book II contains the most specific diatribe against guile and Greece in the episode of Sinon and the Trojan horse. Sinon condemns himself and all Greeks in his blasphemous protestation, "ille, dolis instructus et arte Pelasga, / sustulit exutas vinclis ad sidera palmas. . . ."[12]

Virgil's hatred of guile is given strong Christian moral emphasis in Dante's *Inferno*, especially in the later cantos, where the traitors Ugolino, Fra Alberigo, and finally Brutus and Judas lay claim to the lowest places in Hell. But a strong disapprobation of guileful behaviour does not imply an emphasis on its opposite, sincerity. Though Virgil and Dante approve of sincere and honest behaviour, neither sees it as self-sufficient or even central to ethical conduct.

The unwillingness to rely on a single *idée fixe* as a touchstone of ethical conduct is characteristic of the great poets of the Middle Ages and the Renaissance. Both Dante's comprehensive view of the

---

11. Of course this is not true of Pope and Johnson, for example. But neither are these presented here as strict proponents of sincerity. Both were influenced by it, but Johnson's response is largely in opposition. The full reaction against the sincere ideal by such authors as Swift, Gay, and Sheridan is a subject deserving of full treatment. In a certain sense not one author treated in this essay can be reduced to the sincere ideal without ignoring at least some facets of his work. I do not argue for a monistic interpretation of even the least complicated writers.

12. *Virgil*, ed. H. Rushton Fairclough (Cambridge: Harvard University Press, 1960), p. 304, 2, 152–53.

universe and the Aristotelian ethical ideal of the golden mean find expression in the plays of William Shakespeare.

Indeed, some of Shakespeare's plays can be read as examinations of the consequences of excessive guile or ingenuousness. Othello, for example, is the sincere man, incapable of deceit, who expects that others, and Iago in particular, are as sincere as he. He is culpable to the degree that absolute sincerity precludes wisdom; he is blinded by his virtue to the ways of the world. The plain-dealing Coriolanus is at fault because his single-minded virtue does not permit a wise balance of virtues and a sense of what action is appropriate to a given time. Sincerity tends to be blindly one-sided, as Shakespeare understood. On the other hand, the guileful man is made vulgar by his deceit and is clearly evil. But even here Shakespeare reveals his sense of the complexity of human experience as he sets the guile of Cleopatra against the questionable uprightness represented by Octavian and his sister. No simple moral formula will work, but if we allow for extraordinary variation from play to play, a major motif of Shakespeare's art is the unequal struggle between the ingenuous and the ingenious.

If we search the Hebrew scriptures for the origins of sincerity, we shall find very little to interest us. Indeed the deceptions of Jacob, for example, by which he gains the blessing intended for Esau and overcomes his enemies, seem to have a positive connotation. Jacob's guile was born of an understanding of God's will, a sensitivity to the order of the universe. To Jacob, as to Odysseus, the justice of an end seems to be the only consideration. Means are not subject to moral scrutiny.

It is probable that sincerity of behaviour first became a central ideal with the advent of Christianity, though it is equally probable that Stoic and Epicurean attitudes akin to sincerity reinforced the Christian gain and perhaps made it possible in the first place. Idealization of the simple, honest life in a pastoral setting can be found in the works of Horace, Lucretius, Seneca, Cicero, and Juvenal, among others. These classical pastoral statements were to reinforce and vivify later conceptions of the sincere ideal.

For Puritans of the seventeenth century, Saint Paul, in particular, exemplified the sincere ideal. In the King James Version of the Old and New Testaments, the word "sincere" and its other forms appear only about seventeen times; but ten of these appearances are in Paul's Epistles, where "simplicity and godly sincerity" receive consistent high praise.[13]

The concern of Paul lest the word of God be corrupted[14] and his reliance on the heart devoted to Christ[15] lead, at least by implication, to a doctrine of sincerity. In the Pauline Epistles there is an emphasis on the accurate expression of truth and a full confidence that the truth can be known and expressed. If these Epistles share the ambiguities of the rest of scripture, they did not seem to do so to the Puritan mind. The injunction to be sincere was taken very seriously indeed, as we shall see in the following chapter.

It should not surprise us that Paul or any other scriptural figure could be used as a faction or an age might wish, without regard for scholarly accuracy. Indeed it is astounding to remark that Archbishop John Tillotson regarded the guileful Jacob as a prime example of the sincere man.[16] Such was the newly felt power of the sincere ideal that any important saint or patriarch could be made to exemplify it. Jesus' words on seeing Nathanael, "Behold an Israelite indeed, in whom is no guile," were celebrated by seventeenth- and eighteenth-century divines as indicative of the new Christian ethic.[17] In short, sincerity was to be found at the heart of every piety. In demonstrating this contention, Tillotson defines sincerity as follows:

> Of sincerity, as it regards men; and so it signifies a simplicity of mind and manners in our conversation, and carriage towards another; singleness of heart, discovering itself in a constant plainness and honest openness of behaviour, free from all

13. II Corinthians, 1:12. All Biblical references are to the Authorized King James Version.

14. II Corinthians, 2:17 and Ephesians, 4:29.

15. II Corinthians, 3:2–3. Note also Ephesians, 6:24 and Philippians, 1:10.

16. " Of Sincerity Towards God and Man," 29 July 1694, *Works* (London, 1820), 4, 2. It is possible that Tillotson is influenced by the typological view that Jacob represents the Christian dispensation displacing the Hebrew one (viz. in displacing Esau). Such a reading would necessarily minimize the guile of Jacob in favour of his more attractive features. See Murray Roston, *Prophet and Poet: The Bible and the Growth of Romanticism* (Evanston: Northwestern University Press, 1965), pp. 42–43.

17. John, 1:47.

insidious devices, and little tricks, and fetches of craft and
cunning: from all false appearances and deceitful disguises of ourselves in word or action; or, yet more plainly, it is to speak as
we think, and do what we pretend and profess, to perform and
make good what we promise, and, in a word, really to be what
we would seem and appear to be.[18]

. . . .

And with the sincerity of our piety towards God, let us join the
simplicity and integrity of manners in our conversation with
men. Let us strictly charge ourselves to use truth and plainness
in all our words and doings; let our tongue be ever the true
interpreter of our mind, and our expressions the lively image of
our thoughts and affections, and our outward actions exactly
agreeable to our inward purposes and intentions.[19]

As the intellectuals of the late seventeenth century and the
eighteenth century appropriated this ideal, they found that other
beliefs of the age served to reinforce their new-found truth. It may
prove helpful to outline briefly some of these, since they will play
prominent parts in the detailed analyses to follow.

A motif central to the sincere ideal is the primarily Horatian myth
of retirement, documented so fully by Miss Maren–Sofie Röstvig.[20]
It will be seen that especially among poets, retirement became a sine
qua non for complete moral and poetic development.

Another concept embraced by the sincere ideal is that of liberty.
This Whig battle cry may be connected with those political theor-
ists aptly called the classical republicans.[21] Here Puritan and

---

18. Tillotson, *Works*, 4, 10–11.
19. Ibid., 4, 15.
20. *The Happy Man: Studies in the Metamorphoses of a Classical Ideal.* 2 vols.
(Oslo, 1954, 1958). E. M. W. Tillyard has argued that *Robinson Crusoe* is a work
inspired by the retirement myth, thus providing a link between that myth and Puritanism. See *The Epic Strain in the English Novel* (London: Chatto and Windus, 1967)
and *Some Mythical Elements in English Literature* (London: Chatto and Windus,
1961). Maynard Mack accentuates the retirement theme in *The Garden and the City:
Retirement and Politics in the Later Poetry of Pope, 1731–1743* (Toronto: University
of Toronto Press, 1969).
21. Zera Fink, *The Classical Republicans* (Evanston: Northwestern University
Press, 1945).

republican sentiments unite in such men as Milton, Harrington, and Algernon Sidney. The classical republicans favoured the establishment of a state that would exemplify the best republican governments of Greece and Rome and the ideal of the Venetian republic. The chief sources for this ideal were Polybius, Cicero, Machiavelli, and Contarini. Though there was some difficulty over the pagan orientation of the proposed classical republics, a few writers (Milton particularly) united classical and Hebraic–Christian principles with substantial success. It seems fairly clear that the aspirations of the classical republicans and the Hebraic-oriented Puritans could find common ground under the banner of liberty.

A third theme, often closely connected with retirement, is that of the Second Eden or the New Jerusalem—an expanded social conception of retirement, with paradisiacal overtones. Much of the imaginative vitality of the Second Eden concept came from *Paradise Lost*, as I shall try to prove in later chapters.

Milton's paradisiacal ideals derive from the practical proposals of some associates of his early career and the general utopianism of Puritan thought. Reformers such as Henry Robinson, Samuel Hartlib, John Dury, Comenius, and Milton himself presented in the early days of Puritan success practical schemes for everything from education to fisheries.[22] John Stoughton, associate of Hartlib and Dury, presented his utopian hopes in a book called *Felicitas Ultimi Saeculi* in strains which only the Latin language can afford:

> O quam candida facies veritatis se tum aperiet, mundo, sine velo, sine maculis, quam plene eburnea! quam recta species sanctitatis exhibebit se oculo sine naevo, sine rugis, & quam pure crystallina! quam longa series & tanquam acies jucunditatis, explicabit se in ello Campo Elysio, sub vexillis, quam plane plusquam aurea! quam integre venusta vel elegantissimis formarum spectatoribus eris, o Ecclesia Christi, quam formosa

---

22. For accounts of Henry Robinson see W. K. Jordan, *Men of Substance* (Chicago: University of Chicago Press, 1942) and William Haller, *Liberty and Reformation in the Puritan Revolution* (New York: Columbia University Press, 1955), pp. 159–62. An excellent account of Hartlib, Dury, and Comenius is in H. R. Trevor–Roper, *The Crisis of the Seventeenth Century* (New York: Harper & Row, 1968).

tot numerisque omnibus ad Archetypam scilicet Ideam Pul-
chritudinis absoluta!²³

But such visions give way to more practical considerations later
in Stoughton's work and in Samuel Hartlib's *A Description of the
Famous Kingdome of Macaria.* In this latter pamphlet Hartlib, using
Thomas More's *Utopia* and Bacon's *The New Atlantis* as models
manqués, outlines in a dialogue between a traveller and a scholar the
governmental perfection of the kingdom of Macaria. In that nation
fruit planting, health services, and general prosperity minister to the
physical needs of all citizens. Macaria, the traveller tells the scholar,
"is become like to a fruitfull Garden. . . ."²⁴ When the scholar is
amazed by the assertion that peace has been made permanent, the
traveller tells him why this is so:

> they have a law, that if any Prince shall attempt any invasion,
> his kingdome shall be lawfull prize: and the Inhabitants of this
> happy Countrey are so numerous, strong, and rich, that they
> have destroyed some without any considerable resistance; and
> the rest take warning.²⁵

Here are the beginnings of the myth of prosperity and power which
were to shape Whig ideals in the eighteenth century. We are never
allowed to forget that Macaria is not Macaria at all but rather Hartlib's visionary hope for England. But if, in retrospect, Macaria is
merely visionary, we must remember that for Hartlib it was a very
real possibility, supported by a host of practical proposals. Further,
England was to lead the way to utopia by example and imperialism:

> Traveller: . . . for the Art of Printing will so spread know-
> ledge, that the common people, knowing their own rights and
> liberties, will not be governed by way of oppression; and so, by
> little and little, all Kingdomes will be like to *Macaria.*
> Scholar: That will be a good change, when as well superiors
> as inferiors shall bee more happy: Well, I am imparadised in my

---

23. *Felicitas Ultimi Saeculi* (London, 1640), pp. 17–18.
24. *A Description of the Famous Kingdome of Macaria* (London, 1641), p. 4.
25. Ibid. p. 5.

minde, in thinking that England may bee made happy, with such expedition and facility.[26]

The scholar's "imparadised" state was only the beginning, since in 1641 there was some confidence that such a state could move out from the mind to social and political reality. Milton's "paradise within" is the scholar's state after all social and political hopes had been dashed, with the additional wisdom that the inner state of man is more important than the external one.

Hartlib's egalitarian confidence found its echo in the Leveller movement under the leadership of such men as John Lilburne and William Walwyn. Of the former I shall have something to say when I turn to Puritan autobiography in the next chapter. The less militant, more ingratiating, Walwyn, however, reflects more accurately many attitudes which were later to make up the sincere ideal.

In his early work, *The Power of Love*, Walwyn criticizes in good Puritan style the elaborate costumes of even those who pass as religious persons.[27] Plain manners and plain clothes are his only desire. He comes out strongly for toleration, but puts most of his confidence in "plaine truth" which "will prove all, sufficient for vanquishing of the most artificiall, sophisticall errour that ever was in the world. . . ."[28] Walwyn's classical and humanistic reading (in translation) gives his political thought a civilized and rational quality seldom met with in his associates of the Leveller movement.[29] Untempted by bureaucratic power, Walwyn chooses simplicity of government and of life. The laws of England, he argues, should be reduced to a single volume, and his attacks on Prynne and other parliamentarians stress that they take advantage of the overly complex legal system to gain their selfish ends.

Walwyn, then, has more in common with the educated men who were to become the poets of the sincere ideal than with the rugged militants who were his associates. But even the coarse, self-righteous

26. Ibid., pp. 13–14.
27. *The Power of Love* (1643). Reprinted in William Haller, ed., *Tracts on Liberty in the Puritan Revolution* (New York: Columbia University Press, 1934), 2, 274–75.
28. Ibid., 2, 278.
29. Joseph Frank, *The Levellers* (Cambridge: Harvard University Press, 1955), pp. 30–31.

outcries of John Lilburne anticipate many Whig ideals. Joseph Frank has summarized the Leveller achievement as follows: "by the organization of a party, by the broad dissemination of their ideas, and by the persistent inculcation of a precise program, the Levellers, specifically, if not in these exact terms, attempted to make optimism, secularism, rationalism, and pragmatism the basic elements of a democratic society and the working slogans of England's political development."[30] Professor Frank's comparison of Walwyn's essential rationality with the oblivious piety of George Fox shows that the Puritan mind was moving from objectivity and practical reformation to the subjectivity of self-realization. This tendency I shall elaborate on in the next chapter.

Related to these larger utopian goals are ideals of conduct that will characterize the sincere ideal. First among these is the simplicity of life, speech, and language, valued by Tillotson and Walwyn. For them simple speech is the real language of the heart. This language, rendered spontaneously, expresses the true nature of man as surely as if it were the divine afflatus.

Another characteristic of the sincere ideal is vigorous, sometimes unorthodox, Protestantism, inevitably coupled with virulent anti-Catholic feeling. The imagined Protestantism postulated stands for liberty, utopianism, and simplicity and spontaneity of expression. Roman Catholicism, on the other hand, represents for most enthusiasts of the sincere ideal enslavement of mind and spirit, a corrupt state, and deceit of manner and expression.

This persistent libel directed by English authors against the Catholic Church and Catholic nations can be characterized at its worst by the work of one Gabriel d'Emillianne, who published in 1690 *The Frauds of the Monks*, a dull catalogue of supposed Catholic deceit and superstition. It is likely that in the aftermath of the accession of William and Mary this volume was popular, however, for it was succeeded by *A Journey to Naples* (1691) and *A Short History of Monastical Orders* (1693), mere elaborations on d'Emillianne's initial effort. The point to notice is that the attack is always directed against the falseness and cunning of the Catholic clergy and the gullibility of the

30. Ibid., p. 252.

Catholic faithful, who, in the author's view, insist upon deceiving themselves with images, relics and false pardons. These convenient beliefs permitted those who combined the principles of Protestantism with firm anti-Catholicism to imagine themselves as crusaders against falseness and deceit, rather than as mere bigots. This dark side of sincerity takes effective shape in the establishment of the "Good Old Cause" during the Restoration period and culminates in the Gordon Riots of 1780.

Another theme, closely related to the motif of retirement and classical republicanism, is friendship. This is male friendship, usually, and sometimes consciously opposed to romantic love involving the other sex. Yet despite the high proportion of celibate poets dedicated to the sincere ideal, women receive generally favourable treatment. Although male friendship is at times a higher ideal, women retain an honoured place in the scheme of things, if only as "softer" versions of the male friends. John Pomfret's "The Choice" illustrates this very well. First,

> That Life might be more Comfortable yet,
> And all my Joys Refin'd, Sincere, and Great;
> I'd Chuse two Friends, whose Company wou'd be
> A great Advance to my Felicity.
>
> . . . .
>
> In their Society, I cou'd not miss
> A Permanent, Sincere, Substantial Bliss.
>
> (74–77, 96–97)[31]

But granting this, life still can be enlarged upon:

> Wou'd Bounteous Heav'n once more Indulge, I'd choose,
> (For who wou'd so much Satisfaction lose,
> As Witty Nymphs, in Conversation, give,)
> Near some Obliging, Modest Fair to live;
> For there's that Sweetness in a Female Mind,
> Which in a Man's we cannot hope to find: . . .
>
> (98–103)

31. Ronald S. Crane, ed. *A Collection of English Poems, 1660–1800.* Line numbers are included in the text.

Particularly, this lady should exemplify sincerity:

> I'd have her Reason all her Passions sway;
> Easy in Company, in Private Gay:
> Coy to a Fop, to the Deserving Free,
> Still Constant to her self, and Just to me.
>
> . . . .
>
> Averse to Vanity, Revenge, and Pride,
> In all the Methods of Deceit untry'd: ...
>
> (107–10, 123–24)

It is germane to note that, throughout the history of European literature, sincerity had been an issue in love affairs and other romantic
situations, moral and immoral, arising from the courtly love tradition, which came to be a staple of Restoration dramatic comedy and
fiction. Sincerity in love, often a euphemism for sexual fidelity, provides a significant impetus toward the sincere ideal, precisely because female chastity could be regarded as a virtue even by those who
rejected the laws of religion. Since the sincere ideal, though continually influenced by religious developments, was becoming a secular
ethic, it could find primary inspiration in the secular arts of poetry,
fiction, and drama. Thus the deception involved in explicitly sexual
temptation could unite both secular and religious concerns in a unified, if superficial, vision.

The Whiggish doctrine of progress may be mentioned briefly as
an article of faith to many who profess the sincere ideal. The belief in
sincerity does not always imply a belief in an untainted human
nature. Rather, a more usual view is that man, if not perfectible, can
at least be improved. Thus sincerity becomes an attainable moral
ideal, just as utopia becomes an attainable social ideal. Sincerity and
utopianism usually bore some relationship to one another.

Given the emotional need for optimism in social and political
matters, it is not surprising that exponents of sincerity were greatly
interested in science. Newtonian physics revealed, for many, Nature
in the clarity and simplicity of truth. With all Nature's secrets laid
open, there was nothing to conceal. And Nature was thus an appropriate model for human society.

But as it became apparent that the social system would not conform to the ideal, sincere authors turned to a religio-scientific heaven for the consolation which they failed to find on earth. There in a combined traditional and scientific heaven, all deceit and superstition were overthrown and the previously desired earthly paradise becomes a reality above. John Gay, in an early version of *Rural Sports* (1713), gives pious pause in contemplation of the universe:

Now Night in silent State begins to rise,
And twinkling Orbs bestrow th' uncloudy Skies;
Her borrow'd Lustre growing *Cynthia* lends,
And o'er the Main a glitt'ring Path extends;
Millions of Worlds hang in the spacious Air,
Which round their Suns their Annual Circles steer.
Sweet Contemplation elevates my Sense,
While I survey the Works of Providence.
Oh, could my Muse in loftier Strains rehearse
The Glorious Author of this Universe,
Who reins the Winds, gives the vast Ocean Bounds,
And circumscribes the floating Worlds their Rounds!
My Soul should overflow in Songs of Praise,
And my Creator's Name inspire my Lays.[32]

Gay here anticipates the work of later poets who, failing to find a utopia on earth, sought it in God's perfect Newtonian universe.

The movement of the potential paradise from earth to heaven was for many authors another way of turning concern from social and political realities to their own inner state. Science provided many answers, or so some eighteenth-century thinkers believed; but even the revolutionary Newtonian physics seemed less important to their originator than his conventional moralistic writings. This tendency away from the external world to the inner life of man is well expressed by William Melmoth, who, after praising the achievement of Newton, turns to applaud Shaftesbury:

Yet if so just the fame, the use so great,
Systems to poise, and spheres to regulate,

32. *The Poetical Works*, ed. John Underhill (London: The Muses' Library, 1893), 1, 266.

To teach the secret well-adapted force,
That steers of countless orbs th' unvaried course;
Far brighter honors wait the nobler part,
To ballance manners, and conduct the heart.
Order *without* us, what imports it seen,
If all is restless anarchy within?
Fir'd with this thought great Ashley, gen'rous sage,
Plan'd in sweet leisure his instructive page.
Not orbs he weighs, but marks with happier skill,
The scope of action and the poise of will:
In fair proportion here describ'd we trace,
Each mental beauty, and each moral grace,
Each useful passion taught its tone design'd,
In the nice concord of a well tun'd mind.[33]

This concern for human action and will, a constant eighteenth-century motif, led thinkers to consider carefully the psychological basis of action. A significant result was Hartley's monumental *Observations on Man* (1749) and a formidable line of successors. But even before the term "enthusiasm" had lost its connotation of opprobrium, an ideal of spontaneity was coming into being. If serious writers in the seventeenth century had often served political and partisan causes, their counterparts in the early part of the eighteenth century were beginning to turn away from social concerns to the private inner life of the imagination.

33. Robert Dodsley, ed., *A Collection of Poems by Several Hands* (London, 1748), I, 192.

Reason is a sleepy half-useless thing, till some Passion excite it.

Richard Baxter

2

The Puritan Contribution and Milton

Sincerity in poetry is not a new phenomenon, but critical concern with it is. The growth of this critical concern seems to mark, more and more emphatically, a division between poetry and the real world, or, we may say, between the mind of the poet and the everyday society in which he finds himself.

In the poetry of George Herbert the object of concern is God and man's proper relation to Him. It is the relationship between God and the poet as man which is important, not the poet's relationship to his poem. Since this necessitates a belief in a real world created by God, the poet, even as poet, will be concerned more with the sincerity of his belief than with the expression of that sincerity in the poem. Of Herbert's ultimate religious sincerity we cannot pretend to judge, but it is probably safe to assume a certain disparity between the faith of the priest and the fluctuation of attitudes reflected by the poems. Just how close was the correlation between the religious postures in the poems and Herbert's own understanding of himself we cannot know, nor is it likely that he knew.

Herbert, of course, does not seem to have been beset with the doubts which Donne experienced; but the intensity of emotion evident in his poems is such that there is no sense of a conscious attempt to correlate the poems to a given experience. The poem is itself an experience, perhaps, but it is not necessarily an experience that happened to George Herbert, priest, at a given time. A single poem may represent a whole range of experience, and may be, in effect, a summing up, constituting a new experience that can be called poetical. But whatever the relationship, it is not significant to the poem or to

the poet; they are separate and distinct, except for the certain correlation that only God can know.

I mean to suggest that a poetry which attempts to perfect this
correlation will labour under many difficulties. It will depend on
spontaneity, in the belief that such a "natural" process will hit upon
the true correlation, or it will laboriously work out the details of the
desired correspondence. The sincere poet will choose whichever of
these approaches seems to promise most success, or he may choose
to unite both. This last is the viewpoint most often expressed by
poets of sincerity. In his *Essays on Men and Manners*, William Shenstone remarks that "fine writing is generally the effect of spontaneous thoughts and a laboured style."[1] Indeed, the sincere poet has
before him not only the difficulty of writing a fine poem but the requirement to establish a highly tenuous correlation between thought
and style, feeling and expression. Further, it seems that spontaneity
and a laboured style can act at cross-purposes. Finally one must
yield to the other.

Though it remains a difficult historical problem, it seems likely
that a pervasive concern for sincerity in the composition of literature
began in the introspective religious impulse of seventeenth-century
revolutionary Puritanism. There is some irony here, since Puritanism itself was usually inimical to poetry. But Milton stands as the
exception to the rule and proves by his achievement that Puritanism,
freed of purely practical religious and political concerns, could provide a unique vision for poetry. Indeed, by combining with the
classical tradition, Puritanism played a key role in the development
of eighteenth-century poetry toward a poetry of sincerity. It is
probably safe to say that the poetry of sincerity is largely the outcome of English Puritanism and English classicism acting upon one
another. It is also safe to say that the ideal of sincerity began as an
English phenomenon and grew from that to what Professor Henri
Peyre has called "the most potent idée-force in the literature and
psychology of our age."[2]

Except for Milton, of course, the Puritan contribution in poetry,
at least in Great Britain, was negligible. Richard Baxter, whose theo-

1. *Works*, 2, 152.   2. Peyre, *Literature and Sincerity*, p. 14.

logical talents were enormous, achieved only modest success with the Muse. Baxter's poetry, however, is instructive, for it is a prelude to both the didacticism of much eighteenth-century verse and the concern for self of the poetry of sincerity.

For Baxter, George Herbert is the proper model for a poet: "Herbert speaks to God like one that really believeth a God, [sic] and whose business in this world is most with God. Heart-work and Heaven-work make up his books."[3] Though Baxter's phrasing suggests that he is aware of the difficulties of such a judgement, clearly sincerity is the criterion that he applies to Herbert's poems. He uses the same criterion in preferring Seneca to all his Roman contemporaries, "because he speaketh things by words, feelingly and seriously, like a man that is past jest. . . ."[4] Baxter upholds seriousness and sincerity in moral and religious matters.

Unlike the poetry of his Puritan contemporary in America, Edward Taylor, Baxter's poetry is more a religious exercise than poetry. The *Fragments* are meant specifically as a help to others: "All that I have to say for these Fragments, is 1. That being fitted to women, and vulgar wits, which are the far greatest number, they may be useful to such, though contemptible to those of higher elevation and expectation. 2. And being suited to afflicted, sick, dying, troubled, sad, and doubting persons, the number of such is so great in these calamitous times, as may render them useful to more than I desire. 3. And if my present grief may but excuse the publication, he that needeth them not may let them alone."[5] How successful Baxter was in fulfilling his didactic intentions cannot be estimated, but those intentions were to be echoed later in the work of Isaac Watts and Philip Doddridge, among others. It may be significant as well that Baxter's little book of poems was reprinted in the nineteenth century when the criterion of sincerity reached the zenith of its influence.[6]

Baxter's poems do indeed sound sincere, but at their very best they also sound like Herbert's poetry:

3. "To the Reader," *The Poetical Fragments* (1681; reprinted London, 1821), p. iv.
4. Ibid., p. iv.
5. Ibid., p. v.
6. Note the republication date of 1821 in note 3.

Still when he took me by the hand,
My father on me smiled:
Oft have I broken his command;
And yet he call'd me child.[7]

In a later age similarity to another poet would suggest a lack of
sincerity. But since Baxter finds in Herbert the voice of sincerity, he
seems to assume that poems that approximate that voice are sincere
as well. Though it is Herbert's simplicity which attracts Baxter, he
never achieves in his own poems Herbert's complexity and subtlety
of rhythm. Our final judgement of Baxter's poetry must be that it
prepared the way for much of the clumsy religious verse of the
eighteenth century, which in turn made way for the worst religious
sentiment of the nineteenth century. The unity of poetic and religious sincerity resulted all too often in bathos.

If we except Milton once again, English Puritans were better attuned to the sermon than to poetry. The sermon was of great importance to the Puritan divine. Prophesying represented immediate
contact with the people whom he was trying to wean away from the
regular Church of England sinecure holders, who read their sermons
from prepared texts, or even worse, from the Puritan point of view,
read the sermons of others. To the new breed of preacher spontaneity was important, since it seemed to prove that the message was
coming from the heart. These attitudes were lent impetus by the new
Ramist rhetoric, which emphasized the same simplicity.[8] Thus, like
any other convention, the ideal of sincerity began to develop its own
rhetorical theory.

The invention of the so-called plain style was the first step in the
movement toward the simple and straightforward style of Tillotson,
South, and indeed, Swift. The rationale behind this interest in simplicity and clarity was partly didactic and partly concerned with
sincerity as an independent value. Simplicity of language was to insure that all men, even those lowest on the social ladder, could

7. Baxter, *The Poetical Fragments*, p. 86.
8. For the ramifications of Ramist theory see Perry Miller, *The New England Mind:
The Seventeenth Century* (1939; reprinted Boston: Beacon Press, 1961), pp. 116–53,
and passim. Also Walter J. Ong, *Ramus: Method and the Decay of Dialogue; From
the Art of Discourse to the Art of Reason* (Cambridge: Harvard University Press, 1958).

apprehend the word of God, since after all, each man was the final authority on that word. But further there was the Puritan insistence that every preacher have experienced that which he taught, so that he could speak from the fullness of his heart and so be assured that he taught the word of God.[9]

Poetry and the sermon, important as they are in the development of sincerity, nonetheless take second place to the Puritan treatise on religion and especially the Puritan autobiography or personal apology.[10] Richard Baxter, who has the distinction of contributing to every one of these modes, devotes a substantial section to the delineation of sincerity in his famous treatise *The Saints' Everlasting Rest.* John Howe, a very active Puritan leader after the Restoration, who led an abortive pilgrimage to Holland and gave the sermon at the funeral of Baxter's wife, places sincerity in a central position among virtues: "Sincerity is a most God-like excellency; an imitation of his truth, as grounded in his all-sufficiency; which sets him above the necessity or possibility of any advantage by collusion or deceit; and corresponds to his omnisciency and heart-searching eye."[11] Howe's extremely high regard for sincerity as a religious value is not extraordinary, although few divines take the trouble to define it as explicitly as he does here.

Interest in sincerity seems to have been born of an increasing Puritan concern for self, arising from the important question asked more or less hysterically by every Calvinist, "Am I one of the elect?" But conversion alone was not necessarily a mark of election: it had to be a "sincere" conversion. And so the question became "Am I sincere?"

Confined to the realm of the spirit such a question could be expected to cause psychological difficulties for any human being. But for many Puritans whose enthusiasm was both social and religious, the strain was enormous and sometimes unendurable. When a

9. Miller, *The New England Mind: The Seventeenth Century*, p. 301.

10. The most authoritative work on Puritan autobiography and other biographical modes continues to be William Haller, *The Rise of Puritanism* (New York: Columbia University Press, 1938). A useful recent source of information is Paul Delany, *British Autobiography in the Seventeenth Century* (New York: Columbia University Press, 1969).

11. *The Whole Works* (London, 1822), 3, 231.

complex human being looking for a simple answer to that infernal question "Am I sincere?" began to realize that his motives were hopelessly complicated, the strain must have been extraordinary. Add to this the fact that there was no escape from this question in political or social affairs, and we go a long way toward explaining the intensity of Puritan enthusiasm.

In Puritan autobiography in particular we can see the relationship between concern for personal salvation and interest in social and political affairs. The spiritual torment of the Puritan mind turns to politics for release. But the subsequent violent proselytizing and revolutionary prescriptions only compound the difficulty.

The model for this religious-social-political awareness was Saint Paul, in so many ways the all-in-all to Puritans of the seventeenth century. Paul's life story, his sinfulness prior to his conversion, and his success in establishing the Church throughout the world, while achieving the heights of personal piety, provided a model or type of ideal behaviour. Paul extended personal piety and conversion to the social and political spheres.

The pattern of Paul's experience was shared in turn by countless Nonconformists in England and America. Roger Clap, for example, describes how he committed one of Paul's sins:

But on a time on the Lord's-Day, when I was standing by and seeing some Youths Play, they gave me those *Points* which they played for, to hold for them until their Game was out; and my Conscience not being quiet, God brought that saying of Saul, afterwards Paul, to my Mind, who did acknowledge that he was guilty of the Death of Stephen; "For he stood by, and kept the Garments of them that slew him": I then put down that which I had in keeping for them, and went away. . . .[12]

Thomas Goodwin comments on his conversion patterned on Paul's:

This that was suggested to me was not an ungrounded fancy, but the pure word of God, which is the ground of Faith and

12. *Memoirs of Captain Roger Clap* (1731) in *Collections of the Dorchester Antiquarian and Historical Society* (Boston, 1844), 1, 22–23. Clap wrote his memoirs circa 1680.

Hope. It was the Promise and Performance of God's forgiving of Paul the most heinous Sins, that ever any Convert committed who was saved; for he was the chiefest of Sinners, as himself confesses: And this Instance was directed unto me as the most pertinent to my case, that I could elsewhere have found in the Book of God.[13]

Since Paul was, by his own admission, "the chief of sinners," the very title of Bunyan's *Grace Abounding to the Chief of Sinners* suggests the direct influence of Paul's experience.

Because the autobiographies of Puritan leaders usually dealt with their sufferings at the hands of the establishment, Paul's sufferings in his efforts to convert the world were a handy paradigm. John Lilburne uses this paradigm to express his revolutionary faith: "nor should my many imprisonments be more a blemish unto me, then [*sic*] unto the Apostle Paul, who thought it no dishonour to remember those that somewhat despised him, that he had been in labours more abundant, in stripes above measure, in prisons more frequent, in deaths oft."[14] Henry Burton, who lost his ears to Bishop Laud's cruelty, evaluates his every trial and action by the touchstone provided by Paul's experiences.[15]

This enormous interest in Paul among Puritan divines makes their preoccupation with the problem of sincerity understandable. In the King James Version of the Bible the word "sincerity" and its cognates appear in Paul's writings as often as they do in the entire remainder of the Bible, Old and New Testaments.

Paul normally uses the word in its original sense of "uncorrupt": "And this I pray, that your love may abound yet more and more in knowledge and in all judgment; That ye may approve things that are excellent; that ye may be sincere and without offence till the day of Christ; . . ."[16] In his Epistle to Titus, Paul states that it becomes

13. Thomas Goodwin, Jr., "The Life of Dr. Thomas Goodwin" in *The Works of Thomas Goodwin, D.D.* (London, 1704), 5, xii.
14. "The Just Defence of John Lilburne" (1653) in *The Leveller Tracts, 1647–1653*, ed. William Haller and Godfrey Davies (New York: Columbia University Press, 1944), p. 453.
15. *A Narration of the Life of Mr. Henry Burton* . . . (London, 1643), pp. 34–37.
16. Philippians, 1:9–10.

sound doctrine for a young man to be "in all things shewing thyself a pattern of good works: in doctrine shewing uncorruptness, gravity, sincerity, . . ."[17] But Paul is himself a man of exemplary sincerity, in a more modern sense of the word, and seemed so to dissenting English churchmen. Isaac Watts, in his "Discourses on St. Paul's Divine Commission," characterized the great saint as "a wise, learned, sincere, honest man, . . ."[18] Watts stresses Paul's sincerity throughout both discourses devoted to him.

An important aspect of the Pauline Epistles is that they are addressed to a large audience or to one disciple on whom Paul relies for the performance of Christian action. This epistolary form was adopted by English Puritans, who fairly consistently addressed their apologies to "a very special friend" or to those more general brethren who would support them in their trials. The epistle format gives the author full scope to the personal expression of his grief and actions and at the same time permits him to strike a corresponding chord in the hearts of his fellow men. A sense of community is to be the outgrowth of inner purity and religious passion.

A consummate practitioner of the epistolary apology is John Lilburne, a Leveller, who composed his *Coppy of a Letter written by L.C.L. to one of his special friends* . . . during his imprisonment of 1638–40. It was published some years later, however, for a reason which William Haller makes clear: "It was obviously published in 1645 or 1646 in order that Lilburne in his quarrel of that date with Prynne might avail himself of popular sympathy for his sufferings of 1638–40."[19] This pamphlet, usually called Lilburne's "autobiography," was intended to attract kindred souls to the Leveller cause and to Lilburne's faction in particular. Like so many other Puritans, Lilburne had a vision of the religious commonwealth that he hoped to establish in England, and his pious meditations are meant to show his qualifications for such a task.

The full title of Henry Burton's "autobiography" shows once again the usual scope of Puritan apologies: *A Narration of the Life of Mr. Henry Burton. Wherein is set forth the various and remarkable*

---

17. Titus, 2:7.   18. *Works*, 2, 10.
19. Haller, *The Rise of Puritanism*, p. 436.

Passages thereof, his Sufferings, Supports, Comforts, and Deliverances. The purpose of this work was very much the same as Lilburne's. Burton looks for a sympathetic response in passages such as the following:

> In this interim, I heard of the good pleasure of God, in taking away my deare and only daughter. It was a little before supper that Mr *Lieutenant* began darkly to intimate the same unto me, untill I prayed him to deale plainly with me, which he then did: whereupon craving pardon, I immediately retired to my lodging, and there on my knees gave the Lord solemne thanks, that it had pleased him to translate my daughter, now his alone, into his Kingdome of glory, after he had fitted her to be a Virgin Spouse for her husband Jesus Christ. For a holy and sweet conditioned Maid she was ever from her childhood, being now growne marriageable, and now for ever married unto Jesus Christ.[20]

The confident joy with which Burton says he resigned his daughter to Christ is difficult for the modern mind to grasp. We may see in Burton either a fanatic or a Christian exemplar. But no matter how we judge him, one thing is clear: the physical world has become for him merely a typological pattern of the spiritual world, and it is in the latter that all reality resides. The daughter's death cannot be seen in terms of physical loss for which a certain lamentation is appropriate. Burton does not allow himself the expression of temporal loss. Since for him everything is accounted for in terms of a changeless spirituality, he turns immediately to the spiritual meaning of the temporal event, denying, in effect, its temporality.

Behind this seeming insensitivity to the real, we can see the direction in which the Puritan mind was journeying. Since the temporal world seems to offer the Puritan nothing but persecution and suffering, he turns toward his spiritual vision, finding in that the hope of permanence and truth absent elsewhere. The result of this idealism is that the mind is torn apart in an irreparable division of the spiritual and the temporal. Because his utopian hopes for society are dashed

---

20. Burton, *A Narration*, p. 23.

almost from the beginning in that he expects too much, the Puritan turns more fiercely than ever to the heavenly Eden of the spirit.

Yet even for Burton the point of total withdrawal from reality has not been reached. During the 1640s and, indeed, even later, there were high hopes that a perfect commonwealth might be achieved. But men like Burton and Lilburne were perhaps more harmful to such hopes than helpful. Their often blind, uncompromising zeal and self-righteousness led to divisions of unreconcilable proportions. Richard Baxter places the blame on those he considers extremist:

> And I must add this to the true Information of Posterity, That God did so wonderfully bless the Labours of his *unanimous faithful Ministers*, that had it not been for the Factions of the giddy and turbulent Sectaries on the other side (who pull'd down all Government, cried down the Ministers, and broke all into Confusion, and made the People at their wits end, not knowing what Religion to be of); together with some *laziness* and *selfishness* in many of the Ministry, I say, had it not been for these Impediments, *England* had been like in a quarter of an Age to have become a Land of Saints, and a Pattern of Holiness to all the World, and the unmatchable Paradise of the Earth. Never were such fair opportunities to sanctifie a Nation, lost and trodden under foot, as have been in this Land of late! Woe to them that were the Causes of it.[21]

Of course Baxter's hopes for an "unmatchable Paradise of the Earth" are no more realistic than those of the Levellers, but it is interesting to note that even after the paradise had been lost irreparably, the validity of the original hope was not called in question.

We may, with Baxter, suspect the motives of men such as Lilburne and Burton, but John Bunyan's sincerity seems beyond question. That impression may be due, in part, to the greatness of the writer, but perhaps even more important is his separation from the practical political affairs that seemed to hold promise for Lilburne and Burton. Bunyan's important works are post-Restoration,

---

21. *Reliquiae Baxterianae: Or Mr. Richard Baxter's Narrative of the Most Memorable Passages of his Life and Times*, ed. Matthew Sylvester (London, 1696), p. 97.

and their orientation is spiritual rather than political. Yet his movement toward the spiritual is accompanied by a sense of the Baptist
community to which he belonged. In *Grace Abounding* there is no
longer hope for the "unmatchable Paradise of the Earth." If a
Christian society is to be realized, based on Puritan principles, it
evidently must be congregational in nature, that is, limited to those
who would freely subscribe to such a way of life. The whole of
England, as had been seen during Cromwell's tenure, would not
submit to such visionary schemes. For this reason Bunyan probably
assumed, as Milton did, that his works would find a smaller audience
than Lilburne and Burton had hoped for. Therefore it is somewhat
ironic that Bunyan's works, especially *The Pilgrim's Progress*, have
enjoyed such enormous popularity.

Bunyan's superiority as a writer over most of his Puritan contemporaries would seem to stem from his mastery of the concrete.
Rather than obscure the temporal event by translating it into spiritual terms, Bunyan consistently makes his spiritual conceptions concrete by use of imagery from real experience. This can be illustrated
by the following short passage: "If any of those who were awakened
by my ministry did after that fall back, as sometimes too many did,
I can truly say their loss hath been more to me than if one of my own
children, begotten of my body, had been going to its grave; . . ."[22]
Though in its explicit preference for the spiritual over the physical
this is similar to Burton's reaction to his daughter's death, the supposed physical death is the one that evokes the sympathy of Bunyan's audience, and the vividness of that physical reality is what
communicates force to the spiritual claim.

Indeed, Bunyan often brings us fully into the realm of physical
reality. His love for his poor blind child and his portrayal of his wife
pleading before the magistrate are the very stuff of life. Though
there is a tacit movement toward the spiritual, Bunyan achieves, to
some degree, the ability to see physical things as temporally and
spiritually important at the same time. He can hold in his mind two
diverse and seemingly contradictory views of the same thing without losing his ability to function intellectually and artistically. His

22. *Grace Abounding to the Chief of Sinners* (London: Everyman's Library, 1928),
p. 87.

allegorical technique, at its best, retains the concrete imagery of good Elizabethan and Jacobean verse and of the King James Version of the Bible. Note once again how Bunyan moves from an obscure emotion to the reality of physical terror: "In prayer, also, I have been greatly troubled at this time; sometimes I have thought I should see the devil, nay, thought I have felt him, behind me, pull my clothes."[23]

But despite this natural feeling for the concrete which insures his artistic success, the unmistakable movement of Bunyan's mind is toward abstract spiritual values. The failure of the commonwealth and his own earthly sufferings limited his quest for society to his family and religious community.

Perhaps the most extreme form of religious idealism is to be found in the personal writings of the Quaker, George Fox. Fox begins his *Journal* with a public utterance in the best tradition of Puritan controversial literature. He writes his book "that all may know the dealings of the Lord with me, and the various exercises, trials, and troubles through which He led me, in order to prepare and fit me for the work unto which He had appointed me. . . ."[24]

This autobiography ("journal" is in this case a misnomer) begins as a call to the brethren to unite, but it soon becomes clear that the holy commonwealth is to be found in each individual. Quaker society will be merely a collection of individuals, each guided by his own inner light. In effect, every man becomes equivalent to Jesus Christ himself.

The tendency to translate physical experience into spiritual experience is readily apparent in Fox's autobiography. His constant sufferings, the many attempts on his life, all achieve meaning at the spiritual level and only at the spiritual level. Once again we find the tendency to treat physical existence as if it were a type in scripture and deny not only its apparent physical meaning but its very reality as well: "The judge said . . . 'All the world cannot convince you.' 'Is it likely,' I said, 'the world should convince? The whole world lies

23. Ibid., p. 35.
24. *Journal*, ed. John L. Nickalls (Cambridge: Cambridge University Press, 1952), p. 1.

in wickedness.' "²⁵ Further disputation with George Fox after such an assertion would be useless. Nothing in the world can convince him that his actions are inappropriate. Fox has denied the reality of sensory experience, and in so doing, the relationship of the world to the spirit. In the *Journal* of George Fox, Puritan autobiography has some of its greatest moments and Fox's personal religious sincerity cannot be denied. But in carrying idealism to its highest point, he loses the capacity to deal with the everyday world in a vital and meaningful way. Since each man must follow his own inner light, communication between men of diverse religious beliefs is no longer possible.

This was not, of course, George Fox's intention. He, like the other autobiographers, sought out a community of men and women who might share the same hopes and fears with himself. To attract such a society, the author had to rely most heavily on a quality prized most by modern politicians, that is, sincerity. Puritan auto-biographers almost never indulge in irony or other forms of dis-simulation, and they encourage their disciples to imitate them in this. The hope is to establish a society based on mutual trust and common ideals. Unfortunately sincerity is as strangely protean as the human personality with which it is so intimately connected. As new "truth" appears, the allegiance of sincerity changes. Thus a disciple's sincerity may lead him to reject his teacher's principles and set out in another direction. He, in turn, is subject to the same treatment by his followers. In this way the Puritan sects continued to divide into wholly disunited and ineffective splinter groups, which found com-munication with one another impossible. But despite the inability of most Puritans to understand the nature of sincerity and its ultimate consequences, its contribution to the formation of their dwindling societies was of significance in the next century.

John Milton shared many of the Puritan attitudes described in this chapter and succeeded in translating them into poetry. Just as Richard Baxter longed for his "unmatchable Paradise of the Earth," Milton needed to justify man's loss of Eden and of his second para-dise, the Commonwealth.

25. Ibid., p. 484.

University-educated Puritans such as Burton and Baxter were well versed in the classics, but they were equally reluctant to give their classical learning Christian employment. Most dissenters shared the moralistic viewpoint of John Norris of Bemerton: "For I appeal to the common sense and experience of mankind, whether it be advisable to entertain the gay catching fancies of boys with the amorous scenes of the poets. Whether it be convenient or safe to season their green imaginations with such impure and obscene images as are there set forth to the life: or is not this rather the direct way to corrupt them, to sow in their tender minds the seeds of impurity, and to lay a standing foundation for debauchery?"[26] Since dissenters saw themselves chiefly as teachers and moralists, their regard for the safety of the young would extend to all the members of their flock. It was the attitudes of Norris, not of Milton, which were communicated to those who continued the Puritan tradition in literature.

Though it would be absurd to hold that Milton is untouched by strict Puritan moralism, his imagination is too close to the earlier English Renaissance to be terrified by classical sensuality. And it is this combination of classical and Hebraic-Christian motifs that left a legacy too rich and various for all but his greatest successors to emulate.

Even the greatest of his professed imitators tend to emphasize one of these traditions and avoid the other. James Thomson, for example, is primarily a classicist, and his Christian sympathies are only incidental to his essential deism. William Blake, on the other hand, despises the classics and asserts a scriptural style, although Homeric and Virgilian influence does enter his work.

Paradise Lost, as might be expected, is the work by Milton that contributes most directly to the development of the idea of sincerity. Indeed, it is probably the single most influential work. Milton's other works, poems and prose, seem to have had a negligible effect.

26. *Reflections Upon the Conduct of Human Life* (1691), p. 171. A useful study of the relationship between English Puritans and literature is Lawrence A. Sasek, *The Literary Temper of the English Puritans* (Baton Rouge: Louisiana State University Press, 1961). Covering the sixteenth and earlier seventeenth century is Russell Fraser, *The War Against Poetry* (Princeton: Princeton University Press, 1970).

Milton approaches sincerity more from its opposite, guile, than as a positive isolated virtue. The centrality of Satan in *Paradise Lost* makes guile a chief focus and the object of close psychological examination. Thus the narrator asks and answers his own question concerning the fall of our first parents:

> Who first seduc'd them to that foul revolt?
> Th' infernal Serpent; hee it was, whose guile
> Stirr'd up with Envy and Revenge, deceiv'd
> The Mother of Mankind; . . .
>
> (1, 33–36)[27]

Almost immediately in book 1, we see the essential split in Satan's personality. We are fully aware that he is affecting an attitude at odds with his true inner state:

> So spake th' Apostate Angel, though in pain,
> Vaunting aloud, but rackt with deep despair: . . .
>
> (1, 125–26)

The deceit implicit in this state is promptly translated into national policy by the conclave in Pandemonium. But of course even before the consultation begins, Satan has decided upon the course of action for all:

> our better part remains
> To work in close design, by fraud or guile
> What force effected not: . . .
>
> (1, 645–47)

The magnitude of guile and hypocrisy is illustrated in book 3 when Satan is able to deceive even the archangel Uriel:

> So spake the false dissembler unperceiv'd;
> For neither Man nor Angel can discern
> Hypocrisy, the only evil that walks
> Invisible, except to God alone,
> By his permissive will, through Heav'n and Earth:

---

27. Milton, *Paradise Lost*. References are included in my text.

And oft though wisdom wake, suspicion sleeps
At wisdom's Gate, and to simplicity
Resigns her charge, while goodness thinks no ill
Where no ill seems: . . .

                              (3, 681–89)

Thus the difference between the fallen and the unfallen is described
in terms of guile. But, as we shall see, final happiness in the fallen
world is the result of a properly balanced union of innocence and
experience. The final vision of *Paradise Lost* may be described in
part by the words of Jesus sending forth his disciples: "Behold, I
send you forth as sheep in the midst of wolves: be ye therefore wise
as serpents, and harmless as doves."[28]
Milton does not wait until the fall of Adam and Eve to give the
detailed analysis of Satan's guile specific moral application. He does
so earlier in the Paradise of Fools episode in book 3. The Paradise
of Fools is juxtaposed with Eden and the real Paradise of Heaven itself. Just as Heaven permits no deceit and Eden is transformed by
deceit, the Paradise of Fools is founded on deceit and nourished by
it. The inhabitants of this last state include every shade of the deceived:

                    he who to be deem'd
A God, leap'd fondly into *Ætna* flames,
Empedocles, and hee who to enjoy
Plato's Elysium, leap'd into the Sea,
Cleombrotus, and many more too long,
Embryos, and Idiots, Eremites and Friars
White, Black and Grey, with all thir trumpery.
Here Pilgrims roam, that stray'd so far to seek
In *Golgotha* him dead, who lives in Heav'n; . . .

                              (3, 469–77)

In this passage we have not only the strong anti-Catholic feeling
usual in Milton and in most English poets of sincerity, but also, in
the last two lines cited, the lesson of the entire poem. I take the lines
"Here Pilgrims roam, that stray'd so far to seek / In *Golgotha* him

---

28. Matthew, 10:16.

dead, who lives in Heav'n" to mean that all attempts to experience the life of the spirit to the full on earth are doomed to failure. It follows then that man's dismissal from Eden is proper and that the dream of paradise on earth should be given uncertain reality on the windy outside of Milton's universe.

Again Milton raises the objection that Catholic religious vocation is a form of self-deception:

> And they who to be sure of Paradise
> Dying put on the weeds of *Dominic*,
> Or in *Franciscan* think to pass disguis'd; . . .

> (3, 478–80)

Here Milton may have had in mind the twenty-seventh canto of the *Inferno*, in which Guido da Montefeltro, the great deceiver, after a bad earlier life, becomes a friar to save his soul:

> Io fui uom d'arme, e poi fui cordigliero,
>   credendomi, sí cinto, fare ammenda;
>   e certo il creder mio venía intero,
> se non fosse il gran prete, a cui mal prenda!,
>   che mi rimise nelle prime colpe;
>   e come e quare, voglio che m'intenda.

> (67–72)[29]

I was a man of arms, and then a corded friar, thinking, so girt, to make amends; and indeed my thought had come true but for the Great Priest—may ill befall him!—who put me back in the old sins, and how and wherefore I would have thee hear from me.[30]

The point in Dante, as well as in Milton, is that taking the robes of the friar is not sufficient and that blaming another for one's own sins merely compounds the guilt. But even more, Guido, who by his own admission plays the role of the fox (l'opere mie / non furon leonine, ma di volpe [74–75]), is deceived by the false absolution of Pope

---

29. *La Divina Commedia*. Line references are in my text.

30. Translation by John D. Sinclair, *Dante's Inferno* (New York: Oxford University Press, 1961), pp. 337–39.

Boniface. The deception of Guido and the Pope is great, however, for at Guido's death even Saint Francis is deceived into thinking he is worthy of salvation. But the devil who comes for him is a better judge of the real situation:

"ch'assolver non si può chi non si pente,
    né pentére e volere insieme puossi
    per la contradizion che nol consente."

(118–20)

For he cannot be absolved who repents not, nor can there be repenting and willing at once, for the contradiction does not permit it.[31]

We may see from this that Dante's understanding of sincerity is identified with the traditional religious view that one's outward actions should correspond to the state of one's soul. To wear the garments of piety and be nonetheless a willing sinner is the very height of hypocrisy.

Milton takes Dante's conception a step further. He identifies the religious garb with hypocrisy. If the naked Adam and Eve freely and openly praying to God, without need of the *Book of Common Prayer* or the elaborate vestments of piety, is an ideal of behaviour, then the use of printed texts or religious garb is to be condemned.[32] Indeed we can see from this just why sincerity became important to Puritan thinkers. Its discovery meant that a positive ideal, with the power to banish effectively the arch-enemy deceit as personified in Satan himself, had been found. But since most Puritans held the Catholic Church to be the agent of Satan on earth and the Pope a veritable anti-Christ, it was convenient to characterize that Church as deceitful and to combat it with a free and open soul.

Another major characteristic of those who follow in the line of Milton is their claimed spontaneity of composition. Such an ideal reflects confidence in the immediate human response and has its

31. Ibid., p. 341.
32. See book 4, 740, in which clothes are described as "These troublesome disguises which wee wear." In book 5, 144 *ff.*, Adam and Eve praise God.

source in the classical notion of the poet as a man possessed by a god
or at least receiving inspiration from on high. This privilege Milton
claims for himself, of course, especially as he turns to the challenging
task of relating the fall of man:

If answerable style I can obtain
Of my Celestial Patroness, who deigns
Her nightly visitation unimplor'd,
And dictates to me slumb'ring, or inspires
Easy my unpremeditated Verse: . . .

(9, 20–24)

The importance to Milton of such a psychological state is given full
emphasis when "unpremeditated" is echoed in a passage immediately
following the personal statement. Satan is described as "now
improv'd / In meditated fraud and malice, bent / On man's destruction" (9, 54–56). Succeeding this is a series of images stressing
Satan's deceitful actions. Into Paradise he "by stealth / Found
unsuspected way" (69) and "found / The Serpent subtlest Beast of
all the Field" (85–86), whom he "chose / Fit Vessel, fittest Imp of
fraud" (88–89). If Milton compares his own "unpremeditated"
poetic skills with Satan's "meditated fraud," he also suggests a comparison with Adam's and Eve's praise for "Thir Maker, in fit strains
pronounc't or sung / Unmeditated" (5, 148–49).

To begin to do justice to Milton, it would be necessary to examine
the development of his poetic, moral, and political ideas from their
beginnings to their culmination in his three long poems. That task,
however, is not within the scope of this essay.

In our brief look at *Paradise Lost*, we have determined only that
Milton shares many of the views which I attributed, a priori, to
what I have called sincere poets. Most of all, however, Milton
shares the Puritan confidence in sincerity and in man's capacity for
good. It is reasonable, then, that after his long and fruitless political
struggle to make the Commonwealth a viable institution by which
Paradise on earth might be achieved, a disillusioned Milton should
conclude, as his poetic successors will also conclude, that man should
"not be loath / To leave this Paradise, but shalt possess / A paradise
within thee, happier far" (12, 585–87).

Thus *Paradise Lost* traces the apparent loss of an ideal state only to assert that such a state, rightly understood, is not political, but moral and personal. This, as we shall see, is a paradigm for succeeding poets, who increasingly turn toward the issues of personal morality as they turn away from social and political morality. They are seekers after paradise; but paradise, as Milton discovered, is to be found within.

Sincerity goes farther than Capacity.

William Penn

3

Dissent and Latitude to 1748

ISAAC WATTS

Isaac Watts was a spiritual heir of the Puritan movement. He was born in 1674 and so grew to manhood long after Puritan power in the political and social arenas had begun to wane. His refusal to vary from his family's dissenting principles cost him the opportunity for a university education, but, like most other dissenters of his time, he existed comfortably in Anglican England, as Henry Burton and Lilburne could not have done.

Watts was in the most learned of Puritan traditions. This learning he combined with an intense patriotism, which proved that he was willing to struggle for his rights within the framework of existing society. Just how far Watts was able to unite Puritan ideals with a new and strong loyalty to the crown can be seen in the following passage from a sermon that he preached to the Societies for Reformation of Manners, in 1707:

> Blessed be God, we have a Moses in the midst of us on the top of the hill, a queen of a manly soul upon the throne of our British Israel: She has by her royal proclamations given order to fight with Amalek, to oppose and suppress the armies of iniquity: She still holds up the rod of command; and it may be well called the rod of God, not only because all authority is derived from God as the original source of government; but because here it is held up in his quarrel too. It shall be called a rod of faith and of power, for it has wrought wonders at a distance: This the fields of Blenheim witness, and the plains of Ramillies; wonders of rescue for the German empire, and wonders of liberty for mankind. (*Works*, 2, 755)

Here the vestiges of typological interpretation retain only a rhetorical force. To call Anne "Moses" and the enemy "Amalek" is merely a convenient way of drawing battle lines. But this subdued Puritan enthusiasm has a new rationale in Whiggish liberty. The old cry of religious freedom for dissenters now has a universal application. Indeed, the increasingly secular movement of post-Restoration Puritan thought is evinced by the fact that Watts's concerns for the reformation of manners are practically identical with those to which Steele was to dedicate the *Tatler* less than two years later. In supporting moral reform, Steele comes close to stating the sincere ideal: "The general purpose of this paper, is to expose the false arts of life, to pull off the disguises of cunning vanity, and affectation, and recommend a general simplicity in our dress, our discourse, and our behaviour."[1] Watts centred this reformation of society in religion, but much of the old Puritan rigour was gone, and a general and healthful simplicity was emphasized.

The demise of such conservative myths as the divine right of kings and innate ideas had led to a questioning of scriptural authority.[2] It was not so much that large numbers of persons followed Spinoza and Toland in direct attacks on scripture, but rather that thinkers began to regard the scriptural texts as means to ends instead of ends in themselves. The moral benefits conferred by scripture became for many a more serious question than its literal truth. With the mysterious complexities of typological interpretation clarified out of existence, it became possible to tamper with scripture in order to make it more useful for moral purposes, and Watts accepted this opportunity.

One of Watts's most important projects was the rewriting of the Psalms in English verse for use in churches. Whereas earlier Puritans had laid great stress on preserving the Psalms in a form as close as possible to their Hebrew meaning, Watts based his translations (or, more properly, imitations) on very different principles. Most of

---

1. *The Tatler*, ed. George A. Aitken (London, 1898), 1, 8.
2. See my "Dryden's Debasement of Scripture in *Absalom and Achitophel*," *Studies in English Literature, 1500–1900*, 9 (1969): 395–413. An excellent study of typology in seventeenth-century poetry is Paul J. Korshin, "The Evolution of Neoclassic Poetics," *Eighteenth-Century Studies*, 2 (1968): 102–37.

all he objected to those elements which tended to distract sincere Christians from their professions of faith:

> Experience itself has often shewn, that it interrupts the holy melody, and spoils the devotion of many a sincere good man or woman, when, in the midst of the song, some speeches of *David* have been almost imposed upon their tongues, where he relates his own troubles, his banishment, or peculiar deliverances; where he speaks like a *jewish* prince, a musician, or a prophet; or where the sense is so obscure that it cannot be understood without a learned commentator. (*Works*, 4, xv)

The "Jewishness" of the Psalms was particularly objectionable to Watts, and so he replaced Hebrew allusions with evangelical ones. His central concern is to remove from scripture everything that he regards as particular and idiosyncratic, and so to achieve a kind of universal application. But his sense of universality is subordinated to the utilitarian end of making scripture readily available to those who are simple, evangelical, and English.[3]

To further this emphasis Watts wrote spiritual songs for ordinary persons and hymns that exemplified the ideal of simplicity. In his preface to *Hymns and Spiritual Songs*, he describes his own difficulties of composition:

> I confess myself to have been too often tempted away from the more spiritual designs I proposed, by some gay and flowery expressions that gratified the fancy; the bright images too often prevailed above the fire of divine affection; and the light exceeded the heat: yet, I hope, in many of them the reader will find, that devotion dictated the song, and the head and hand were nothing but interpreters and secretaries to the heart: . . .
> (*Works*, 4, 150)

Here sincerity in composition is an explicit ideal. Watts hopes both that the reader will find evidence of sincerity in the poems and

---

3. For a good account of eighteenth-century translations of the Psalms see Moira Dearnley, *The Poetry of Christopher Smart* (London: Routledge & Kegan Paul, 1969), pp. 226–45.

that he will, in turn, be encouraged to a similarly devout response to spiritual subjects.

In his usual pedagogical role, Watts speaks to the children of God in their own language, confident that such language comes from the sincere heart. It is not surprising, then, that his poetic compositions for children should differ little from those for adults. Simplicity, sincerity, piety, and hard work are stressed in his *Divine Songs for Children*, a volume ridiculed by Dickens but singled out for praise by both Philip Doddridge and Samuel Johnson, which sought to instil in the very young a serious sense of Christian responsibility. More important to this study, however, is Watts's *Horae Lyricae*, his book of poems written for the sophisticated reader.

The preface to the *Horae Lyricae*, written in 1709, is of importance in the history of English poetry. It marks a significant attempt to return poetry to the service of religion. Watts states the problem in his opening paragraph:

> It has been a long complaint of the virtuous and refined world, that poesy, whose original is divine, should be enslaved to vice and profaneness; that an art, inspired from heaven should have so far lost its memory of its birth place, as to be engaged in the interests of hell. How unhappily is it perverted from its most glorious design! How basely has it been driven away from its proper station in the temple of God, and abused to much dishonour! The iniquity of men has constrained it to serve their vilest purposes, while the sons of piety mourn the sacrilege and the shame. (*Works*, 4, 317)

Since poetry has been debased in ungodly usage, Watts observes, a subtle change in attitudes toward poetry has followed:

> This profanation and debasement of so divine an art has tempted some weaker Christians to imagine that poetry and vice are naturally akin; or, at least, that verse is fit only to recommend trifles, and entertain our looser hours, but it is too light and trivial a method to treat any thing that is serious and sacred. (*Works*, 4, 318)

Watts counters this notion with the insistence that the Bible, after all, is poetry:

'Tis strange that persons that have the Bible in their hands
should be led away by thoughtless prejudices to so wild and
rash an opinion. Let me entreat them not to indulge this sour,
this censorious humour too far, lest the sacred writers fall
under the lash of their unlimited and unguarded reproaches.
(*Works*, 4, 318)

Watts further insists upon the use of poetry in intensifying religious
devotion:

If shorter sonnets were composed on sublime subjects, such as
the Psalms of David and the holy transports interspersed in the
other sacred writings, or such as the moral Odes of Horace and
the ancient lyrics, I persuade myself that the Christian preacher
would find abundant aid from the poet, in his design to diffuse
virtue and allure souls to God. (*Works*, 4, 323)

Such ideas were not new with Watts: he relied on Blackmore and
Dennis for part of his theory and on John Norris of Bemerton for
part of his practice. But Watts was the first to combine theory and
practice in the production of some fairly good poems.

Thus the notion of sincerity in religion was brought over into the
realm of poetry. To be sure, the poetry is religious, and Watts
would have argued against any sharp distinction between poetry
and religion, as we have seen. But this denial of a distinction is important. Where poetry is divorced from serious matters, such as
religion and philosophy, it will tend to be affected, trivial, pretty,
and little more. It is only when poetry is allowed to have serious
concerns that sincerity is demanded of the poet and the poem. A poet
who professes a serious moral purpose must believe what he communicates as truth. It is then that the problem of correlating
one's true sentiments with the meaning of the finished poem
arises.

Watts believed that he had attained this correlation in at least one
group of his poems:

The "Poems sacred to Virtue, &c." were formed when the
frame and humour of my soul was just suited to the subject of
my verse. The image of my heart is painted in them, and if they

meet with a reader whose soul is akin to mine, perhaps they may agreeably entertain him. (*Works*, 4, 324)

Here Watts unites sincerity with the Puritan's desire for an audience. The audience will consist of kindred souls and the bond of that relationship will be mutual trust and confidence. In other words, the poet's sincerity will entitle him to the regard of others.

A part of this sincere attitude, necessary both in poetry and social affairs, is seriousness. Satiric irony, trope in the Ramist system, is eschewed:

> When I have felt a slight inclination to satire or burlesk, I thought it proper to suppress it. The grinning and the growling Muse are not hard to be obtained; but I would disdain their assistance, where a manly invitation to virtue, and a friendly smile, may be successfully employed. Could I persuade any man by a kinder method, I should never think it proper to scold or laugh at him. (*Works*, 4, 325)

The desire for audience is related to a concern for the establishment of a good society—a desire that was not new with the Puritans, but was exemplified by them, and which Watts inherited from them. This deep concern for the betterment of society which we noted in his sermon "To Encourage the Reformation of Manners" becomes the subject of poetry in the *Horae Lyricae*:

> Perhaps there are some morose readers that stand ready to condemn every line that is written upon the theme of love; but have we not the cares and the felicities of that sort of social life represented to us in the sacred writings? (*Works*, 4, 325)

Watts believes that mutual trust and love will make a better society possible. The external society is not, however, his central concern; the salvation of one's soul is most important. But the salvation of souls is easier in an uncorrupt society congenial to such an end.

Although Watts professes an artless sincerity in what he writes, his lyrics preserve something of the finished simplicity of the seventeenth century. Milton was Watts's great model, but he learned much from Cowley, whom he imitated assiduously. It was Milton's religious fervour, originality, and comprehensiveness of vision, more than his style, which excited Watts's imagination. In the ode "The Adventurous Muse," Milton receives treatment tantamount to apotheosis:

> Immortal bard! Thus thy own Raphael sings,
>   And knows no rule but native fire:
> All heaven sits silent, while to his sovereign strings
>   He talks unutterable things;
> With graces infinite, his untaught fingers rove
>   Across the golden lyre;
> From every note devotion springs,
> Rapture, and harmony, and love,
>   O'erspread the listening choir.

(Works, 4, 399)

If this is sincere praise, we can still recognize that it is cast in a highly formal and rhetorical style of poetry. Indeed this is characteristic of Watts in general. The hymns and divine songs for children are presented in language more appropriate to the vulgar and to children, respectively, but even their simplicity is couched in a polished and studied rhetoric characteristic of the seventeenth century but suggesting later developments in the eighteenth. His work in the funeral elegy is particularly interesting in this regard.

In the short prefatory letter to his ambitious "Funeral Poem on the Death of Thomas Gunston, Esq.," Watts has some remarkable things to say about his own relation to the composition of the poem:

> Had I been a common mourner at the funeral of the dear gentleman deceased, I should have laboured after more of art in the following composition, to supply the defect of nature, and to feign a sorrow; but the uncommon condescension of his friendship to me, the inward esteem I pay his memory, and the vast and tender sense I have of the loss, make all the methods of art needless, whilst natural grief supplies more than all. . . . And I transcribe nature without rule, and represent friendship in a mourning dress, abandoned to deepest sorrow, and with a negligence becoming woe unfeigned.
> Had I designed a complete elegy . . . and intended it for

public view, I should have followed the usual forms of poetry,
so far at least as to spend some pages in the character and
praises of the deceased, and thence have taken occasion to call
mankind to complain aloud of the universal and unspeakable
loss. But I wrote merely for myself as a friend of the dead, and
to ease my full soul by breathing out my own complaints. I
knew his character and virtues so well, that there was no need
to mention them while I talked only with myself; for the
image of them was ever present with me, which kept the pain
at the heart intense and lively, and my tears flowing with my
verse. (*Works*, 4, 437)

This is one of the clearest statements of a sincere intention in the
early eighteenth century. Of course such a statement is not at odds
with classical precedent. Rather it is the emphasis that is important.
We may, if we choose, regard Watts's remarks as merely conventional; but even if we do, we cannot deny that the problem of sincerity was very real to him and required a solution.

The poem itself, despite the alternating and even sporadic use of
different verse forms (blank verse, couplets, alternating rhymes, and
occasional alexandrines), is classical and Miltonic and reveals a
knowledge and command of contemporary poetic diction:

Of blasted hopes, and of short withering joys,
Sing, heav'nly muse. Try thine ethereal voice
In funeral numbers and a doleful song;
Gunston the just, the generous and the young,
Gunston the friend is dead. O empty name
Of earthly bliss! 'tis all an airy dream,
All a vain thought! Our soaring fancies rise
On treacherous wings! and hopes that touch the skies
Drag but a longer ruin thro' the downward air,
And plunge the falling joy still deeper in despair.
(*Works*, 4, 438)

In an elegiac ode written about twenty years later on the death of
his patron and friend Sir Thomas Abney, Watts again indulged
himself in what he considered grief-inspired, spontaneous verse.
Here are some of his prefatory remarks:

There are some occurrences that can of themselves rouse the muse from the deepest sleep. Poesy is not always under the command of the will. As there have been occasions heretofore when I have wished to write, but the imagination has refused to attend the wish; so there are seasons when verse comes almost without a call, and the will might resist in vain. A few such seasons have I met with in the course of my life, and some of them have found me even in the chambers of death. When I have spent days in the midst of mourning, and the whole soul hath been turned to sorrow, the harp hath sounded of its own accord, and awakened all the doleful strings. Such was the hour when your dear and honoured brother [preface addressed to Abney's wife, the sister of Gunston] Mr. Thomas Gunston departed this life; and such is the present providence. Uncommon worth forsaking our world, strikes all the powers of nature with sentiments of honour and grief, and the hand and the heart consent to raise a monument of love and sorrow.

Accept then, honoured madam, these lines of elegy, as a sincere pledge of the greatest veneration which my heart pays to the memory of Sir Thomas Abney. (*Works*, 4, 545–46)

There are several possible reasons behind these extraordinary professions of sincerity. First, Watts may be merely following the Horatian convention, "si vis me flere, dolendum est / primum ipsi tibi." Second, he may be deceived by his own enthusiasm into believing that these professions are authentic. Third, he may be indulging himself in irony similar to Pope's "I lisp'd in Numbers, for the Numbers came." And, fourth, he may indeed be assessing his experience with exactitude.

The third possibility can probably be ruled out by a consideration of Watts's tone. Nowhere in his work do we find evidence for such a pervasive and complicated irony, and indeed, if we are to substantiate irony here, we should have to believe that nearly everything he wrote is ironic.

The first possibility is verified by the fact that Watts is following conventions established in the works of many of the greatest poets and given current validity by Milton himself. But the use of a convention is not to the seventeenth and eighteenth centuries ipso facto proof of disingenuousness. Indeed it was an assumption of Aristotelian rhetoric and echoed by Milton in his "An Apology for Smectymnuus" that only a good man could be truly eloquent.[4] A particularly striking figure of personification might argue for a passionate sincerity in its composition. Most modern commentators on sincerity find it in just such intensity. Professor Spacks, writing on Pope, comments, "The sincerity of the *Epistle to Dr. Arbuthnot* is sincerity of purpose, attested by passionate conviction of utterance. It is the sincerity of the moral imagination at work."[5] To use a convention is often to bring the force of an entire tradition to a single utterance. Surely such intensity can be sincerely felt.

But the question remains whether Watts was self-deceived or correct in attributing sincerity to himself and attaching literary merit to that state. The answer may lie in the developing conception of sincerity.

Shakespeare was probably content to regard his plays as the product of a feigning art. Nowhere in his greatest work does Shakespeare affect a sincere intention, although profundity is everywhere. In the inimitable art of Shakespeare nothing is promised and everything is performed. But in the work of most of his contemporaries only an indifferent and anonymous achievement remains.

For Milton and his successors the case is different. Milton sought long and self-consciously for a subject before *Paradise Lost* took substantial shape. Even as the poem took form, it justified itself as much by significant intention as by significant achievement. Even the state of mind of the author, as revealed consciously in the poem, served as proof that the poem deserved to be. But the evidence of the greatness of *Paradise Lost* is that it needs no such personal justification.

In the work of lesser poets like Watts, the intention and the poet's state of excitement are all too often the poem's chief justification. Wordsworth's claim for his *Lyrical Ballads* is relevant to much of Watts's poetry: "the feeling therein developed gives importance to

4. John Milton, *Prose Writings* (London: Everyman's Library, 1958), p. 57.
5. Patricia Meyer Spacks, "In Search of Sincerity," *College English*, 29 (1967–68): 598.

the action and situation, and not the action and situation to the feeling."[6]

It seems reasonable that we should regard sincerity as at least an adjunct to Watts's art. The subject of the preface cited above and of the ambitious elegy which followed, Sir Thomas Abney, was Watts's close friend and protector. The Abney family was in effect the only family Watts had during his adult life, and when he died in 1748, he had lived with them for thirty-six years. Watts's sobriety and goodness are attested to by so many reliable witnesses that it is difficult to believe that he might have regarded convention as a sufficient excuse to express insincere sentiments. But even more important, if we are to find much value in the poetry of Watts, we shall have to find it in the feeling, which gives importance to the action and situation. This feeling comes from the sense of self which the poet reveals in his poems and is not created subjectively by the reader. In Milton's *Paradise Lost* or Blake's *Milton* our sense of the poet in the poem is so crucial that without it the poems could hardly be the same. In the poetry of Isaac Watts, on a much diminished scale, the same is true.

Watts, however, does belong to two poetic worlds: he distinguishes between his moments of spontaneity in verse and his usual process of composition. For him spontaneity indicates that his poetry is sincere.

Spontaneity is a difficult concept for even the poets who claim to experience it. Watts describes it in the imagery of a musical instrument: "the harp hath sounded of its own accord, and awakened all the doleful strings" (of elegy). We might agree that spontaneity suggests a flow of language beyond the normal powers of a given poet. The implication, then, is that the source of language is something other than the poet's conscious mind. Watts would probably agree with David Perkins's assertion, "If a writer can catch experience as it is before he reflects upon it, and his feelings in the same instant of time, he is touching on the purest source of whatever knowledge and understanding he can hope to have."[7]

6. *Literary Criticism of William Wordsworth*, ed. Paul M. Zall (Lincoln: University of Nebraska Press, 1966), p. 43.
7. *Wordsworth and the Poetry of Sincerity*, p. 23.

The question as to whether Watts was deceived in his beliefs about sincerity and spontaneity is difficult to answer. Though my own rationalist leanings tempt me to claim that he was, such an accusatory pronouncement would be out of order here. The primary task is to understand, and in the case of authors observing the sincere ideal, that must be done on their own terms. To deny the sincerity of these authors is to deny the rationale and integrity of their art. That is not an action to be taken lightly.

BENJAMIN HOADLY

Since dissenters continued to remain outside the main literary and political circles in the early eighteenth century, sincerity, with all its implications, was only beginning to have an impact on the reading public. The latitudinarian theology of John Tillotson introduced some principles of the sincere ideal into the English Church, and gradually, certain Puritan attitudes as well became institutionalized within that Church to bring about the full compromise in religion marked in politics by the revolution of 1688. Moderation and compromise were to be the order of the day. Strict nonjurors and liberal extremists alike were disapproved of by the majority of Englishmen. "Enthusiasm" retained its strictly pejorative connotation.

One Churchman, however, who would not compromise his liberal principles was Benjamin Hoadly, successively bishop of Bangor, Hereford, Salisbury, and Winchester. In his capacity as bishop of Winchester, a position he held for about twenty-five years, he exerted enormous influence, particularly because he maintained the strong support of George II. The liberality of his religious convictions went beyond that of most dissenters, a fact which made him attractive to many deists, whose approbation he found something of an embarrassment.

The Hoadly family was for two generations rather remarkable. Benjamin's brother, John, while archbishop of Dublin, incurred for a brief time the wrath of Swift, and Benjamin's two notable sons, John and Benjamin, were professional writers and dramatists. Benjamin edited the complete works of his father in 1773.

Hoadly's influence on the literature of the eighteenth century is difficult to estimate since he was not himself specifically literary. However, he seems to have patronized poets and other literary figures rather consistently. Shaftesbury, for example, regarded Hoadly as a kindred spirit, for he mentions him approvingly in a letter denouncing Atterbury and other nonjurors.[8] Mark Akenside, another author of deist leanings, praises Hoadly as a defender of civil and religious liberty in an ode addressed to him.[9] The contributions of Shaftesbury and Akenside to the development of the sincere ideal were undoubtedly influenced by Hoadly's doctrine of sincerity in religion. This revolutionary doctrine, coming as it did from within the established Church, heartened deists and others of the dispossessed.

Although earlier works suggested the direction that his thought was taking, the first important statement of Hoadly's doctrine of sincerity was in the tract "A Preservative against the Principles and Practices of the Non-jurors," written in opposition to a posthumous work by the nonjuror George Hickes. Hoadly's work, published in 1716, denied, in vigorous terms, the right of James II to the throne of England. Arguing that it is a king's duty to preserve and assist his subjects, he concludes, "In reason, you will see it plain, that any prince, who hath principles in him, that oblige him, in point of conscience, to destroy us, is incapable to preserve, and make us happy."[10] An implication of this position, which Hoadly showed particular acumen in ignoring, is that utility thus becomes the criterion in selecting a king. But Hoadly was much more the utilitarian than the idealist when it came to politics, and this led him to support a strict Erastian ideal, which asserts the right of the king to eliminate Churchmen who support opposing political factions. Such views were particularly pleasing to George I, who was rather unsure of himself and in need of such support. Hoadly's opinions earned him the wrath of his fellow Churchmen and led him to the highly prized seat of Winchester. Ignoring the numerous Biblical texts cited by

8. *Letters of the Earl of Shaftesbury to a Student at the University* (1716) in *Letters of the Earl of Shaftesbury* (1750), p. 43.
9. "Second Book of Odes," Ode VII, 1754.
10. *The Works*, 1, 566. I have regularized an extremely erratic text.

Lancelot Andrewes, William Laud, and other seventeenth-century clerics to prove the superiority of ecclesiastical authority over that of the king, Hoadly cites instead Solomon's removal from office of the high priest Abiathar for supporting the claim of Adonijah to the throne (*The Works*, 1, 583–84).[11]

Hoadly often endangers his position by relying thus on Scripture, since Scripture does not, in most cases, support his position. Yet he is very masterly, throughout his work, in selecting those few Biblical examples that will lend credence to his own beliefs. Although his denial of the authority of the Church leads him that way, Hoadly was far from willing to abandon Christianity for deism, and so it was necessary to avoid the arguments from natural religion and observe the traditional mode of argument from Scripture.

The trend of Hoadly's thought, however, is away from what he regarded as theological quibbles toward social relationships, which he rightly believed were in need of improvement. To this end, it should be noted, he supports, at least tacitly, the principle of violent revolution. In his "Sermon on St. Paul's Behaviour towards the Civil Magistrate, July 26, 1708," he invokes Paul's example in asserting the need to claim one's civil rights: "Let those learn it from St. Paul who will not bear it from others, that rights and privileges, liberty and property and the like, are not words fitted only to raise the spirits of the people, and to foment disturbances in society; but that they are things worth contending for" (*The Works*, 2, 122). Here in 1708 are some of the accents of the revolutionary movements of the later part of the century, but it is interesting to note that these accents are as well those of seventeenth-century revolutionary Puritanism. A year earlier Hoadly had asserted that "the great end of government is the happiness of the governed society" (*The Works*, 2, 111), and though his cries were unheeded at the time, their echoes were to be commonplace later on.

Hoadly cannot bear the tyranny of authority, and almost any kind of temporal authority is, for him, tyrannous. In his eyes the authority of the Church is temporal and as such limits the spiritual jurisdiction of Christ. Such a position leads easily to the idea that every man is a

---

11. The text is I Kings, 2:27.

law unto himself, a notion not unlike George Fox's concept of the inner light. Hoadly propounds the principle of sincere conscience in his "Preservative against the Principles and Practices of the Non-jurors":

> Everyone may find it, in his own conduct, to be true, that his title to God's favour cannot depend upon his actual being, or continuing, in any particular method; but upon his real sincerity in the conduct of his conscience, and of his own actions under it. You adhere, for instance, to the communion of the Non-jurors. Why? Plainly, not because it is the true, Christian communion; (for that it may be, in itself, without your adhering to it;) but because, you judge, and esteem it so to be, upon your most serious consideration; and conduct yourself sincerely by this dictate of your conscience. Your title to God's favour therefore, cannot depend simply upon your adhering to this Communion; because the very adhering to this Communion, if it were against your conscience, would entitle you to His anger: But must depend upon it, considered as a conduct honestly entered into, by the dictate of your conscience. The favour of God, therefore, follows sincerity, considered as such. And consequently, equally follows every equal degree of sincerity. (*The Works*, 1, 592–93)

In 1717 in "A Sermon Preached Before the King," Hoadly denied the need for the Church of England or any other Christian church:

> the Kingdom of Christ, which is the Church of Christ, is the number of persons who are sincerely and willingly, subjects to Him, as law-giver and judge, in all matters truly relating to conscience, or eternal salvation. (*The Works*, 2, 408)

Hoadly's intellectual antecedents are difficult to determine, since he openly follows no earlier thinker. Locke is evidently an important influence, for *The Reasonableness of Christianity* provides criteria for membership in the Church similar to Hoadly's. But Locke is the more conservative, since he insists that acceptance of Christ is necessary. Hoadly, on the other hand, relies on a person's sincerely believing that he is a member of the Church, with what necessary beliefs beyond that he does not make clear.

Hoadly is all the more difficult to place in a tradition since, to escape the vitriolic attacks against him, he sought to ally himself with earlier Churchmen of unquestioned reputation. He declares that William Chillingworth anticipated his doctrine of sincerity:

> The following sentence is quoted out of Mr. Chillingworth, to make a part of this profane catechism, with great dislike: Which I now produce, because it was much in favour of a doctrine about sincerity, which has of late received great discouragement. "I am verily persuaded that God will not impute Errors to *Them*, as Sins, who use such a Measure of Industry in finding Truth, as *Humane Prudence* and Ordinary Discretion, (their Abilities and Opportunities, their Distractions and Hindrances, and All other Things considered,) shall advise them unto, in a matter of such Consequence." Whether I have put this point in so loose terms; or whether Mr. Cheynel has more zealously condemned Mr. Chillingworth for this, as an encourager of all indifference in Religion, or even infidelity; than others have lately condemned me, let the world determine. We must stand or fall together. And this is my comfort, that so great a man, at a time when he was professedly thinking and writing upon this important subject, could find no other rest for the souls of men, but this doctrine of true sincerity in our searches after religious truths: little thinking that hereafter there would arise, amongst the followers of those who patronized him, and licensed his doctrine, any persons who would join with his rigid enemies, in condemning what was then approved by the greatest Churchmen, and solemnly licensed at the University of Oxford. (*The Works*, 2, 621)[12]

Hoadly cites Chillingworth for the very reasons that he would not have dared to cite Locke. But Chillingworth's statement is hardly the expression of a doctrine of sincerity; it is merely indicative of faith in God's good judgement. The author of *The Religion of*

---

12. "A Letter to the Reverend Doctor Snape Prefixed to Francis De La Pillonniere's Reply to Dr. Snape's Vindication."

Protestants a Safe Way to Salvation did not make sincerity itself the object of belief.

Indeed Hoadly's arguments and his attempt to align the non-jurors with the Puritan Cheynel had little or no effect on the reception his works received. His doctrines came under the most virulent attack by a number of high Churchmen, including Francis Atterbury and Thomas Sherlock. But by general agreement among historians of the Bangorian Controversy, William Law's answers to Hoadly were the most brilliant of all.

Fortunately for Hoadly's cause, Law's contributions to the controversy went almost unnoticed, since Law was a young unknown and Hoadly did not take the trouble to answer him. Although Sherlock, fulminating against Hoadly, supposed that he could not answer Law's arguments, it is more likely that practical reasons entered into consideration: Hoadly was attacked by so many that he could recognize only the most eminent. Nevertheless it was Law who, putting aside the personal malice which bristled in most of the attacks on Hoadly, went to the heart of the good bishop's contradictions: "Indeed, my Lord, you have only taken the main supports of our religion away: You have neither left us Priests, nor Sacraments, nor Church: Or what is the same thing, you have made them all 'trifles and dreams' [Hoadly's terms for the badges of ecclesiastical authority]. And what has your Lordship given us in the room of all these advantages? Why, only sincerity: This is the great universal atonement for all."[13]

Despite the ability of Hoadly's opponents and the inconsistency of his own arguments, the doctrine of sincerity, along with the other concomitant liberal ideals which he espoused, made an enormous impression on eighteenth-century England. This can be attributed largely to the fact that the climate of opinion was favourable to the reception of such attitudes. But even so, Hoadly has a serious claim to originality. He possessed the genius to intuit and share the feelings of a large number of Englishmen who were not prepared to renounce religious liberty forever in reaction to the Puritan revolution. Moreover, since almost sixty years had passed since Cromwell's regime

13. William Law, "The Bishop of Bangor's Late Sermon and his letter to Dr. Snape in Defense of it, Answered," *Works* (London, 1762), I, 17–18.

had been superseded, the moratorium on demands for tolerance and religious liberty (insofar as such a moratorium had existed) was at an end. Not that the years before Hoadly's rise to fame had not been periods of stir; they had been, but in the works of Benjamin Hoadly a consensus which had remained underground, so to speak, came at last to the surface. His brother prelates vigorously opposed him, but the strong approval of his views by George II kept his enemies from destroying him. And since an eminent prince of the Church was now the spokesman for a popular viewpoint, it could no longer be ignored, even by conservative Churchmen. Had Hoadly not been stigmatized by the round censure of some important contemporaries, he would probably be acknowledged as the father of the more liberal tendencies within the English Church today.

As is true of so many liberal intellectuals, Hoadly's liberalism went far beyond the consensus that gave him support. But the public mind bent on a revolution in politics, morals, or social order does not follow its leaders into the ramifications of ideology. Sincerity and personal presence seem to be the important characteristics of the most effective leaders, and offering, as Hoadly did, the simple concept of sincerity, which everyone thinks he understands, seemed to promise some success. But Hoadly was no demagogue. His motives tended toward a commendable meliorism. His efforts in religious controversy were, paradoxically, the direct result of his attempts to avoid controversy. Theology seemed to him less important than peace among men.

Long after the Bangorian Controversy was forgotten, however, Hoadly's sincere ideal continued to flourish in the religious and moral lives of men and, of course, in literature. Eventually it was to assume the force of an unquestioned assumption about ethics and art—a concept so completely integrated in the psyche of man that he seldom pauses to reflect upon it. The following passage from *The Gentleman's Magazine* of 1736 shows that sincerity had, for some, already become that unquestioned assumption about which one might reflect only to admire:

'Tis an eminent and signal honour to Christianity, that it lays the chief stress on Sincerity, and inculcates that, as the only

necessary recommendation to the esteem, friendship, and
communion of our fellow-Christians, which entitles to the
favour of God, and the rewards and blessings of eternity.—
'Tis vastly more honourable to Christianity, to suppose, that
all those, who in the Temper of their minds are qualified to receive, and improve, in a proper manner, the privileges of the
Gospel, have a right to partake of them; than 'tis to assert, that
they are excluded upon no foundation but a mere arbitrary
appointment.—Whatever naturally tends to promote Peace
and Concord, must redound more to the honour of our
Religion, than that which has a direct tendency to create ani-
mosities and divisions; which are the necessary consequences of
narrowing our communion, more than a regard to Sincerity,
and common Christianity, requires.[14]

Here the social emphasis of sincerity in the eighteenth century is
made plain. Sincerity is the synthesizing virtue; it promises and is
that human state in which everything is made whole.

14. *The Gentleman's Magazine* (1736), 6: 22.

The plainest Authors that write as they speak, without the Disguise of pompous Elegance, have ever been accounted the best by all good Judges.

John Toland

4

The Prelapsarian World of the Deists

In *The Reasonableness of Christianity as Delivered in the Scriptures* (1685), John Locke, insisting on the pre-eminence of Reason, undertakes to show that Christian tenets are fully comprehensible by that faculty. This he does by reducing these tenets to one, viz. that Christ is the Messiah. This, and this alone, is the necessary belief for the Christian:

> considering the frailty of man, apt to run into corruption and misery, he [God] promised a deliverer, whom in his good time he sent, and then declared to all mankind, that whoever would believe him to be the Savior promised and take him (now raised from the dead and constituted the Lord and Judge of all men) to be their King and Ruler, should be saved. This is a plain, intelligible proposition, and the all-merciful God seems herein to have consulted the poor of this world and the bulk of mankind. These are articles that the laboring and illiterate man may comprehend.[1]

Locke meant, as Leslie Stephen has pointed out, that "a belief in Christ involved a belief in all the doctrines known to come from Christ."[2] But the point was missed by many of Locke's followers, if not by Locke himself. The reduction of Christian beliefs to one opens the way to rejection of that last belief, just as the opening of a

---

1. *The Reasonableness of Christianity as Delivered in the Scriptures* (1695), ed. George W. Ewing (Chicago: Gateway Edition, 1965), p. 193.
2. *History of English Thought in the Eighteenth Century* (1876; reprinted New York: Harbinger–Harcourt, Brace, 1962), I, 80–81.

file on a chessboard can lead to checkmate. Locke's position leads directly to the views of latitudinarians, unitarians, and deists, which set aside the one last Christian principle allowed by Locke.

Another breach in the fortress of tradition came in Locke's rational pleas for toleration, especially in his *Letter Concerning Toleration*. This helped lead the way to a freedom of religious and philosophical speculation heretofore unknown. With the gradual erosion of external authority, traditional views were overturned in the introspective intellectualism inherited by Locke from Descartes. Locke's fascination with psychological processes contributed greatly to this development, which led to theories of imagination, association, and sympathy later in the eighteenth century. This psychological interest received its impetus from Locke, but earlier Puritan concerns with the internal state and personal sincerity provided it with a strong groundwork.

This internalization of focus was important to the deists in their relentless search for "truth." Truth was surely their object, but it was difficult to define, except in the most general terms. Though at first deists sought truth in Nature, often through natural science, most came eventually to Pope's realization that the proper study of mankind is man. Man is, after all, an aspect of the truth which is Nature, and so the universal could be studied in the particular. The principal concern of deists became the internal faculties of man, such as his moral sense or imagination.

The deist controversialists provide us with a rather bare outline of the sincere ideal. First of all, they oppose all deceits and frauds, but especially those associated with "Popery." The concept of religious mysteries is particularly aggravating, as Charles Blount makes clear: "The Morality in Religion is above the Mystery in it; for . . . The Universal sense of Mankind in the Friendships Men make, sheweth this; for who does not value good Nature, Sincerity and Fidelity in a Friend, before subtilty of Understanding."[3] For the deists the proof of truth was simplicity, sympathy, openness, and light, in short, a neoclassical version of the sincere ideal, with scriptural influence scrupulously avoided. In recounting the history

3. *The Miscellaneous Works of Charles Blount* (1695), p. 91.

of Christianity, John Toland shows how religion may diverge from truth:

> Thus lest *Simplicity*, the noblest Ornament of the Truth, should expose it to the Contempt of Unbelievers, *Christianity* was put upon an equal Level with the *Mysteries* of *Ceres*, or the *Orgies* of *Bacchus*. Foolish and mistaken Care! as if the most impious Superstitions could be sanctif'd by the Name of *Christ*. But such is always the Fruit of prudential and condescending Terms of Conversion in Religion, whereby the Number and not the Sincerity of Professors is mainly intended.[4]

The attitudes of the deist controversialists are simple enough. Christianity as practised by those of "Popish" predilection is mysterious, superstitious, and deceitful. The Natural Religion to which deists adhere is, on the other hand, a clear and distinct idea in which truth is reflected whole. In his "Clito: a Poem on the Force of Eloquence," Toland indicates what the "all-perfect *Deity*" really wants of man:

> His sacred Temple's e'ery good Man's Heart,
> Where his choice Gifts he freely dos impart;
> But they deserve and share his first Applause,
> Who stake their Lives in their dear Contry's Cause.
> An honest Mind is the best Pray'r he needs;
> Paid with good Works, for him no Victim bleeds.[5]

A good heart, patriotic fervour, an honest mind, and all will be well.

The deist controversialists provide us with many aspects of the sincere ideal, but their contribution is limited by the argumentative form which their work usually takes. Deism shows to better advantage in the writings of those deists whose interests were artistic: Shaftesbury, Thomson, and Mark Akenside. In these authors, and particularly the poets, the deistic myth is given full imaginative rein. Since deism is myth, not reality, the poets are able to give it the

4. *Christianity Not Mysterious: or, a Treatise Shewing that there is Nothing in the Gospel Contrary to Reason, Nor Above It* (1696), pp. 160–61.
5. "Clito: a Poem on the Force of Eloquence" (London, 1700).

most positive and thorough expression. After a short examination of
Shaftesbury, we shall study the poets in some detail.

SHAFTESBURY

Shaftesbury's specific commentary on the concept of sincerity is
negligible; yet the word is found constantly in his writings. A comment in a letter to John Locke in 1694 may serve to show how far he
was from limiting the meaning of sincerity: "Goodness and sincerity, and a great many other things of that kind, would sound just
as well as good nature and simplicity. . . ."[6]
  Never a theoretical principle, sincerity was, from youth on, a
governing virtue in Shaftesbury's life. When he was only eighteen,
Lord Ashley wrote to his father, expressing great concern over the
deterioration of his brother Maurice's personality:

> Without examining him too severely, or relating what particu-
> larly I have observed or have been informed of, I would only
> offer to your lordship to reflect on the change of his temper
> from what it was a year or two ago. Whether that perfect good
> nature, that trusty sincere plain dealing, disinterest and without
> craft, and that benign bookish temper, whether all this has con-
> tinued in him. Where are all the marks of those mighty im-
> provements that must have been produced in him, if it had
> continued but in any measure? Whether or not your lordship
> finds that there be now in his temper some contraries too ob-
> servable; something of a surliness and a rugged conversation,
> not so open, free, or true-hearted, or so free from design,
> pique, and little equivocation and trick; and whether all the
> bookish inclinations have not had a severe check in him.[7]

Could an eighteen-year-old be more emphatically redundant about
the sincere ideal than is Ashley in his "trusty sincere plain dealing,
disinterest and without craft . . ."?

---

6. *The Life, Unpublished Letters, and Philosophical Regimen of Anthony, Earl of
Shaftesbury*, ed. Benjamin Rand (New York: Macmillan Company, 1900), p. 298.
Hereafter cited as *Philosophical Regimen*.
  7. Ibid., p. 282.

Shaftesbury's early respect for sincerity and its concomitant virtues came later to be connected with his ethical and aesthetic theories. His admiration for the Stoics and Socrates, whom he describes as "the divinest man who had ever appeared in the heathen world," aligns him with philosophers whose high seriousness in the quest for truth places them among the world's first "sincere" men. Socrates is pre-eminent in deist thought, just as Saint Paul takes first place among the Puritans.[8]

Shaftesbury's intention was, as Socrates' had been, to educate the ignorant to understand themselves. As Paul Hazard has put it: "How should we seek for happiness? How, but by humanizing people, if one may be permitted the phrase, by divesting them of their affected gravity, their hypocrisy, of the sort of puffed-uppedness that blinded them to what their feelings really were."[9] When such feelings have been clarified, and are allowed to make the rational choice for which they are fitted, they will inevitably choose what is good; for beauty, proportion, and harmony are naturally desirable, and the good partakes of these qualities.

The dependence upon natural religion, coupled with the complete rejection of Church tradition is a kind of ultimate Protestant position, born of a distrust of all human authority. All that is necessary, then, is that the doors of perception be cleansed to permit man to recognize in Nature what he has overlooked for centuries. Indeed, Shaftesbury's problem, like that of Blake and other Romantic poets, is the problem of perception. But Shaftesbury does accept a classical and literary tradition, which enables him to solve his problem through education:

'Tis undeniable . . . that the perfection of grace and comeliness in action and behaviour can be found only among the people of a liberal education. (*Characteristics*, 1, 125)

Good taste and breeding, then, overcome all difficulties:

To philosophise . . . is but to carry good-breeding a step

8. *Characteristics of Men, Manners, Opinions, Times*, 1, 23.
9. *The European Mind, 1680–1715*, trans. J. Lewis May (1935; reprinted Cleveland: Meridian–World, 1963), p. 296.

higher. For the accomplishment of breeding is, to learn whatever is decent in company or beautiful in arts; and the sum of
philosophy is, to learn what is just in society and beautiful in
Nature and the order of the world.

'Tis not wit merely, but a temper which must form the well-
bred man. In the same manner, 'tis not a head merely, but a
heart and resolution which must complete the real philosopher.
(*Characteristics*, 2, 255)

Just as the philosopher is required to be sincere, the poet must, at
least, advocate virtuous principles:

'Tis manners which is wanting. 'Tis a due sentiment of morals
which alone can make us knowing in order and proportion, and
give us the just tone and measure of human passion.

So much the poet must necessarily borrow of the philosopher
as to be master of the common topics of morality. He must at
least be speciously honest, and in all appearance a friend to
Virtue throughout his poem. (*Characteristics*, 1, 181)

Though the implication is that poets should strive to transcend
these minimum requirements, Shaftesbury draws an important distinction between the work and its author. If the work is moral in
character, the author's possible licentiousness is not the reader's
concern, or at least it is not a concern in relation to the work. In
making this distinction Shaftesbury maintains, at this stage of his
argument, a basically Renaissance attitude toward poetry. But he
takes it only to reject it, for the example of *Paradise Lost* suggests
that poetry should take the direction of apologetics and personal
writing:

Upon the whole, since in the two great poetic stations, the epic
and dramatic, we may observe the moral genius so naturally
prevalent; since our most approved heroic poem has neither the
softness of language nor the fashionable turn of wit, but
merely solid thought, strong reasoning, noble passion, and a
continued thread of moral doctrine, piety, and virtue to recommend it; we may justly infer that it is not so much the
public ear as the ill hand and vicious manner of our poets which
needs redress. (*Characteristics*, 1, 180)

The best way to insure writing moral poetry is to combine know-ledge of the heart with technical skill. The inward colloquy may bring about such balance:

> And thus at last we are returned to our old article of advice: that main preliminary of self-study and inward converse which we have found so much wanting in the authors of our time. They should add the wisdom of the heart to the task and exer-cise of the brain, in order to bring proportion and beauty into their works. (*Characteristics*, 1, 180)

This concern for the heart and a high regard for sincere, spon-taneous expression, despite neoclassical strictures, lead Shaftesbury to elaborate what is essentially a doctrine of sincerity:

> The poets even of the wanton sort give ample testimony of this slavery and wretchedness of vice. They may extol voluptuous-ness to the skies and point their wit as sharply as they are able against a virtuous state. But when they come afterwards to pay the necessary tribute to their commanding pleasures, we hear their pathetic moans and find the inward discord and calamity of their lives. Their example is the best of precepts, since they conceal nothing, are sincere, and speak their passion out aloud. And 'tis in this that the very worst of poets may justly be pre-ferred to the generality of modern philosophers or other formal writers of a yet more specious name. *The muses' pupils never fail to express their passions and write just as they feel.* 'Tis not, indeed, in their nature to do otherwise, whilst they indulge their vein and are under the power of that natural enthusiasm which leads them to what is highest in their performance. They follow Nature. They move chiefly as she moves in them, without thought of disguising her free motions and genuine operations, for the sake of any scheme or hypothesis which they have formed at leisure and in particular narrow views. (*Character-istics*, 2, 347)[10]

Thus sincerity in poetry is merely the act of following Nature. In

10. The italics are mine.

other words, it is human nature to be sincere. In this the poet imitates the Creator:

> a poet is indeed a second Maker; a just Prometheus under Jove. Like that sovereign artist or universal plastic nature, he forms a whole, coherent and proportioned in itself, with due subjection and subordinacy of constituent parts. . . . The moral artist who can thus imitate the Creator, and is thus knowing in the inward form and structure of his fellow-creature, will hardly, I presume, be found unknowing in himself, or at a loss in those numbers which make the harmony of a mind. (*Characteristics*, 1, 136)

M. H. Abrams is quite right in pointing out that Shaftesbury's notion of "plastic" is neoclassical in conception, and probably bears little resemblance to the organic formative theories of the Romantics.[11] Nevertheless, in considering the qualities of the ideal poet, Shaftesbury is looking beyond the poets of his own time. In the past, only Homer and Shakespeare could meet his standards of sincerity. Homer, he believes, shows a kind of negative capability: "The poet, instead of giving himself those dictating and masterly airs of wisdom, makes hardly any figure at all, and is scarce discoverable in his poem. This is being truly a master" (*Characteristics*, 1, 129-30). But somehow this quality leads to a greater identity, since it is in accord with Nature. The ancients, Shaftesbury submits, unlike the moderns, "could with just reason bear to see their natural countenances represented" (*Characteristics*, 1, 131).

Shaftesbury goes on to deplore the superficial individuality of modern authors, which is "designed to draw the attention from the subject towards himself . . ." (*Characteristics*, 1, 131). In this way mannerism replaces Nature—a violation of neoclassical principles. The task of the true poet is to create harmony within the broad scheme of general nature.

The social orientation of *Characteristics* gives way to a more individualistic, stoical point of view in Shaftesbury's *Askémata*, or exercises. The desire for harmony with Nature remains, however,

---

11. M. H. Abrams, *The Mirror and the Lamp* (New York: Oxford University Press, 1953), p. 201.

and this deistic attitude is expressed in terms of sympathy.[12] But Nature, with which we sympathize, is distinguished from that which is superficial or false. This permits a key distinction between self and society, or rather two kinds of society:

> Cut off tenderness of a certain kind; cut off *familiarity*, and that sympathy of a wrong kind. Learn to be with self, to talk with self. Commune with thy own heart; be that thy companion. For what other is there? See what thou has [sic] got by seeking others. Is this *society*? Is it genuine and of a right kind, when it is that fond desire of company, that seeking of companionship, and that want of talk and story? Is this what prompts thee in the case? Is this the affection that draws thee to the sociable acts and commerce with mankind? What is this but sickness of a dangerous kind? . . . Friendship has nothing to do here. See with whom this is in common. See the nation and people that are the most insatiable in this way. . . . And see in what place this reigns the most: the court and places near the court; the polite world; the great ones.[13]

Here society is redefined. The corruption of polite company is to be eschewed and communion with the heart to be sought. This does not, I think, exclude the company of friends whose objects of concern are serious and who might well contribute to moral improvement. Nevertheless the desirability of retreat from the world is clearly stated. The good man will discover a community in himself, if he can discover no kindred souls, and that community will observe the sincere ideal.

JAMES THOMSON

James Thomson is representative of so many important attitudes in the eighteenth century that he is impossible to characterize in any simple way. Politically he was a Whig, though more reflective than many of his fellow Whigs. Philosophically he was a deist, though

---

12. *Philosophical Regimen*, pp. 17–18.   13. Ibid., p. 144.

The Seasons has been read as a Christian poem. His poetic style reflects both an adherence to neoclassical principles and a marked originality of poetic outlook. In short he is a complex figure. After the publication of "Winter" in 1726, James Thomson began to enjoy a notoriety greater than any author has a right to expect. Particularly notable was the generous approbation of Aaron Hill, whose position as an older man and established literary figure made his concern particularly welcome. The warmth of the ensuing friendship between these two was the result of a meeting of kindred souls whose views on literary and moral subjects were similar. In a letter to David Mallet (through whom Hill and Thomson were brought together), Hill expressed his view of "Winter":

> The meanest Truth I can say of it is, that the Fancy is vast, & lively; and The Judgment Calm & Solid.—The Images burn, & live: & the Expressions paint & embody.
>
> There is an Elegance, & Clearness, in the Language which I shou'd never have done wondering at, if It were not still more distinguishable by a Certain Fullness, & luxuriant Richness, without Waste, which I have very rarely met with; and which can never be too much commended.—There is also a Magnanimity, and moral Dignity of Sentiment, that glitters aptly, and endears the Author, while it ornaments the Poem.[14]

It should be noted that Hill, as is usual with him, emphasizes the sentiments that he expects to find in a literary work.

This letter was shown to Thomson by Mallet, and the young poet immediately expressed to Hill the excited thanks that might be expected from a young author on receiving the kindness of an admired older one:

> I will not affect a moderate Joy at your Approbation, your Praise: It pleases, it delights, it ravishes me! Forgive me for the Lowness of the Truth, when I vow, I'd rather have it than the Acclamations of Thousands: 'Tis so sincere, so delicate, so distinguishing, so glowing, and, what peculiarly marks and endears it, so beautifully generous.

14. James Thomson, *Letters and Documents*, ed. A. D. McKillop (Lawrence: University of Kansas Press, 1958), p. 23.

That great Mind, and transcendent Humanity, that appear in the Testimony you have been pleas'd to give my first Attempt, would have utterly confounded me, if I had not been prepar'd for such an Entertainment, by your well-known Character; which the Voice of Fame, and your own masterly Writings, loudly proclaim.[15]

The accents of praise are here exaggerated and sentimental, but this is precisely the point. Thomson's protestations of a commitment to sincerity remove all barriers to full expression. Hill, himself, was given to such excessive warmth, as his later correspondence with Samuel Richardson was to testify. Hill and his circle were consciously creating a climate of kindness and benevolence which had as its object nothing less than the reformation of manners based on the universal cultivation of social love. Thomson examines and praises Hill's exemplification of this virtue:

> The Social Love, of which you are so bright an Example, tho' it be the distinguishing Ornament of Humanity, yet there are some ill-natur'd enough to degrade it into a Modification of Self-love, according to them, its Original.
>
> These Gentlemen, I am afraid, mingle their Tempers too much with their Speculations.
>
> Self-love is, indeed, indispensably necessary for the Well-being of every Individual, but carries not along with it an Idea of moral Beauty and Perfection; whereas Social Love is of quite another Nature; the just and free Exercise of which, in a particular manner, renders one amiable, and divine. The accomplish'd Man I admire, the honest Man I trust; but 'tis only the truly-generous Man I intirely love. Humanity is the very Smile and Consummation of Virtue; 'tis the Image of that fair Perfection, in the Supreme Being, which, while he was infinitely happy in himself, mov'd him to create a World of Beings to make them so.[16]

The influence of Shaftesbury is evident here in the emphasis on social love and in the concern for Beauty as a moral value. In his own

15. Ibid., p. 24.   16. Ibid., pp. 25–26.

way, Thomson answers Hobbes's view that man was capable of self-love only. This is made clearer in another enthusiastic letter to Hill written shortly after the two met for the first time:

> There is downright Inspiration in your Society: It enlarges and exalts all the Powers of the Soul, chases every low Thought, throws the Passions into the most agreeable Agitations, and gives the Heart the most affecting Sentiments—'Tis moral Harmony![17]

We move in this passage from a concern for society as a whole to the limited literary society, of which Hill was a leading light. This small group and others like it became increasingly important to Thomson and his friends. Such groups were not identical with the Kit-Kat club, for example, although they have much in common with it, and probably derived from that coffee-house club. The new "society" was to serve a grander purpose than being a platform for wit. It was to be an epitome of sense and sophistication, to be sure, but even more important, it would provide for its members the opportunity to cultivate the most highly regarded virtues of the heart. Thus Hill and his group had a firm moral purpose in mind which lent to their meetings a tone of high seriousness absent from most earlier clubs. This seriousness of purpose was the natural inclination of the young James Thomson.

"Winter" was published before Thomson's introduction to Hill, but not before his acquaintance with his fellow Scotsman David Mallet. Mallet enjoyed a previous connection with Hill, and it was perhaps through Mallet that Thomson imbibed some of his attitudes. Another literary figure known to Thomson before his acquaintance with Hill was Richard Savage, who embodied all the cultivated, liberal attitudes which Thomson wished to develop in himself. Just how much Thomson learned from Savage is difficult to say, but Savage's example did make a favourable impression.

Subsequent to Aaron Hill's praise of "Winter," Thomson wrote a preface to the second edition of the poem in which he sought to embody the poetic principles of Hill and his group, a set of prin-

17. Ibid., p. 27.

ciples to which Thomson had not been previously averse. They are in many respects similar to those espoused earlier by Dennis, Blackmore, and Watts. The preface is an apology which argues for the importance of serious poetry. For Thomson any attack on poetry of this kind is an attack on all that is valuable in civilized society:

> It is declaring against the most charming power of imagination, the most exalting force of thought, the most affecting touch of sentiment—in a word, against the very soul of all learning and politeness. It is affronting the universal taste of mankind, and declaring against what has charmed the listening world from Moses down to Milton. In fine, it is even declaring against the sublimest passages of the inspired writings themselves, and what seems to be the peculiar language of heaven.[18]

This last remark is reminiscent of Watts's position in his preface to the *Horae Lyricae*, a position that was to become even clearer to the rational man later in the century when Robert Lowth delivered his significant *Lectures on the Sacred Poetry of the Hebrews*. Indeed Thomson's preface is so clearly in this tradition that some of his additional comments are worth quoting at length:

> let poetry once more be restored to her ancient truth and purity; let her be inspired from heaven, and in return her incense ascend thither; let her exchange her low, venal, trifling, subjects for such as are fair, useful, and magnificent; and let her execute these so as at once to please, instruct, surprise, and astonish: and then of necessity the most inveterate ignorance, and prejudice, shall be struck dumb; and poets yet become the delight and wonder of mankind.
>
> But this happy period is not to be expected, till some long-wished, illustrious man of equal power and beneficence rise on the wintry world of letters: one of a genuine and unbounded greatness and generosity of mind; who, far above all the pomp and pride of fortune, scorns the little addressful flatterer; pierces through the disguised designing villain; discountenances all the reigning fopperies of a tasteless age: and who,

18. James Thomson, *The Complete Poetical Works*, p. 239.

stretching his views into late futurity, has the true interest of
virtue, learning, and mankind entirely at heart—a character so
nobly desirable that to an honest heart it is almost incredible so
few should have the ambition to deserve it. (p. 240)

Perhaps in his enthusiasm Thomson was thinking of Hill or expressing hopes for himself when he wrote these words. But whatever he had in mind, the visionary search for society is central to this
preface.

If the poet, then, is to choose the "great and serious subjects"
which will serve as a basis for the renovation of society, it still remains to decide what these subjects are. Thomson, citing Virgil's
Georgics and the Book of Job, selects the works of Nature:

> I know no subject more elevating, more amusing; more ready
> to awake the poetical enthusiasm, the philosophical reflection
> and the moral sentiment, than the works of Nature. (pp. 240–41)

The emotions that Nature arouses in man are connected with the
spontaneity of poetic production:

> How gay looks the Spring! how glorious the Summer! how
> pleasing the Autumn! and how venerable the Winter!—But
> there is no thinking of these things without breaking out into
> poetry; which is, by-the-by, a plain and undeniable argument
> of their superior excellence. (p. 241)

Thomson is instructive as he clarifies the main conditions for the
production of spontaneous Nature poetry:

> For this reason the best, both ancient, and modern, Poets have
> been passionately fond of retirement, and solitude. The wild
> romantic country was their delight. And they seem never to
> have been more happy, than when, lost in unfrequented fields,
> far from the little busy world, they were at leisure, to meditate,
> and sing the Works of Nature. (p. 241)

The myth of retirement is linked by Thomson to both Nature as a
subject for poetry and spontaneity as a poetic ideal. But Thomson is
not in need of Urania or the Divine Spirit for inspiration and consequent spontaneous verse. The sufficiency of the simple, rural setting

makes an elaborate theory of spontaneity unnecessary. With Nature and retirement present to the poetic mind, Thomson maintains, there is no holding poetry back.

C. A. Moore has shown that Thomson was consistently uncritical of his own times and tended to overestimate the possible effects of minor political change and Ralph Cohen has indicted his "knowledge of man."[19] These limitations make Thomson very much a man of his time. But it is usually unfair to expect any but the greatest of men to be at serious variance with their own times, especially when the attitudes of the age are appealingly sentimental. Further, it is probably an error to believe that Thomson thought his views had much practical political value. As I have suggested, Thomson espoused an idealistic vision which finally transcended the prime political considerations of his time. His poetry became the means by which he articulated that vision.

This explains, in part, his interest in various versions of the prelapsarian myth. Although original sin, in a strict Christian sense, is not his concern, he regards his contemporary world as fallen from an earlier state of bliss characterized by innocent and guileless behaviour. The task for men of his time, and for poets in particular, is to recapture in some way that primeval situation. Like the Puritans, Thomson begins with an unrealistic confidence that paradise can be won by political and social means. But as he becomes more familiar with life, practical expedients give way to imaginative ones.

But Thomson's poetical visions, unlike his political ones, are not based on self-delusion. His final outlook is less optimistic than is usually supposed. The following pages are devoted to that viewpoint, as it is revealed in Thomson's poetry.

"Spring" begins with a severe reminder that winter has not left us:

As yet the trembling year is unconfirmed,
And Winter oft at eve resumes the breeze, . . .

(18–19)[20]

---

19. C. A. Moore, "Whig Panegyric Verse, 1700–1760," *PMLA*, 41 (1926): 362–401. Ralph Cohen, *The Unfolding of the Seasons* (Baltimore: The Johns Hopkins Press, 1970), p. 329.
20. All references to Thomson's poetry are to *The Complete Poetical Works*.

Thomson's lingering over the most ruinous of the seasons may surprise us, since spring represents for him the only season enjoyed in Paradise. But, as we shall see, winter represents the situation in contemporary Europe, and is always present throughout *The Seasons*.

First, however, a prelapsarian paradise is contemplated, when "reason and benevolence were law"(257). But this world is no longer with us, and at the present time evil is rife:

> But now those white unblemished minutes, whence
> The fabling poets took their golden age,
> Are found no more amid these iron times,
> These dregs of life! Now the distempered mind
> Has lost that concord of harmonious powers
> Which forms the soul of happiness; and all
> Is off the poise within: the passions all
> Have burst their bounds; and Reason, half extinct,
> Or impotent, or else approving, sees
> The foul disorder.
>
> (272–81)

The important phrase, "and all / Is off the poise within" should be noted especially, since it reveals Thomson's diagnosis of society's illness. The problem is individual and internal. The solution, then, must be self-renovation.

The seasons themselves are a particularly appropriate theme, since, expressing change and mutability, they represent the state of the fallen world since the deluge:

> The Seasons since have, with severer sway,
> Oppressed a broken world: . . .
>
> (317–18)

In this broken world man is worse than the wildest beasts. Thomson notes that "Ensanguined man / Is now become the lion of the plain, / And worse" (340–42). Nature teaches that the wild animals obey their instincts when they ravage:

> But man, whom Nature formed of milder clay,
> With every kind emotion in his heart,

And taught alone to weep,—while from her lap
She pours ten thousand delicacies, herbs
And fruits, as numerous as the drops of rain
Or beams that gave them birth,—shall he, fair form!
Who wears sweet smiles, and looks erect on Heaven,
E'er stoop to mingle with the prowling herd,
And dip his tongue in gore.

(349–57)

Thus man has possibilities that he has not realized in the present age, possibilities testified to by past ages, by the innate goodness of his heart, and his very place of pre-eminence in the creation.

A further indication of man's depravity is his cruelty in the slaughter of domestic beasts: "This," Thomson writes, "the feeling heart / Would tenderly suggest: . . ." (370–71). But he is not yet prepared to condemn even this completely:

High Heaven forbids the bold presumptuous strain,
Whose wisest will has fixed us in a state
That must not yet to pure perfection rise:
Besides who knows, how, raised to higher life,
From stage to stage, the vital scale ascends?

(374–78)

This notion of the limits of human perception gives Thomson the advantage of questioning most of his assertions, thereby keeping him secure from fanaticism. Thus he seems to enjoy some insight into a higher state of man. His "feeling heart," educated to Reason by Nature, returns to an earlier, more innocent, time. But he restrains himself from assenting to Pythagorean transmigration:

but 'tis enough,
In this late age, adventurous to have touched
Light on the numbers of the Samian Sage.

(371–73)[21]

Although he questions his own assumption with some regularity,

21. For an examination of this passage see Cohen, *The Unfolding of the Seasons*, p. 36.

Thomson does not enjoy calling "the feeling heart" in question. He escapes this necessity to some extent by blaming the age for his incapacity. Further, the concern for animals is less a sympathetic sentimentalism than an expression of concern for the moral imbalance in man which permits him to be cruel. This continues throughout the century and explains in part why Cowper could complain about the slaughter of animals and yet enjoy his beef. Although both Thomson and Cowper would be shocked at the thought, presumably the attainment of the sincere ideal would cleanse moral intentions to such purity that almost any atrocity could be committed with impunity. Thus a war conducted by the sincere society could be a very fine thing indeed.

In "Summer" and "Autumn," Thomson gives us several vignettes of pastoral innocence: the stories of Celadon–Amelia and Damon–Musidora in "Summer" are obviously unsatisfactory; while that of Palemon–Lavinia realizes a successful pastoral ideal.

Celadon and Amelia relive the prelapsarian condition:

> They loved: but such their guileless passion was
> As in the dawn of time informed the heart
> Of innocence and undissembling truth.
>   ("Summer," 1177–79)

The guileless innocence of the lovers is common to Thomson's pastoral paradises, just as guile is an important characteristic of the fallen world. While the lovers are together "creative Love / Still bade eternal Eden smile around" (1193–94). Thus the lovers create, as a poet might, their own situation through "creative Love." This echoes the Miltonic notion that the mind creates its own heaven or hell and implies that where things are amiss, the mind, and not the environment, should be renovated.

As the story proceeds the lovely Amelia is suddenly struck dead by a lightning bolt, and so Eden is demolished. One can only guess at Thomson's meaning in doing this. Perhaps he is merely following the story as he knew it. But more likely he is suggesting that pastoral paradises are not immune to disaster. Indeed, the vignette seriously questions the possibility of such a paradise. The stark and shocking pessimism of this story's senseless conclusion seems to suggest that

Thomson's dreams never approached reality for him, that his assays into the realm of the ideal were excursions into a fantasy world which his rational, neoclassical attitudes finally triumphed over. In the very last lines of *Liberty*, he breaks an even more optimistic and serious vision of social perfection:

> As thick to view these varied wonders rose,
> Shook all my soul with transport, unassured
> The Vision broke; and on my waking eye
> Rushed the still ruins of dejected Rome.

$$(5, 717-20)$$

The conclusion, then, of a poem often cited as an example of Whiggish optimism is a broken vision and a waking scene of ruins and a dejected city. Aaron Hill perceived the impossibility of Thomson's vision, while extolling its grandeur. He wrote of *Liberty* in a letter to Thomson: "I look upon this mighty work, as the last *stretched* blaze of our expiring genius. It is the dying effort of despairing and indignant virtue. . . ."[22]

There is in "Summer" another pastoral story. Damon seeks out his beloved Musidora, but, finding her bathing, dares not gaze upon her. Musidora, with "admiration of her lover's flame, / By modesty exalted" (1358-59), puts on her garments "which blissful Eden knew not" (1351), and carved in a tree a message for Damon: "the time may come you need not fly" (1370).

The obvious meaning of this bizarre tale is that Musidora may in time marry Damon, in which case he will have the right to view her nakedness. But it may also mean that in this world—unlike blissful Eden—shame is a reality, and a better world is envisioned in which such precautions need not be taken. The optimism is, of course, couched in metaphor, since Thomson does not wish for a world of nudists. Thomson approves of modesty, to be sure; Adam and Eve of *Paradise Lost* showed before their fall due modesty. The issue in "Summer" is the necessity of flight, which would not exist if virtue were completely sound.

Thomson is certainly indebted for his view of Paradise to Milton,

---

22. Aaron Hill, *The Works*, I, 248.

whose achievement, later in the poem, is praised as the culmination
of classical poetry:

> A genius universal as his theme,
> Astonishing as chaos, as the bloom
> Of blowing Eden fair, as heaven sublime!

("Summer," 1569-71)

The reference to Eden in the original text of the poems makes clear
the fact that Milton's Eden was on Thomson's mind when he compared the Celadon–Amelia and Damon–Musidora settings with Eden.

In "Autumn" we find a more successful paradise. The story of
Palemon and Lavinia differs in many ways from the pastorals in
"Summer." Lavinia begins in a destitute state, and is, at last, rescued
from poverty and solitude by marriage to Palemon, prototypal of
Pamela. The happy couple then coalesces into a utopian ideal:

> [They] flourished long in tender bliss, and reared
> A numerous offspring, lovely like themselves,
> And good, the grace of all the country round.

(308-10)

Here there is no discordant note, unless it be Lavinia's original
poverty. Yet even that emphasizes her innocence. She and her mother

> Almost on nature's bounty fed,
> Like the gay birds that sung them to repose,
> Content, and careless of to-morrow's fare.

(189-91)

Thomson's puritan ideal of prosperity makes Palemon's position
more attractive, however:

> The pride of swains
> Palemon was, the generous and the rich,
> Who led the rural life in all its joy
> And elegance, such as Arcadian song
> Transmits from ancient uncorrupted times,
> When tyrant custom had not shackled man,
> But free to follow nature was the mode.

(217-23)

It is fairly clear that this story does not take place in the "ancient uncorrupted times," since we learn that Lavinia and her mother "shunned the cruel scorn / Which virtue, sunk to poverty, would meet / From giddy fashion and low-minded pride" (186–88), a problem that would not have occurred in the prelapsarian world. Yet here the pastoral retreat is untouched, or almost untouched, by the realities of life.

The inconsistency of this story with the idylls in "Summer" points up the difficulty of defining Thomson's purpose. But this much may be said: all the stories assist in defining an imaginative ideal: in "Summer" reality breaks in; in "Autumn" the ideal is left unscathed. We cannot expect Thomson to destroy or mutilate every ideal scene that he draws, to accord with our sense of the tragic. Thomson's world-view does allow for tragedy in the conflict between heroic man and certain inscrutable forces of Nature, and he does qualify some of his idylls enough to rescue him from the charge of blind optimism. Yet his optimism, often ill-advised, takes the sharpness from incipient tragedy by suggesting that no ill is irremediable.

Thus far it is clear that Thomson recognizes a discrepancy between the ideal prelapsarian world and contemporary Europe. We shall now inquire into the remedies that he proposes. First of all, we should note that he has no simple answers. "Industry" is the key term, but it is a term that has a number of complex meanings:

All is the gift of industry,—whate'er
Exalts, embellishes, and renders life
Delightful.
("Autumn," 141–43)

Thomson returns to the notion expressed in "Spring" that the seasons are oppressors of man, and suggests that industry overcomes this oppression:

Pensive Winter, cheered by him,
Sits at the social fire, and happy hears
The excluded tempest idly rave along;
His hardened fingers deck the gaudy Spring;
Without him Summer were an arid waste;

Nor to the Autumnal months could thus transmit
Those full, mature, immeasurable stores
That, waving round, recall my wandering song.

("Autumn," 143–50)

But industry is as all encompassing a term as virtue itself. It includes agriculture, the mechanic arts, commerce, poetry, the fine arts—in short any ennobling or civilizing influence. Thus in *The Castle of Indolence* the bard who accompanies the Knight of Art and Industry sings:

Let godlike reason from her sovereign throne
Speak the commanding word *I will!* and it is done.

(Canto 2, 62)

Thus industry is activity leading to good.

One critic has accused Thomson of inconsistency on the grounds that "implicit in the high regard for civilized human accomplishment is condemnation of man in his natural state."[23] This criticism depends for its validity on what is meant by "natural state." Thomson certainly rejects savage primitivism. But the fact that he expunged from the original text of "Spring" lines 296–323 does not mean that he rejected the ideal of the Golden Age.[24] For Thomson the Golden Age was a prelapsarian state to which eighteenth-century man could not aspire. One means of restoring human equipoise was to cultivate the civilizing arts. Although he probably did not accept the concept of original sin in a literal sense, he was drawn to the Miltonic portrayal of the fall and the notion that the effects of the fall could be mitigated by education and civilization, in short, Reason. In considering the virtues of the Golden Age, Thomson is only drawing into clear relief the vices of his own times, and showing what a falling off there has been. To recommend a return to that prelap-

23. Patricia Meyer Spacks, *The Varied God: A Critical Study of Thomson's The Seasons* (Berkeley: University of California Press, 1959), p. 171.
24. See Otto Zippel, ed. *The Seasons* (Berlin, 1908), pp. 18–19, and Mrs. Spacks *The Varied God*, p. 162.

sarian state would be absurd, and Thomson makes no such recommendation.

Rather, in rejecting the false dichotomy between the Golden Age and civilized corruption, Thomson envisions an order in accord with the eighteenth-century world as he understands it. He prefers industrious rural areas to industrious urban ones, and at the same time recognizes the importance of cities and seaports to rural prosperity. Cities, Thomson would say, tend to be corrupt, but it is the corruption that is to be condemned, not the city itself. In viewing the rise of the Calvinist Swiss cities, Liberty (the allegorical figure) praises them: "unguilty cities rise, / Cities of brothers formed—" (*Liberty*, 4, 330–31). Cities are good, then, in so far as they preserve the virtues of the countryside.

Thomson clarifies his position when he apologizes for his poetry by citing Virgil's example:

> Such themes as these the rural Maro sung
> To wide–imperial Rome, in the full height
> Of elegance and taste, by Greece refined.
>
> ("Spring," 55–57)

Thomson's ideal combines the best of urban and rural qualities. He exemplifies it in Cincinnatus, who leaves the plough to rule the state, returning afterward to his rural retreat, or in Cato, the prototype of virtue in government. The following passage clarifies his understanding of the necessary connection between urban commercial centres and rural prosperity:

> Ye generous Britons, venerate the plough;
> And o'er your hills and long withdrawing vales
> Let Autumn spread his treasures to the sun,
> Luxuriant and unbounded. As the sea
> Far through his azure turbulent domain
> Your empire owns, and from a thousand shores
> Wafts all the pomp of life into your ports;
> So with superior boon may your rich soil,
> Exuberant, Nature's better blessings pour

O'er every land, the naked nations clothe,
And be the exhaustless granary of a world!

("Spring," 67–77)

This benevolent imperialism has annoyed many critics; but it
should be remembered that these notions are part of an ideal vision
and do not represent a practical programme.

Though the epithet "rural" as applied to Virgil has the superficial meaning of the Virgil of the Georgics and Bucolics, Thomson
extends that meaning to identify the great Roman poet with the
rural setting. By doing this he suggests the elegance and sophistication which he expects to accompany country virtue. Thus the refined "rural" voice is the one to which the urban centres ought to
pay heed. For Thomson the Golden Age has passed, never to come
again, but certain aspects of that age could be captured and trans-
mitted by the poetic imagination, functioning under the proper
conditions.

Thomson, however, was basically a neoclassicist who accepted,
more innocently than Pope or Swift, the ideals of Reason and
Honour. He was a serious-minded man to whom all but the mildest
satire was foreign. He did not himself write satire, if we except the
playful banter in parts of The Castle of Indolence, and he seems not to
have had a mind conformable to the satiric enterprise. He was horri-
fied by situations in which his ideals and reality were at odds; but
although he continued to hold to those ideals, his appraisal of them
was sensible. He was not the gullible optimist he is often taken for.
Almost every effusion of optimism in The Seasons is balanced by a
realistic view of vice in the world. Thomson has grand ideals, often,
and holds them high, but he is not blinded to the impracticality of
those ideals. Indeed, The Seasons is in many ways an attempt to
reach a realistic viewpoint without a complete compromise of
principle.

For Thomson one of the central problems in the eighteenth-
century world, particularly in courts and cities, is the lack of moral
sincerity. "Guile" is a common term in Thomson's vocabulary, and
he uses it to describe almost every situation where virtue has failed.
Thus the fall of man is characterized by "winding wiles, / Coward

deceit, and ruffian violence" ("Spring," 302–23). On the other hand, the praiseworthy youth of Britain are

In genius and substantial learning, high;
For every virtue, every worth, renowned;
Sincere, plainhearted, hospitable, kind, . . .

("Summer," 1473–75)

And where poetry is lacking there is "Nothing, save rapine, indolence, and guile" ("Summer," 1771). These examples could be multiplied greatly by drawing on all of Thomson's poems.

Socrates represents for Thomson, as for Shaftesbury, the best exemplification of the sincere ideal.[25] His firm dedication to plain truth led to the development of Greek philosophy, unequalled in any succeeding age or nation. Here is high praise for the Greeks in the spirit of the classical republicans:

They, ever candid, reason still opposed
To reason; and, since virtue was their aim,
Each by sure practice tried to prove his way
The best. Then stood untouched the solid base
Of Liberty, the liberty of mind.

(*Liberty*, 2, 243–47)

Thus liberty of mind, perhaps the greatest liberty of all, is equated with complete openness of mind and freedom from superstitious restraint. Had Thomson foreseen the inroads that modern propaganda has made on "liberty of mind," he would have valued it all the more. Here is the sincere ideal at its apogee, where complete sincerity is indeed possible.

If, as I have tried to show, the fine combination of urban sophistication and rustic virtue represents Thomson's social ideal, the question of the model on which society is to be remade must still arise. The answer is not simple, since Thomson's attitude vacillates between his grand ideal in which all of society participates and the

25. Professor Cohen raises the question of Thomson's deist leanings. I agree with him that Thomson has clear Christian interests, but not so clear as he supposes. Of course Christian–Deism is not unheard of in the eighteenth century, witness Pope's *Essay on Man*. For Cohen's view see *The Unfolding of the Seasons*.

more realistic view of the small, closed society of intellectual friends. The two views can be united to some extent, but still unsatisfactorily, when eminent politicians and men of the world are included in the closed society.

Thomson's solution belongs to the imagination. First, retirement from the world is necessary; the poet enters woodland gloom:

> These are the haunts of meditation, these
> The scenes where ancient bards the inspiring breath
> Ecstatic felt, and, from this world retired,
> Conversed with angels and immortal forms, . . .
>
> ("Summer," 522–25)

Reminiscent of some of Wordsworth's experiences in *The Prelude*, Thomson is moved by Nature to ecstatic song:

> Deep-roused, I feel
> A sacred terror, a severe delight,
> Creep through my mortal frame; and thus methinks,
> A voice, than human more, the abstracted ear
> Of fancy strikes—
>
> ("Summer," 540–44)

The voice then articulates Thomson's poetic aspirations, which he in turn relates to social concerns:

> "Be not of us afraid,
> Poor kindred man! thy fellow-creatures, we
> From the same Parent-Power our beings drew,
> The same our Lord and laws and great pursuit.
> Once some of us, like thee, through stormy life
> Toiled tempest-beaten ere we could attain
> This holy calm, this harmony of mind,
> Where purity and peace immingle charms.
> Then fear not us; but with responsive song,
> Amid these dim recesses, undisturbed
> By noisy folly and discordant vice,
> Of Nature sing with us, and Nature's God.
> Here frequent at the visionary hour,
> When musing midnight reigns or silent noon,

Angelic harps are in full concert heard,
And voices chaunting from the wood-crown'd hill,
The deepening dale, or inmost sylvan glade:
A privilege bestow'd by us alone
On contemplation, or the hallow'd ear
Of poet swelling to seraphic strain."

("Summer," 544–63)

This is poetry reliant on a vision of the ideal, and Thomson freely acknowledges his attempt to transmute reality by means of the imagination. As guides to behaviour he presents in *Liberty* idealized visions of Greece and Rome. These visions are transported to the present in the following lines, referring to Pitt and Cobham's seat at Stowe:

While there with thee the enchanted round I walk,
The regulated wild, gay fancy then
Will tread in thought the groves of Attic land; . . .

("Autumn," 1054–56)

Here in the company of friends the ideal life can be re-created and shared:

Retirement, rural quiet, friendship, books,
Ease and alternate labour, useful life,
Progressive virtue, and approving Heaven!
These are the matchless joys of virtuous love; . . .

("Spring," 1162–64)

The importance of friends in this scheme of things throws some light on Thomson's characterizations of the persons to whom each of his "Seasons" is dedicated. The Countess of Hartford, Dodington, Onslow, and Wilmington exemplify the virtues which the poems praise. These dedicatory individuals are, to some extent, then, controlling figures in *The Seasons*.

Thomson's use of poetic inspiration to achieve this imaginative ideal should be commented upon further. The Greek and Roman worlds are for him founts of inspiration. Thus he refers to the Greek landscape as "mountains and streams where verse spontaneous

flowed, . . ." (*Liberty*, 2, 95). Homer is the one source of true inspiration and he himself experienced it undefiled. Liberty addresses
the blind bard:

> Heroic song was thine; the fountain-bard,
> Whence each poetic stream derives its course!
> Thine the dread moral scene, thy chief delight!
> Where idle fancy durst not mix her voice
> When reason spoke august, the fervent heart
> Or plained or stormed, and in the impassioned man,
> Concealing art with art, the poet sunk.
>
> (*Liberty*, 2, 272–78)

Nature, Reason, whatever forces in the world are of importance,
speak to the poet, and from that impassioned union of head and
heart springs the poetic creation. Thus the true poetry to which
Thomson aspires is described in Liberty's words to Homer:

> The sweet enforcer of the poet's strain,
> Thine was the meaning music of the heart.
> Not the vain trill, that, void of passion, runs
> In giddy mazes, tickling idle ears;
> But that deep-searching voice, and artful hand,
> To which respondent shakes the varied soul.
>
> (*Liberty*, 2, 285–90)

Thomson's view of Homer is echoed in a book by Thomas
Blackwell, *An Enquiry into the Life and Writings of Homer*, published in 1735, the same year as *Liberty*. Blackwell locates the sincere
ideal in Homer's time and civilization, and sees the blind poet as its
full expression. Here, in part, is his description of Homer's society:

> *They lived naturally*, and were governed by the *natural Poise* of
> the Passions, as it is settled in every human Breast. This made
> them speak and act, without other Restraint than their own
> native Apprehensions of *Good* and *Evil, Just* and *Unjust*, each
> as he was prompted from *within*. These Manners afford the most
> *natural* Pictures, and proper Words to paint them.
> They have a peculiar Effect upon the Language, not only as

they are natural, but as they are ingenuous and *good*. While a Nation continues simple and sincere, whatever they say has a *Weight* from *Truth*: Their Sentiments are strong and honest; which always produce fit Words to express them: Their Passions are sound and genuine, not adulterated or disguised, and break out in their own artless Phrase and unaffected Stile.[26]

Blackwell is more the primitivist than Thomson, and sees even the guile of Homer's Greeks as sincere:

the *Grecian's* Wiles are plain and natural; either Stratagems in War, or such Designs in Peace as depend not upon forming a *Party* for their execution. He excells in the simple instructive parts of Life, the Play of the *Passions*, the Prowess of *Bodies*, and those *single Views* of Persons and Characters, that arise from untaught, undisguised Nature.[27]

For Blackwell Homer lived at precisely the right moment for poetry, when humanity was properly balanced between naked barbarity and total feigning.[28]

Despite the fact that it was the first poem of *The Seasons* to be written, "Winter" unites all of these seemingly disparate ideas. Since winter is the most cruel of the seasons and the most likely to foster despair, it is fitting that Thomson epitomize his viewpoint in that poem.

"Winter" opens on a particularly serious note in which the sad aspect of the season sets the tone for the entire production:

See, Winter comes to rule the varied year,
Sullen and sad, with all his rising train—
Vapours, and clouds, and storms. Be these my theme.
These, that exalt the soul to solemn thought
And heavenly musing.

(1–5)

The power of winter is indeed terrible, but the horrors are, in another sense, "congenial" (6), since they encourage meditation on

---

26. *An Enquiry into the Life and Writings of Homer* (1735), p. 55.
27. Ibid., p. 326.   28. Ibid., pp. 327–28.

heavenly subjects. Thus the narrator's purpose is to reconcile the apparent harshness of Nature with the virtuous possibilities of man. The reconciliation will be made in civilized societies like those of Greece and Rome described in *Liberty*. The poem, then, is a kind of theodicy in which Nature and God are closely identified and in which the organization of society plays a key role.

In the midst of winter's most awful storms, Thomson elaborates upon his rural retreat and scholarly association with the great sages of the ancient world:

> Sages of ancient time, as gods revered,
> As gods beneficent, who blessed mankind
> With arts and arms, and humanized the world.
>
> (433–35)

Homer, Virgil, and "the British Muse" are joined together and praised for their harmony: "First of your kind! society divine" (541). The achievement of such a meditative life in a closed society will lead to a widening of understanding:

> Hence larger prospects of the beauteous whole
> Would gradual open on our opening minds;
> And each diffusive harmony unite
> In full perfection to the astonished eye.
> Then would we try to scan the moral world,
> Which, though to us it seems embroiled, moves on
> In higher order, fitted and impelled
> By wisdom's finest hand, and issuing all
> In general good.
>
> (579–87)

Here is an anticipation of the poem's conclusion in which everything will be found to be reasonable and orderly.

But Thomson must return to the central problem of the poem, which is the destruction and death represented by winter:

> Behold, fond man!
> See here thy pictured life; pass some few years,
> Thy flowering Spring, thy Summer's ardent strength,

And pale concluding Winter comes at last
And shuts the scene.

(1027–32)

At this point of ultimate decline and despair, all vanities of human
life have disappeared, and only "Virtue," if one has been fortunate
enough to cultivate it, remains:

All now are vanished! Virtue sole survives—
Immortal, never-failing friend of man,
His guide to happiness on high.

(1039–41)

Thus the ending of the poem moves toward a kind of guarded optimism, springing from an understanding of the total scheme of
things and the prospect of eternity. As the great eternal scheme becomes clearer to "reason's eye," it can

see now the cause
Why unassuming worth in secret lived
And died neglected: why the good man's share
In life was gall and bitterness of soul: . . .

(1052–55)

The poem, which has concerned itself with winter as death, now
moves toward a conception of the meaning of death. At last the refined reason can grasp the unity of the universe:

Ye good distressed!
Ye noble few! who here unbending stand
Beneath life's pressure, yet bear up a while,
And what your bounded view, which only saw
A little part, deemed evil is no more:
The storms of wintry time will quickly pass,
And one unbounded Spring encircle all.

(1063–69)

The "one unbounded Spring" is an ambiguous eternity, a reinvoca-
tion of Paradise; yet there is nothing overly optimistic about this
poem. Indeed, as I have observed in other poems, every optimistic

statement is countered by an observation which tends to call it in
question. Even this ending is not without a note of despair. In its
1744 version "Winter" expresses a disillusionment discernible when
compared with the 1726 text. For example, the earliest version is unambiguous in its assertion of eternity:

> Time swiftly fleets,
> And wish'd *Eternity*, approaching, brings
> Life undecaying, Love without Allay,
> Pure flowing Joy, and Happiness sincere.
>
> (1726 text, 402–5)

For many reasons, not the least of which was his unsuccessful
courtship of Elizabeth Young, Thomson underwent a change over
the almost twenty years from 1726 to 1744 when *The Seasons* was
put in its final form. There is in the later "Winter" a greater emphasis on retirement. Pope and the recently deceased James Hammond are introduced as friends in retirement, and indeed the entire
retirement passage is expanded greatly. In addition, the bleak descriptive passages are often increased in violence, intensity, and
length. Thus Thomson's progress in "Winter" would seem to show
in just eighteen short years the same tendencies toward introversion
discovered in the Puritan mind. The young poet, though not
worldly, had higher hopes for the world than does the older Thomson. By 1744 Thomson's hopes for the improvement of society at
large resided almost solely in the little group of friends which he had
valued even before the first publication of "Winter." But despite
the fact that his group contained a number of notables to whom his
own notoriety gave him access, the effect of these men on the world
was seen to be negligible. It may well be that the ineffectiveness of
the literary group gave rise to Thomson's increasing tendency to
withdraw into himself. But in addition to any such reasons, there
were personal reasons as well. The poet's view of society has
narrowed to a small circle of friends and even they do not receive
his unqualified expression of confidence.

Such developments, however, often make a poet more serious
about his purposes than he might otherwise have been. In a limited
society of personal friends, thus under the pressure of social re-

jection, dishonesty or malignity of any sort was intolerable. Complete trust and sincerity were demanded. But as these high standards of behaviour were violated and the poet became more and more his own audience, the problem of sincerity increased. For now the poet found himself in a Puritan struggle for his own soul.

MARK AKENSIDE

Although Mark Akenside's poetic theory derives from the works of both Addison and Shaftesbury, the influence of Addison has been shown to be relatively superficial.[29] It is rather the combination of Platonic and Stoic elements in the works of Shaftesbury which finds expression in Akenside's poetry. Also, the influence of Milton, although not specifically ideational, is ever-present in ways other than stylistic.

The Pleasures of Imagination must be regarded as Akenside's masterpiece. It exists, of course, in two versions, the first published in 1744 and the second, much revised text, in 1774, after Akenside's death. In the original version of the poem, Akenside entered upon a task that had not been undertaken before:

> With what attractive charms this goodly frame
> Of nature touches the consenting hearts
> Of mortal men; and what the pleasing stores
> Which beauteous Imitation thence derives
> To deck the poet's or the painter's toil,—
> My verse unfolds.
>
> (1, 1–6)[30]

Thus the nature and function of the imagination will be the theme, and it will be explored in all its manifold aspects.

A certain frame of mind is necessary, as we shall see, for the full

29. Robert Marsh, "Akenside and Addison: The Problem of Ideational Debt," *Modern Philology*, 59 (1961): 36–48.

30. References to Akenside's poetry are to *The Poetical Works*, ed. Alexander Dyce. Citations to *The Pleasures of Imagination* are by book and line numbers; page numbers only are cited for the odes.

perception of these truths. First, Harmony is called upon to descend
(1, 20), for with Harmony comes,

> Majestic Truth; and where Truth deigns to come,
> Her sister Liberty will not be far.
>
> (1, 23–24)

These are all, for Akenside, essential qualities, of which more will be
said later.

After further expatiating on the uniqueness of his poetic task, he
considers the ultimate source of his inspiration:

> From Heaven my strains begin; from Heaven descends
> The flame of genius to the human breast,
> And love and beauty, and poetic joy
> And inspiration.
>
> (1, 56–59)

Since poets, in creating poetry, imitate the divine Creator Himself,
it is necessary to contemplate the character of that Creator:

> Ere the radiant sun
> Sprang from the east, or 'mid the vault of night
> The moon suspended her serener lamp;
> Ere mountains, woods, or streams adorn'd the globe,
> Or Wisdom taught the sons of men her lore;
> Then liv'd the Almighty One: then, deep-retir'd
> In his unfathom'd essence, view'd the forms,
> The forms eternal of created things;
> The radiant sun, the moon's nocturnal lamp,
> The mountains, woods, and streams, the rolling globe,
> And Wisdom's mien celestial. From the first
> Of days, on them his love divine he fix'd,
> His admiration; till in time complete
> What he admir'd and lov'd, his vital smile
> Unfolded into being. Hence the breath
> Of life informing each organic frame,
> Hence the green earth, and wild resounding waves;
> Hence light and shade alternate, warmth and cold;

And clear autumnal skies and vernal showers,
And all the fair variety of things.

(1, 62–78)

Thus the poet, in order to imitate the Creator in these serious affairs, must prepare himself by assimilating certain qualities of mind. The capacity to do this does depend on natural talents, however, underscoring the aristocratic quality of Akenside's philosophy (1, 96–98). But given the requisite talents, the mind of man seems naturally fitted to look upon the mysteries of nature and respond to them:

so did Nature's hand
To certain species of external things,
Attune the finer organs of the mind:
So the glad impulse of congenial powers,
Or of sweet sound, or fair proportion'd form,
The grace of motion, or the bloom of light,
Thrills through Imagination's tender frame,
From nerve to nerve: all naked and alive
They catch the spreading rays; till now the soul
At length discloses every tuneful spring,
To that harmonious movement from without
Responsive.

(1, 113–24)

The mind then reacts almost exactly in the way that Divinity responded at the world's creation:

Then the inexpressive strain
Diffuses its enchantment; Fancy dreams
of sacred fountains, and Elysian groves,
And vales of bliss; the intellectual power
Bends from his awful throne a wondering ear,
And smiles; the passions, gently sooth'd away,
Sink to divine repose, and love and joy
Alone are waking; . . .

(1, 124–31)

If the poet is to be God-like in his creative activity, it follows from

this that his life reflect in every aspect the positive virtues attributed
to God. There is no difficulty at all in knowing these virtues, for
they are those prized by classical antiquity. Thus in the "Hymn to
Science," Akenside prays:

> O let thy powerful charms impart
> The patient head, the candid heart,
>   Devoted to thy sway;
> Which no weak passions e'er mislead,
> Which still with dauntless steps proceed
>   Where reason points the way.
>
> (p. 442)

"Candid" is one of Akenside's favourite adjectives of moral description. Susie I. Tucker states that its "usual eighteenth-century sense
is that of kindness," but she cites several other meanings as well, including that of Dyche and Pardon, "plain downright dealing."
Glossographia Anglicana Nova defines candid as "White, also Innocent," suggesting its latinate meaning close to that of "sincere." But
"benevolence" is probably the best definition of candour in a majority of cases,[31] and is often the chief meaning in Akenside's use of
the word. It is likely that this complex of meaning attracted Akenside. In his quest for harmony and unity, an all-encompassing word
such as candour is very useful indeed.

If patient head and candid heart are the qualities which the poet
must possess, we are not surprised when the reader of *The Pleasures
of Imagination* is addressed as one "Whose candid bosom the refin-
ing love / Of Nature warms, . . ." (1, 134–35). Here candid seems to
mean pure and, therefore, receptive, in addition to its other usual
meanings, many of which may be operant. An individual must
possess the capacity or internal harmony necessary to comprehend
Nature, and this capacity consists, at least in part, of an open, un-
bigoted mind. The notion of the initial gift is curiously like the
Calvinistic view of grace, which cannot be earned but must be a free
gift of God. This idea of initial selection probably did not disturb

31. Susie I. Tucker, *Protean Shape* (London: The Athlone Press, 1967), pp.
212–14.

Akenside's sensibilities, since, after all, he had been raised in a dissenting family. But accepting the circular argument that Nature selects for illumination those whom she (or God) has previously selected, Akenside makes it clear that illumination comes only to the gifted ones willing to make the necessary effort.

Thus virtue becomes for all exceptional men the main object of their lives; they are to progress toward perfection and divinity in a way which may remind us of God's prelapsarian plans for man in *Paradise Lost*:

> Say, why was man so eminently rais'd
> Amid the vast Creation; why ordain'd
> Through life and death to dart his piercing eye,
> With thoughts beyond the limit of his frame;
> But that the Omnipotent might send him forth,
> In sight of mortal and immortal powers,
> As on a boundless theatre, to run
> The great career of justice; to exalt
> His generous aim to all diviner deeds;
> To chase each partial purpose from his breast;
> And through the mists of passion and of sense,
> And through the tossing tide of chance and pain,
> To hold his course unfaltering, while the voice
> Of truth and virtue, up the steep ascent
> Of nature, calls him to his high reward,
> The applauding smile of Heaven?
>
> (1, 151–66)

This essentially prelapsarian vision of man is much the same as Milton took before the Commonwealth finally crumbled. Unlike the religious poets of the earlier seventeenth century who emphasized the sinful nature of man, Milton stressed the noble, independent qualities. In a sense Milton's more secular view is also more positive, since Donne and Herbert held that man's state on earth was essentially a debased one. For Milton man becomes more capable of noble action when he is on his own, to a certain degree independent of God, though reliant on Him.

In Akenside the idealistic vision is carried much further. God

becomes less anthropomorphic, more impersonal, and more a
generalization of individual characteristics to which man should
aspire. He is then a generalized statement of Truth, Virtue, Beauty,
Goodness, and everything else which naturally attracts the virtuous
man. That movement toward perfection, which is God, is made
clear in the following passage:

> For from the birth
> Or mortal man, the Sovereign Maker said,
> That not in humble nor in brief delight,
> Not in the fading echoes of renown,
> Power's purple robes, nor pleasure's flowery lap,
> The soul should find enjoyment; but from these,
> Turning disdainful to an equal good,
> Through all the ascent of things enlarge her view,
> Till every bound at length should disappear,
> And infinite perfection close the scene.
>
> (1, 212–21)

To this perfection we are led by Nature, whose own beauty and perfection attract us:

> The generous glebe
> Whose bosom smiles with verdure, the clear tract
> Of streams delicious to the thirsty soul,
> The bloom of nectar'd fruitage ripe to sense,
> And every charm of animated things,
> Are only pledges of a state sincere,
> The integrity and order of their frame,
> When all is well within, and every end
> Accomplish'd.
>
> (1, 364–72)

Akenside justifies his own poetic endeavour by confounding Beauty,
Truth, and the Good:

> Thus was Beauty sent from Heaven,
> The lovely ministress of Truth and Good
> In this dark world; for Truth and Good are one,

And Beauty dwells in them, and they in her,
With like participation.

(1, 372–76)

It is important to Akenside, even more than to Keats, that these qualities be related, since his poetic apprehension of beauty has both a moral (Good) and an anagogic (Truth) dimension. Akenside's generalizing tendency to unite all particulars in a monadology allows his rhetoric almost any illogicality. In a completely unified universe almost anything is very like everything else. But his scheme has a rationale: Fancy can be deceptive and sometimes will be mistaken about Beauty. But true Beauty can be identified by inquiring: "Where is the sanction of eternal Truth, / Or where the seal of undeceitful good?" (1, 382–83). Thus Beauty initially identifies the purview of Truth and Good, but after that initial encounter, we must go on to see them for ourselves. If we do not perceive them, it is possible that we did not, in the first case, descry true Beauty. But for Truth and Good, Beauty is a necessary determinant.

This leads Akenside to reject the gloom of superstition, which he associates with Gothic (Roman Catholic) religion. For Akenside, as for Shaftesbury and Thomson, Truth is airy, clean, and well-lighted. "Graves, and hoary vaults, and cloister'd cells" (397) are symbolic of unnatural and deceitful activities, and as such are hateful to a man of "sincere" conviction. Ancient Greece and Rome, or Akenside's romantic conceptions of them, provide open vistas:

From the grove
Where Wisdom talk'd with her Athenian sons,
Could my ambitious hand entwine a wreath
Of Plato's olive with the Mantuan bay,
Then should my powerful verse at once dispel
Those monkish horrors; then in light divine
Disclose the Elysian prospect, where the steps
Of those whom Nature charms, through blooming walks,
Through fragrant mountains and poetic streams,
Amid the train of sages, heroes, bards,
Led by their winged Genius, and the choir
Of laurell'd science and harmonious art,

Proceed exulting to the eternal shrine,
Where Truth conspicuous with her sister-twins,
The undivided partners of her sway,
With good and beauty reigns.

(1, 402–17)

A consideration of the ancients calls up for Akenside, as it did for
Thomson, the themes of friendship and retirement:

<blockquote>
is aught so fair
As virtuous friendship? as the candid blush
Of him who strives with fortune to be just?
The graceful tear that streams for others' woes?
Or the mild majesty of private life,
Where Peace with ever-blooming olive crowns
The gate; where Honour's liberal hands effuse
Unenvied treasures, and the snowy wings
Of Innocence and Love protect the scene?
</blockquote>

(1, 503–11)

This is the scene where true virtue is possible, and, for Akenside,
Beauty is of no worth without a moral orientation:

<blockquote>
For what are all
The forms which brute, unconscious matter wears,
Greatness of bulk, or symmetry of parts?
Not reaching to the heart, soon feeble grows
The superficial impulse.
</blockquote>

(1, 526–30)

Truth attracts its adherents by a kind of moral magnetism, which
presupposes a pure heart:

<blockquote>
But beyond
This energy of Truth, whose dictates bind
Assenting reason, the benignant Sire,
To deck the honour'd paths of just and good,
Has added bright Imagination's rays:
Where Virtue, rising from the awful depth
Of Truth's mysterious bosom, doth forsake
</blockquote>

The unadorn'd condition of her birth;
And, dress'd by Fancy in ten thousand hues,
Assumes a various feature, to attract,
With charms responsive to each gazer's eye,
The hearts of men.

(1, 543–54)

It is, for example, "the ingenuous youth" whose attention is most readily captured (555). But Akenside's liberal political outlook can be seen in his admitting to such insight the patriot for whom virtue

raises the majestic sword
Of public Power, from dark Ambition's reach
To guard the sacred volume of the laws.

(1, 564–66)

Throughout *The Pleasures of Imagination*, Akenside is himself taking the patriot's part, since his task in roaming the classic fields is to

Transplant son.e living blossoms to adorn
My native clime: while, far above the flight
Of Fancy's plume aspiring, I unlock
The springs of ancient wisdom. . . .

(1, 597–600)

At the outset of book 2, Akenside laments the fact that poetry and science were long under the restraining control of "Gothic night," i.e. the Roman Catholic Church. But he looks forward to a new English age of light:

But now, behold! the radiant era dawns,
When freedom's ample fabric, fix'd at length
For endless years on Albion's happy shore
In full proportion, once more shall extend
To all the kindred powers of social bliss
A common mansion, a parental roof.

(2, 42–47)

This is, of course, a common motif in eighteenth-century poetry. Pope's *Windsor Forest* and the early editions of Thomson's *Seasons* reflect something of the same optimism. Akenside's optimism is particularly apparent in his odes, where British economic expansion and all the first principles of morality are linked together. Northrop Frye has commented on this phenomenon:

> The English are famous for transforming their economic and political ambitions into moral principles, and to the naive mercantile jingoism of the eighteenth-century, which assumed that freedom of action was the same thing as material expansion, there seemed nothing absurd in thinking that the unchecked growth of England's power involved the emancipation of the world. At any rate, Akenside, in his *Ode to the Country Gentlemen of England*, seems to have had a vague idea that war with France is somehow connected with the principles of Freedom, Truth and Reason as well as Glory, and refers to the Hundred Years' War as a crusade in favor of these principles.[32]

What may seem to be outrageous attitudes make sense within the sincere ideal, however. France was the nation of servility and deceit, the very antithesis of virtue. Further, the economic expansion of England was usually seen as an opportunity for the propagation of moral ideals. Though these ideals were sometimes perverted in the struggle for political and economic power, for the poets, at least, the ideals came first and tended to justify any means used to disseminate them. But most important it should be remembered that much of the jingoism in Akenside and other authors is related to the moral idealism of the sincere ideal, which is essentially an imaginative construction.

In *The Pleasures of Imagination*, Akenside has retreated to the subjective imagination, which he argues has a clear relation to objective reality. Nevertheless, his recognition of the magnitude of the moral reformation necessary before the "radiant era" will indeed dawn must have been depressing to him. At the conclusion of book 2, Akenside catalogues at length tyrannies of various sorts, which he finds rampant among his contemporaries. Although one may not think so, some patriots do remain, however:

32. *Fearful Symmetry: A Study of William Blake* (Princeton: Princeton University Press, 1947), p. 179.

"The baleful dregs
Of these late ages, this inglorious draught
Of servitude and folly, have not yet,
Blest be the eternal Ruler of the world!
Defil'd to such a depth of sordid shame
The native honours of the human soul,
Nor so effac'd the image of its Sire."

(2, 765–70)

These are the words of no less an authority than the allegorical "Genius of humankind," who presents to the poet rather abundant extra-sensory perceptions. Whatever optimism we may discover here is clearly qualified by the oppressing facts of the situation. Akenside's excesses are exhortations to glory, not celebrations of success. It is clear that Akenside, were he a mere jingo, would have been happy with the successes enjoyed by the English during his lifetime. That he was not suggests that he did not approve of British imperialism as he saw it practised. He believed that British expansion could be a good thing only if moral ideals were held high. But instead he witnessed cynical greed and hypocrisy everywhere. This led him to assert ideals of strength and power, which were to be aimed at the French as representatives of all that was wrong both at home and abroad. The military ideal in Akenside's poetry is the exemplification of guileless male assertion, in the traditional heroic mode. In a world of deceptions such forthrightness could be looked upon with admiration. Further, in the eighteenth century a civilized human being could look upon war with greater equanimity than we can do today. This does not mean necessarily that he was less civilized than we, but perhaps that war in the eighteenth century was more civilized than war today.

The major purpose of book 2 is to show that all passions, even disturbing ones, lead to insight, and that this testifies to the unity of the world and of mankind. This is an important point in Akenside's argument, since it leads to a basic trust in man's temperament, a position which he clarifies in book 3.

At the outset of book 3, Akenside shows once again that error is the result of inordinate Fancy:

> where the powers
> Of Fancy neither lessen nor enlarge
> The images of things, but paint in all
> Their genuine hues, the features which they wore
> In Nature; there Opinion will be true,
> And Action right. For Action treads the path
> In which Opinion says he follows good,
> Or flies from evil, as the scene
> Was drawn by Fancy, lovely or deform'd:
> Thus her report can never there be true
> Where Fancy cheats the intellectual eye. . . .
>
> (3, 18–29)

Thus Akenside can adopt Shaftesbury's attitude toward ridicule, since ridicule serves to aid Reason and "depress / The giddy aims of Folly" (3, 264–65).

The Imagination, however, leads him who possesses it to a kind of joy, which Akenside likens to "a visionary paradise" (3, 511). Taste itself comes from Heaven:

> What then is taste, but these internal powers
> Active and strong, and feelingly alive
> To each fine impulse? a discerning sense
> Of decent and sublime, with quick disgust
> From things deform'd or disarrang'd, or gross
> In species?
>
> (3, 515–20)

But though the rude rustic is capable of enjoying Nature's beauty, Akenside, good classicist that he is, feels that Heaven's bounty is not enough:

> But tho' Heaven
> In every breast hath sown these early seeds
> Of love and admiration, yet in vain,
> Without fair culture's kind, parental aid,
> Without enlivening suns and genial showers,
> And shelter from the blast, in vain we hope

The tender plant should rear its blooming head,
Or yield the harvest promis'd in its spring.

(3, 535–42)

Thus culture, not here defined, is necessary to the realization of
Akenside's ideal. And it is this neoclassical position which keeps him
from a wholly subjective outlook. Yet the nature of "culture" is not
at all clear. Indeed as the century wore on the notion of unified culture became less and less a reality or possibility. Puritanism had
taken its toll; and the unity of opinion which the Church had fos-
tered was wavering indecisively. Even the Church itself, purged of
the extreme liberals after the Restoration, had now a Benjamin
Hoadly and soon a Richard Watson to show. Akenside's rejection of
Christianity leads him to seek a kind of substitute paideia, to be derived from the learned contemplation of the ancient Greeks.

Far from solving the problem of authority, however, Akenside, by
an almost arbitrary invocation of a specific tradition, leaves the way
open to accept or reject it with impunity. The fact that he suggests
the tradition is associated with Truth seems not to make it any less
arbitrary. To convince men to reject the tradition of which they are
the immediate product and then to ask them to overleap the centuries to kinship with the classical world (or rather an imaginative
version of it) is an ambitious task. Even if men can be impelled to
such action by identifying conservative Christianity with "monkish
glooms" and other horrors, the success of the action cannot be predicted. Indeed, as Akenside admits, only the highly educated can be
received in the formation of such a society. The deist group, then,
becomes a small, closed society of scholars and poets, cut off entirely
from the ordinary run of mankind. For such persons a neoclassical
deism might be satisfactory. But the inroads that such positions were
making on conservative religious thought were noticeable to those
even whose education did not fit them for deism. Thus the Anglican
Church was undermined in a number of ways by intellectuals, reformers, and fanatics of various hue. Such was the legacy of the New
Science and Puritanism. But there was no conspiracy to be deplored.
The tendencies could be found in every walk of life as a deep-seated
reality in human nature, a commodity noted less for its stability than

for its variety of response. It would be folly to believe that the Church had ever exerted total dominance over English society; but by the publication date of the first version of *The Pleasures of Imagination*, things were further out of control than at any time since the Puritan Revolution.

The doctrinal changes that Akenside makes in the second version of his major work emphasize earlier tendencies toward reliance on the subjective impulse. Akenside clarifies this position and seems on his way in the incomplete fourth book toward elaborating a poetic theory stressing personal factors. More specifically, his kinship with dissent can be seen in his psychology of the inner light inspired from on high. Truth and his verses come, in effect, from the same source:

> May the destin'd verse
> Maintain its equal tenor, though in tracts
> Obscure and arduous! May the Source of light
> All-present, all-sufficient, guide our steps
> Through every maze! and whom in childish years
> From the loud throng, the beaten paths of wealth
> And power, thou didst apart send forth to speak
> In tuneful words concerning highest things,
> Him still do thou, O Father, at those hours
> Of pensive freedom, when the human soul
> Shuts out the rumour of the world, him still
> Touch thou with secret lessons: call thou back
> Each erring thought; and let the yielding strains
> From his full bosom, like a welcome rill
> Spontaneous from its healthy fountain flow!
>
> (2, 29–41)

The antecedent of "him" is not clear, but it seems to be "Source of light," which in context may remind us of Christ. But whatever it is, the Miltonic similarities are apparent. This is not merely imitation of Milton, however. Akenside assumes the existence of an inner light and personal inspiration, which is both pagan and Puritan.

Perhaps Akenside's most explicit statement of faith in the subjective impulse comes in the revised edition of his poem. Presupposing a proper apprehension of Truth, impulse becomes "sacred law":

But man, whose eyelids Truth has fill'd with day,
Discerns how skilfully to bounteous ends
His wise affections move; with free accord
Adopts their guidance; yields himself secure
To Nature's prudent impulse; and converts
Instinct to duty and to sacred law.

(2, 185–90)

This impulse is not independent of Truth and the over-all scheme of
the universe, but rather is in accord with them:

Hence Right and Fit on earth: while thus to man
The Almighty Legislator hath explain'd
The springs of action fix'd within his breast;
Hath given him power to slacken or restrain
Their effort; and hath shown him how they join
Their partial movements with the master-wheel
Of the great world, and serve that sacred end
Which he, the unerring reason, keeps in view.

(2, 191–98)

This is clear assurance of the sanctity of the human heart and hence
the truth of the subjective impulse. If a coherent world order assists
in coordinating various impulses, then there is little reason to
question the truth of our sincere effusions. Truth, of course, is an
essential criterion; and this prevents Akenside from taking the extreme subjective viewpoint that we saw earlier in Hoadly. But Truth,
when universal, is ambiguous, and, when scientific, is inaccurate.
Akenside's criterion of Truth could be of very little practical value
in controlling most subjective impulses. Though still a classicist pro-
fessing an adherence to Reason, Akenside, by rational procedure,
shows a confidence in the human emotions which became characteristic of many thinkers in the eighteenth century. Often this new
trust was approached rationally or even called Reason; but it recognizes the revolutionary character of its implications. Indeed, just as
one of Akenside's favourite terms is "freedom," the new tendency
toward trust in the emotions is often seen as the freeing of mankind
from old bonds. Emotion wells up in man for various reasons,

social, political, religious. To sanctify this emotion by calling it truth is to justify its release. Thus the rational arguments for kingship and privilege give way to the feelings of the multitude. Akenside's retreat from the world, whether real or imagined, serves as a critique of the contemporary social order. Corruption there was in abundance, and there seemed to be little hope for radical improvement. Perhaps, reasoned Akenside and men like him, the rational faculty had gone wrong or Truth did not govern Reason as had been thought. This was surely so; but another problem was apparent: the human heart was not sufficiently consulted. This was a significant, seemingly original, observation, which was to be followed by a renaissance and deification of subjective impulse. Thus the floodgate of the human spirit was opened, and it was to prove a formidable tide indeed.

After *The Pleasures of the Imagination*, Akenside's two books of odes are his most important achievement. Though very different in purpose from the long poem, the odes reflect attitudes examined earlier. Now, however, everything is in lyrical form. The odes are, in short, paeans to the freshness of open vistas and the clarity of ingenuous minds. Here is the conclusion of Ode 5 of book 1, entitled "Against Suspicion":

> Let universal candour still,
> Clear as yon heaven-reflecting rill,
>   Preserve my open mind;
> Nor this nor that man's crooked ways
> One sordid doubt within me raise
>   To injure human kind.
>
> (p. 289)

These metaphors reflect Akenside's love of English liberty, asserted in Ode 8, "On Leaving Holland":

> I go where Liberty to all is known,
> And tells a monarch on his throne,
> He reigns not but by her preserving voice.
>
> (p. 298)

Ode 10 "To the Muse" is in some ways reminiscent of Coleridge's

"Dejection." It begins with a lament over declining poetic powers and concludes with new inspiration, signalling the return of the Muse.

Benjamin Hoadly was a direct object of Akenside's admiration. In a 1754 ode, the good bishop is seen as representing honest forthrightness:

> O! never, Hoadly, in thy country's eyes,
> May impious gold, or pleasure's gaudy prize,
> Make public virtue, public freedom, vile;
> Nor our own manners tempt us to disclaim
> That heritage, our noblest wealth and fame,
> Which thou hast kept entire from force and factious guile.
>
> (p. 358)

Again, the enemy of freedom is guile, characterized by all the most abhorrent metaphors associated with Roman Catholic or High Church principles.

But the optimistic view of Akenside's odes and "Hymn to Science" can be seen in proper perspective when we contemplate the sad prospect revealed in the unfinished Ode 15 of book 2, "On Domestic Manners":

> I
> Meek Honour, female shame,
> O! whither, sweetest offspring of the sky,
> From Albion dost thou fly;
> Of Albion's daughters once the favourite fame?
> O beauty's only friend,
> Who giv'st her pleasing reverence to inspire;
> Who selfish, bold desire
> Dost to esteem and dear affection turn;
> Alas! of thee forlorn
> What joy, what praise, what hope can life pretend?
>
> II
> Behold; our youths in vain
> Concerning nuptial happiness inquire:
> Our maids no more aspire

The arts of bashful Hymen to attain;
    But with triumphant eyes
And cheeks impassive, as they move along,
    Ask homage of the throng.
The lover swears that in a harlot's arms
    Are found the self-same charms,
And worthless and deserted lives and dies.

(p. 377)

Here in Akenside's despair regarding the efficacy of existing institutions, we find the source of his attempt to re-create England in a classical mould. Perhaps his ninth inscription contains the best summary of his poetic attempt:

Me though in life's sequester'd vale
The Almighty Sire ordain'd to dwell,
Remote from glory's toilsome ways,
And the great scenes of public praise;
Yet let me still with grateful pride
Remember how my infant frame
He temper'd with prophetic flame,
And early music to my tongue supplied.
'Twas then my future fate he weigh'd,
And this be thy concern, he said,
At once with Passion's keen alarms,
And Beauty's pleasurable charms,
And sacred Truth's eternal light,
To move the various mind of Man;
Till, under one unblemish'd plan,
His Reason, Fancy, and his Heart unite.

(pp. 407–8)

Thus the variety of creation and the various mind of man were to be united in the sincere ideal. This was, of course, no easy task, and Akenside cannot be said to have succeeded. His achievement, however, is often underestimated.

HENRY BROOKE

The development of scientific learning in the seventeenth century had an important effect on poetry, from which it has never wholly recovered. Poetry had, of course, been criticized in earlier ages for being at variance with religious truth; but as science progressed in the seventeenth century its defects became even more obvious: it was demonstrably at odds with the actual world of sense.

It is common for a new body of knowledge to displace old ones in popular opinion, even when there is no real justification for such a displacement. The excitement of discovering facts unknown before can result in a fanaticism which conflicts with the cool dispassion of scientific inquiry. Yet such fanaticism was rampant in England at the end of the seventeenth century.

Baconian dicta were enjoying great currency; particularly attractive was the empirical method, which seemed to obviate the desirability of abstruse speculation. Since the empirical method, as some thought, would render useless the time-honoured rationalism of conservative churchmen, it is not surprising to note that many dissenters and others of liberal religious persuasion rallied under the banner of science. This concern accorded as well with political attitudes. If "trimming" and sincere, above-board handling of political affairs were considered desirable and, indeed, imperative, the same was true with regard to knowledge. It was hoped that science would provide a certainty that would put an end to disagreement. The fear of religious and political cavils is reflected in both science and government.

Samuel Parker, for example, took to examining Platonic ideas "to be fully satisfied of their Truth and Sincerity."[33] He was not satisfied, of course, since, as R. F. Jones points out, he "expresses dissatisfaction with any theory that goes beyond the sensuously obvious."[34]

Robert Hooke, another Baconian, seeking to eschew imagination

---

33. R. F. Jones, *Ancients and Moderns: A Study of the Rise of the Scientific Movement in Seventeenth-Century England* (1961; reprinted Berkeley: University of California Press, 1965), p. 189.
34. Ibid., p. 189.

and contemplation, submits that what is needed for a reformation of philosophy is "a *sincere Hand*, and a *faithful Eye*, to examine, and to record, the things themselves as they appear. . . ."[35] Hooke further asserts that science has been too much the work of "the *Brain* and the *Fancy*."[36]

Clearly the emphasis here is on sensory apprehension, which seemed to these thinkers as straightforward as possible. Here, they believed, all disagreements could be resolved in a harmony of empiricism. Many poets responded to this challenge, not by denying the relevance of scientific method, but by adopting it as a subject for poetry. Important contributions to this attempt were made, among the deists, by Thomson, Akenside, and Henry Brooke.

Henry Brooke, author of *The Fool of Quality*, wrote earlier in his career one of the most interesting examples of scientific poetry, *Universal Beauty, A Philosophical Poem in Six Books*, published in 1735. Its purpose is to prove the deistic premise that the study of Nature leads to an assurance of God's existence. If we follow light,

> Thus, born on airy wings the radiance flies,
> Quickening the vision of poetick eyes;
> Whence we may pierce into the deep profound,
> And, searching, view the wondrous system round:
> For wide as universal Nature spreads,
> Light's sacred fount its streaming lustre sheds . . .
> . . . .
> But whence the Light's invigorating force,
> Its active energy, or secret source,
> Must be ascribed to that Eternal Spring,
> Whom First, and Last, and ever Blest we sing—.
>
> (2, 51–56, 65–68)

Every one of Brooke's analyses, whether it be biological, geological, or astronomical, leads to this very same conclusion: God is the source of everything.

Brooke has little of interest to say regarding the imagination. Poetry concerns him less than does science, and seems for him

---

35. Ibid., p. 196.   36. Ibid., p. 196.

merely a pleasant mode of discourse. Besides that, his verse is often quite obscure, not to mention deficient. As Miss Nicolson has pointed out, Brooke's notes are a more comprehensible treatment of science than the poem itself.[37] Yet a few tendencies in Brooke, elaborated greatly by Thomson and Akenside, should be examined to show the relative unanimity of interest among the deist poets and to point up the special concern for science which often characterized proponents of the sincere ideal.

If Brooke has no especial regard for the imagination, he does have esteem for the human mind:

> Mysterious Thought! swift Angel of the mind!
> By space unbounded, tho' to space confined,
> How dost thou glow with just disdain, how scorn,
> That thought could ever think thee earthly born?
>
> (1, 56–60)

By "mysterious" Brooke seems to mean "spiritual," but its characterization as an angel of light eliminates all hint of religious mystery and "monkish glooms." Thought comprehending thought as a kind of otherness is an oddity, but for Brooke the grand sweep of intellect, not the details, is what counts. Indeed, man's extraordinary mind gives him direct access to the spirituality of Nature:

> The florid theatres, romantick scenes,
> The steepy mountains, and luxuriant plains,
> Delicious regions! plants, woods, waters, glades,
> Grotts, arbours, flowrets, downs, and rural shades,
> The brooks that sportive wind the echoing hills,
> The pearly founts, smooth lakes, and murmuring rills—
> Myriads of Edens! blissful, blissful seats!
> Arcadian groves, sweet Tempe's blest retreats,
> Delightful Ennas, and Hesperian isles,
> And round, and round throughout, Elysium smiles—
> Consummate joy, peace, pleasure without end,
> Thro' mansions numberless their guests attend. . . .
>
> (1, 137–48)

37. M. H. Nicolson, *Newton Demands the Muse: Newton's Opticks and the Eighteenth Century Poets* (Princeton: Princeton University Press, 1946), p. 58.

Brooke's quickly and easily moving couplets evoke a Miltonic paradise of classical and Hebrew elements. The entire poem may be said
to describe a prelapsarian world of wonder in which God is everywhere.

   Though the world, for Brooke, is more the object of science than
of poetry, for God Himself is "the Almighty Alchemist" (2, 193),
his poetic rapture in contemplation of Nature is sometimes evident.
And the world may indeed be in some sense a poem:

   Thus Beauty mimicked in our humbler strains,
   Illustrious, thro' the world's great poem reigns!

                                        (3, 1–2)

The following lines as well outwing the merely scientific:

   Our transient optick o'er the surface plays,
   And Nature's superficial mien surveys;
   But rare with deeper inquisition pryes,
   Where Beauty's wrapt, recluse from vulgar eyes,
   Essential, sits on Truth's Eternal Throne,
   And universal reigns o'er worlds unknown;
   Displays her sway thro' unimagined scenes,
   Elysian tracts, and philosophic plains:
   These, these are climes of ever-living joy;
   Truth ne'er can satiate, Reason ne'er can cloy.
   O worthy! far more worthy to explore,
   Than treasured lustre of Peruvian ore;
   Or supererogated store, acquired
   By pilgrimage, to saintship long expired.
   In Nature's realms no wretched levees wait,
   No monarchs hold their arbitrary seat;
   Far different law her beauteous empire sways,
   And Order dictates her unerring ways.

                                        (3, 165–82)

Here is the deists' Garden of Eden, described with some relationship to scientific truth. Brooke's outlook allows for none of the
pessimism noted in Thomson and Akenside, but that is largely be-

cause Brooke deals only in science, avoiding the difficulties of social and political problems. But in his poetic flights and realistic concern, Brooke is actually retreating from the real problems of the sincere ideal, which are social and political. His imaginative inquiry into "pure" science leaves all other considerations behind, and in discovering that Nature is unified and God is reflected in it, he, in effect, reduces everything to that insight. But Brooke finds more in science than can be reasonably allowed to it. The imaginative conception of unified Nature leaves many important questions unanswered.

Brooke's true poet, then, is the scientist to whom all Nature is an open book. The active mind is emphasized, but the chief reason for trusting man's mind is that it, as is true of everything else, reflects the mind of the maker:

Hence, hence, alone, the final causes tend,
And reach unerring each appointed end;
The maze of endless implication wind,
Directed by the clue of All Perceiving Mind.
Hence from the Seraph's intellectual ray,
To reason's spark that guilds our sensual clay;
To life (scarce conscious) in the instinctive brute;
To reptile, plant, and vegetating root;
The features in conspicuous semblance shine,
And speak, thro' all, One Parent All Divine.

(3, 218–27)

By comparison with Shaftesbury, Thomson, and Akenside, Brooke's imaginative achievement is negligible. In making science the central focus of his poetry, he has severely limited his perspective. Yet in *Universal Beauty* we can see that the empiricism of seventeenth- and eighteenth-century science bore some relationship to the sincere ideal. It is not surprising then to realize that science was largely in the hands of dissenters, who sought in that discipline the clear certainty that their brethren sought in their hearts.

Brooke's hopes for science, like the more politically and socially oriented optimism of Thomson and Akenside, are visionary. For him the possibilities of scientific inquiry provided a way out of the difficulties of modern life. He did not expect to find the disparate and often chaotic materials of the real universe, but rather a unified and ideal world. Thomson and Akenside, of course, also showed interest in science, motivated largely by their concern for Nature; but for them science was only a part of a larger imaginative scheme. Brooke considers Nature much more minutely, hoping to find in the plain "certainty" of scientific exploration that prelapsarian paradise for which all his fellow deists sought.

This Verse little polish'd thô mighty sincere . . .

Prior

5

The Augustan Impulse to 1744

JOSEPH ADDISON AND THOMAS TICKELL

Joseph Addison's role in the development of sincerity in poetry and society is difficult to estimate since his writings give little clue. Those writings reveal him to be a careful, somewhat pedantic, neoclassicist. Yet his personal example seems to have provided an impetus to others who made more important literary contributions to the assertion of the subjective impulse.

In a letter to Ambrose Philips, Addison showed his renovating tendency when he noted the inadequacy of poetry in 1704: "Our poetry in England at present runs all into Lampoon which has seldom any thing of true satire in it besides Rhime & Ill nature."[1] This concern for satire was extended to all poetry; and with the start of his contributions to the *Spectator*, poetry of a more "serious," moral kind received his attention and, subsequently, the approbation of a public whose taste Addison was helping to form.

Though his interest in ballads suggests a premature romanticism, his critiques of the ballad "Chevy-Chase" are strictly in the classical mode, and contribute little to the development of the subjective impulse as a criterion of judgment or composition. But in his paper on the ballad of the "Two Children in the Wood," a specific concession is made: "This Song," he writes, "is a plain simple Copy of Nature, destitute of all the Helps and Ornaments of Art."[2] Addison continues, apologizing somewhat, "There is even a despicable Simplicity

---

1. *The Letters of Joseph Addison*, ed. Walter Graham (Oxford: Clarendon Press, 1941), Letter 43, 10 March 1704.
2. *Spectator* 85. *The Spectator*, ed. Donald F. Bond, 5 vols. (Oxford: Clarendon Press, 1964).

in the Verse; and yet, because the Sentiments appear genuine and unaffected, they are able to move the Mind of the most polite Reader with inward Meltings of Humanity and Compassion." Later in the century simplicity, perhaps even "despicable Simplicity," would seem to be the proper mode of sincere verse.

But Addison, like Shaftesbury, requires only the Longinian *appearance* of "genuine and unaffected" sentiments. The question of sincerity was still too much the province of Puritanism and enthusiasm to receive active concern from neoclassicists, who continued to maintain traditional values, whether social, religious, or poetical.[3] Yet his interest in the sublime; his concern for the secondary function of the imagination, emphasizing the activity of the mind; and his favourable view of Milton and his poetic ideals provide a climate congenial to the development of sincerity as an ideal.

At the same time his attention to "the faery way of writing" suggests another tendency in poetry, which is, in some respects, inimical to the clarity and clear perspective demanded by sincerity. The fact that Addison looks with equanimity on the imaginative concern with demons and other objects of superstition marks a tendency that goes beyond the sincere ideal to more explicitly Romantic notions.

But even supernatural motifs assume two possible meanings in eighteenth-century literature. Poets such as Thomson and Akenside, explicit children of the Enlightenment, reject the supernatural as mere superstition. But later in the century it could be identified with simple nature, as in Collins's "Ode on the Popular Superstitions," or could become an enthralling bogey against which sincere and open Englishmen (and Englishwomen) pitted themselves, as in the gothic novels of Ann Radcliffe.

Aside from his writings, Addison assumed a meaning to some of his contemporaries which can only be described as mythical. This meaning is probably most clearly represented in Edward Young's *Conjectures on Original Composition*, where Addison is praised for his "warm, and feeling heart," a quality which at least some of his earlier contemporaries would seem to deny to him. But for Young

3. Lee Andrew Elioseff, *The Cultural Milieu of Addison's Literary Criticism* (Austin: University of Texas Press, 1963), p. 67.

the fact that his "feeling heart" is not evident in his works is attributable to his concealing that natural warmth when "he should have let loose all his fire, and have show'd the most tender sensibilities of heart."[4] In short, Young praises him less for what he was than for what he might have been.

Thus a partly imaginary Addison becomes for succeeding generations an exemplum of the good man and feeling poet, Pope's Atticus notwithstanding. As Young argues:

> It is for our honour, and our advantage, to hold him high in our esteem: For the better men are, the more they will admire him; and the more they admire him, the better will they be. (*Conjectures*, p. 45)

Young goes on to face the primary objection to Addison and discovers that it is no objection at all:

> And yet (perhaps you have not observed it), what is the common language of the world, and even of his admirers, concerning him? They call him an *elegant* writer: that elegance which shines on the surface of his compositions seems to dazzle their understanding, and render it a little blind to the depth of sentiment, which lies beneath: Thus (hard fate!) he loses reputation with them, by doubling his title to it. (*Conjectures*, p. 43)

Young summarizes Addison's achievement with the words: "heads, indeed, are crowned on earth; but hearts only are crowned in heaven . . ." (*Conjectures*, p. 48).

Yet it would be idle to deny Addison real as well as mythic importance. He participated with Steele in periodical essay ventures to renovate the manners of the age,[5] provided a high standard for religious poetry in his own hymns, and by popularizing *Paradise Lost*, brought into vogue the only poem which united in greatness principles of dissent and neoclassicism. Milton had invigorated neoclassicism with a certain Puritan vitality and made Puritan attitudes

4. *Conjectures on Original Composition*, ed. Edith J. Morley (Manchester: Manchester University Press, 1918), p. 38.
5. Steele's own contribution to the sincere ideal is to be found chiefly in his dramatic works. Though the drama is beyond the purview of this study, I comment briefly upon it in my conclusion.

respectable by the elegance of his style, the catholicity of his learning, and the force of his genius. As is often the case, a great poet requires a critic of genius to present his poetry to best advantage. Addison performed this function so well as to change the shape of his age.

Thomas Tickell (1685–1740) shared many of Addison's interests and was one of his closest friends. It is fitting then that Tickell's greatest triumph came in the writing of his elegy "To the Earl of Warwick on the Death of Mr. Addison," a poem which contributed greatly to the development of the Addison myth.

Pope's promotion of the view that Tickell's version of *The Iliad* was mainly the work of Addison has been damaging to Tickell's reputation. Even if we manage to dismiss this view, it is difficult to avoid the irrational suspicion that Addison's hand is in everything Tickell wrote. But with Addison entirely out of the picture, the elegy stands apart as proof of Tickell's ability, as Dr. Johnson makes amply clear. Johnson, who was, of course, dissatisfied with *Lycidas*, indicates his taste for sincere elegy by overrating Tickell's poem: "To these works [Addison's] he prefixed an elegy on the author, which could owe none of its beauties to the assistance which might be suspected to have strengthened or embellished his earlier compositions; but neither he nor Addison ever produced nobler lines than are contained in the third and fourth paragraphs, nor is a more sublime or more elegant funeral poem to be found in the whole compass of English literature."[6]

Tickell opens his poem, published in 1721, more than two years after Addison's death, with a conventional protestation of sincerity and excessive grief:

> What mourner ever felt poetic fires!
> Slow comes the verse, that real woe inspires:
> Grief unaffected suits but ill with art,
> Or flowing numbers with a bleeding heart.

$$(5-8)^7$$

At first glance it may seem that the poet is saying that his grief, or at

---

6. *Lives of the English Poets*, 2, 310.
7. R. S. Crane, ed., *A Collection of English Poems, 1660–1800*.

least his period of mourning, is over, for at last an elegy has been written. But a more careful reading reveals that the opposite is true: the grief remains and becomes the force behind the creation of the poem.

At the outset Tickell is too much the neoclassicist to believe that good poetry can be the artless production of sincere grief; but as the poem takes shape, its success, giving the lie to this "false surmise," proves the existence of a sincere poetry.[8] This procedure of Tickell's may remind us of Coleridge's in "Dejection" and Wordsworth's in the Immortality ode, in which lamentations over failing imaginative powers rise to the highest poetical achievement.

In the description of Addison's midnight burial, anticipating some of the effects of the "graveyard" school of poetry and Thomas Gray's Pindaric style, the poet once again claims to comprehend the full impact of grief:

> Can I forget the dismal night, that gave
> My soul's best part for-ever to the grave!
> How silent did his old companions tread,
> By mid-night lamps, the mansions of the dead,
> Through breathing statues, then unheeded things,
> Through rowes of warriors, and through walks of kings!
>
> (9–14)

Echoing the early request (line 3) that Warwick not blame the Muse's silence, but "bemoan" it, Tickell emphasizes the truth of his sorrow:

> To strew fresh laurels let the task be mine,
> A frequent pilgrim, at thy sacred shrine;
> Mine with true sighs thy absence to bemoan,
> And grave with faithful epitaphs thy stone.
>
> (23–26)

The key figure of the poem, however, is not the poet but Addison, who, at every point and in every particular, is both theme and example. The consciousness of the poet reaches out to grasp and

8. For an analysis of the figure "surmise" see Geoffrey H. Hartman, *Wordsworth's Poetry, 1787–1814* (New Haven: Yale University Press, 1964), pp. 8 *ff.*

possess the virtues represented by the poem's subject. The poet participates in the moral action of realizing fully the perfection of the personified ideal and by so doing becoming one with it. The shade of Addison haunts the poet like a vision of a better world:

> That awful form (which, so ye heavens decree,
> Must still be lov'd and still deplor'd by me)
> In nightly visions seldom fails to rise,
> Or, rous'd by fancy, meets my waking eyes.
> If business calls, or crowded courts invite,
> Th' unblemish'd statesman seems to strike my sight;
> If in the stage I seek to soothe my care,
> I meet his soul, which breathes in *Cato* there;
> If pensive to the rural shades I rove,
> His shape o'ertakes me in the lonely grove:
> 'Twas there of Just and Good he reason'd strong,
> Clear'd some great truth, or rais'd some serious song;
> There patient show'd us the wise course to steer,
> A candid censor, and a friend severe; . . .
>
> (67–80)

In this passage Addison stands as the "sincere" (unblemished) statesman, the moralist, combining urbanity with rural virtue (Cato), and the poet–philosopher with truth squarely in view. For Tickell, Addison is more the moral censor and less the man of sensibility that he was to be for Young, but in 1721 moral rigour was more important than it would be in 1759, when sentimentalizing was in vogue. But if Addison represents the neoclassical virtues of reason, statesmanship, scholarship, and censorious morality, the outline of the sincere ideal is found in him as well. Stressing imagination, sensibility, retirement, and friendship, Joseph Addison seemed to combine all that was best in man. If his loss might temporarily evoke in his mourners some of the virtues he possessed, so much the better. But in considering his power to do this, the sense of loss is redoubled:

> There taught us how to live; and (oh! too high
> The price for knowledge) taught us how to die.
>
> (81–82)

Here the poet, imitating a moment of passionate grief, breaks the couplet with a form of asyndeton. The couplet alludes to Addison's dying words to Warwick: "See in what peace a Christian can die," words which Young says were related to him by Tickell (who was present at the deathbed) "before his eyes were dry" (*Conjectures*, p. 47).

The real loss, however, is not of Addison but rather of the moral perfection that he represents. The sincere mode is largely elegiac, even when it is not formally so, and the loss of Addison may be likened to the loss of other sincere, ideal states.

"RETIREMENT: A DIVINE SOLILOQUY"

A poem by an anonymous versifier provides a link between the "Augustans" and "Deists" studied in this work. Though Christian in its main emphasis, "Retirement: A Divine Soliloquy" presents a paradisiacal vision that has much in common with deistic and classical perspectives. Chronologically earlier than most of the deist poems, it suggests the importance of Christian influence on English Deism. In arguing that much of the influence on Thomson is not strictly deistic, Ralph Cohen has shown that traditionally Christian motifs are compatible with some of the more radical aspects of natural religion.[9]

Published in 1722, "Retirement" is evidently modelled on Pomfret's "The Choice," which served the eighteenth century as an English model of the myth of retirement. Our poet makes his debt to Pomfret clear when he concludes with a triplet apostrophe to God:

Thy Face unveil'd shall see in heavenly Bliss;
Of which, my Choice, my Rural Paradise,
Like Glass to Gems a faint Resemblance is.

(p. 24)[10]

9. See Chapter 4, n. 25.

10. The relationship of this poem to science has been explored in William Powell Jones, *The Rhetoric of Science* (London: Routledge & Kegan Paul, 1966), p. 149.

At the outset the action of the poem is stated in an apostrophe to flight from the evils of contemporary society:

> Haste, O my Soul, and let thy winged Speed,
> The Flight of Halcyon's from a Storm exceed,
> For lo! the Skies are black with Winds and Rain,
> The World is all as one tempestuous Main;
> A gen'ral Storm of Party Rage and Strife,
> Sits brooding o'er the Land, and blackens Life.
>
> (p. 1)

Expressed here are the very difficulties which Pope and Thomson were to feel so acutely. The solution is, of course, removal to a pastoral retreat, which the poet relates specifically to New Testament imagery in the mode of Philip Doddridge:

> Ye tender Lambs which feed in Pastures green!
> In you my Saviour's Innocence is seen:
> Ye murmuring Doves which coo and bill by Turns!
> In you Love's chastest Fire for ever burns;
> Ye Beasts of Prey by Gratitude made tame!
> Are all their Maker's Praise, of Men the Shame.
>
> (p. 3)[11]

In the natural paradise of a rural retreat the senses and, more important, the soul are treated to ecstatic experiences. Here the poet addresses his lady love, who is identified with his soul:

> Thy nobler Flame, thy Heav'n-born Spirit there,
> More like thy Maker's Image shall appear.
> Whilst unconfin'd the tow'ring Muse shall stretch
> Uncommon Plumes, uncommon Wisdom fetch,
> From all the Creatures, as the lab'ring Bee
> Does Honey from the smallest Flow'r or Tree.
>
> (p. 6)

Thus the beauty of the natural surroundings will, it is hoped, im-

---

11.Doddridge was a hymnologist of note and associate of Isaac Watts.

prove her soul and his poetry. The latter, at least, is extremely
desirable.

The poem moves forward with a pseudo-scientific examination of
natural objects, which pales in a comparison with what Brooke was
to do in *Universal Beauty*. But the concern for science is present
nevertheless, and it leads (as in Brooke) to what approaches pan-
theism.

Once having proved by scientific method that Nature is grand,
the poet proceeds to compare the retreat to Eden. Again the lady is
addressed:

There is still Life, beneath the spangled Roof
Of Heav'ns high vaulted Canopy aloof;
A Jubilee of Rest thou may'st begin;
Live to thy God, and die to Care and Sin.
Such was the blest Abode, the happy Clime,
Where our first Parents sweetly spent their Time
In mutual Love and Innocence, among
The shady Bow'rs and Trees, and flow'ry Throng
Of Eden's Paradise, before they fell.
And turn'd their Heav'nly Garden into Hell.

(p. 15)

The first paradise was turned to Hell by sin; but the second Eden of
retirement will be closed to both care and sin. This second earthly
paradise is stressed once again in the lines that follow:

Thither again, my Soul, if thou wouldst know
What Innocence and Love is, thou must go;
And there, if thou wouldst turn that Hell again
To Paradise on Earth, thou must remain.

(p. 15)

This is not merely a pastoral retreat but a paradise of spiritual tran-
quillity, a representation of the state of the soul. Indeed, Thomas
Parnell saw the second Eden as an imaginative and spiritual ideal
only:

Lovely, lasting peace, appear!
This world itself, if thou art here,

Is once again with Eden blest,
And man contains it in his breast.[12]

The poet of "Retirement" does, of course, make clear the limits of the terrestrial paradise when he compares it to Heaven as glass to jewels (p. 24).

There are laments in "Retirement" over the "cannibal" activities of human society (a notion which he shares with Thomson) and the widespread rejection of the Church (pp. 17–18). This latter regret indicates that we have no deist on our hands, for no deist would feel so strongly about the Church's difficulties.

And finally our poet adopts David as a poetic exemplum, thus following a dissenter tradition and looking forward to an increased admiration of Hebrew poetry as expressed in Lowth's *Lectures on the Sacred Poetry of the Hebrews* (p. 24).

Though this poem deserves no attention on its poetic merits, it is, nevertheless, a curious mixture of attitudes that were to characterize sincere poetry throughout the century. It articulates the myth of retirement, to which it links the notion of terrestrial paradise. This second Eden, however, seems to be essentially a spiritual state. Further, in a general way, the poem suggests that Nature exerts a power of inspiring poets.

Many of these ideas we have discovered already among the dissenters and deists. They will reappear in the poetry of some of the "Augustans" and particularly in the verse of the later century. The sincere ideal was a secular moral standard which seems to have appealed to persons of varied religious and philosophical persuasions.

ALEXANDER POPE

Pope may seem to many readers out of place in a study of the sincere ideal; and not too many years ago such inclusion might have been unthinkable. But Pope scholarship is moving ahead with a rather extraordinary revaluation, which can be seen chiefly in the writings

12. "A Hymn to Contentment," *The Poetical Works*, ed. George A. Aitken (London: Aldine Edition, 1894), p. 98.

of Geoffrey Tillotson and Maynard Mack.[13] These scholars have called into question the traditional view of Pope as the "wasp of Twickenham," an unpleasant, indeed, mendacious little man, whose motives for writing poetry in no way approximated the sincere ideal. It is safe to say that this popular opinion has been thoroughly discredited. The publication of Pope's correspondence in Sherburn's great edition has done much to reclaim his right to personal respect. John Butt, reflecting on the letters and citing testimony from Spence's *Anecdotes*, concludes that Pope's professions of concern for his friends and his many long-term friendships cannot allow us to accept the traditional view of his character: "We cannot surely believe that Pope made a life-long habit of insincere professions of friendship, and that his intimates—the characters of a great many of whom are known independently of these letters—were so much afraid of him as to pretend a devotion that they did not feel."[14]

The word sincerity is a constant in Pope's correspondence, from the early letters to Wycherley to the very last letters he wrote. It is employed most often with relation to friendship, as, for example, when Pope praises Henry Cromwell's "Friendship, Justice, & Sincerity,"[15] or professes his own sincerity: "And you may be confident, if my Opinion can be of any sort of consequence to any thing, that I will never be Unsincere, tho I may be often mistaken. To use Sincerity with you is but Paying you in your own Coin, from whom I have experienced so much of it; and I need not tell you how much I really Esteem and admire nothing in the World so much as that Quality" (*Corr.*, 1, 97). Indeed, it would seem from succeeding

13. See especially Geoffrey Tillotson, *Pope and Human Nature* (Oxford: Clarendon Press, 1958) and Maynard Mack, *The Garden and the City* (Toronto: University of Toronto Press, 1969). Also, Maynard Mack, "The Shadowy Cave: Some Speculations on a Twickenham Grotto" in Carroll Camden, ed., *Restoration and Eighteenth-Century Literature* (Chicago: University of Chicago Press, 1963) and "A Poet in His Landscape: Pope at Twickenham" in Frederick W. Hilles and Harold Bloom, eds., *From Sensibility to Romanticism* (New York: Oxford University Press, 1965). For an inquiry from another point of view see Thomas R. Edwards, *This Dark Estate: A Reading of Pope* (Berkeley: University of California Press, 1963).
14. "Pope Seen Through His Letters" in James L. Clifford, ed., *Eighteenth-Century Literature* (New York: Oxford–Galaxy, 1959), p. 66.
15. Alexander Pope, *The Correspondence*, 1, 67. Cited as *Corr.* in the text.

correspondence that sincerity was Pope's best-loved virtue. Not
that he always managed to be true to it; that is not the point. He did,
however, try to live up to the ideal of sincerity, and his poetry is, in
large measure, an attempt to define that ideal.

Studies devoted to Pope's and Swift's use of the persona or mask
have been of great value in the criticism of eighteenth-century literature. Many nineteenth-century assumptions about the characters of
authors as seen in their poetry were ludicrous to say the least.
Persona studies entirely discredited such views and led to the sound
evaluation of eighteenth-century poetry as the highly sophisticated
art it often is. But distinguishing the persona from the personality
does not solve the irksome problem of their relationship. Irvin
Ehrenpreis has questioned the popular assumptions about personae:

> Only as a relationship between a real speaker and a real listener
> can meaning exist. In drama and prose fiction or epic, where
> separate speeches illustrate separate characters, the whole narra-
> tive must be read as a parable whose implications can be
> gathered from the light in which the various elements appear.
> The author is speaking this parable to the audience. In didactic
> or lyric poetry, as in the reflective or polemical essay, the
> author must be regarded as the speaker. He may talk ironically;
> he may imitate a man he despises; he may ask you to sneer at
> the fool he is copying; he may in mockery talk like his foolish
> audience. But unless we treat the material as indicating, how-
> ever indirectly, what the author believes and is, we do not dis-
> cover the meaning of the work; and if we miss its meaning, we
> cannot judge its form.[16]

The fact that a poet's "real self" cannot be defined confidently
makes the problem an extremely vexing one. Proponents of sincerity, however, have generally assumed that they knew what that
self was. But one of the reasons why a true poetry of sincerity is impossible is that there is probably no definable, static self. In fact
Thomas Edwards argues that Pope's use of the persona is sometimes
an attempt to get closer to his real feelings and personality: "The

16. "*Personae*" in Carroll Camden, ed., *Restoration and Eighteenth-Century Literature*. See n. 13 of this chapter.

'Pope' of *Arbuthnot*, the *Epilogue*, and the other Horatian satires *is* Pope—Pope provisionally freed from the irksome restraints of social and political moderation so that his deepest commitments may get something like pure expression."[17] Such an observation cannot be defended, of course, except by an appeal to the reader's understanding of Pope. But it is not necessary to believe that one thing is the "real" Pope and another not. Pope had a multi-faceted personality and probably did not recognize a clear-cut distinction between himself and his Horatian persona, except in some fairly obvious cases where there is an exaggeration of character resulting in the utterly grotesque. The assumption of the Horatian character was not at variance with the facts of Pope's ideally evaluated personality. This is not to deny that Pope was a master in the use of the poetic persona. It is simply to say that from what we know of his letters and of contemporary testimony concerning him, the Horatian Pope of the satires is very like the Pope who passed in the world as a real man.

Pope's misunderstanding with Wycherley in 1710 led him to several professions of his own "plain-dealing" in the affair. The relationship is curiously coloured by the fact that Wycherley was the creator of Manly, a Restoration prototype of plain-dealing. In a letter to Cromwell, Pope defends himself against the possible charge of insincerity: "Indeed to believe nobody, may be a Maxime of Safety, but not so much of honesty. There is but one way I know of Conversing safely with all men, that is, not by concealing what we say or do, but by saying or doing nothing that deserves to be conceal'd, & I can truly boast this Comfort, in my affairs with Mr. W" (*Corr.*, 1, 102). Pope constantly resorted to this kind of defence during his career. The fact that such a defence was necessary may incline us to be suspicious of him, but we should remember that it would have taken a very bad man indeed to deny with so much pathos the continual charges made against him. The fact was that he could appeal for justice to those friends who knew him best. And that he received comfort from them indicates that he was not totally in the wrong. Pope was so desirous of his friends' respect that he patiently and

17. *This Dark Estate*, p. 110.

painfully sought to justify himself in their eyes. That he was reasonably successful in this enterprise is testified to by the many life-long friendships he was able to maintain.

Surely some of Pope's actions are open to question; I am not here seeking total exoneration for him. But as Norman Ault has shown with regard to the Cibber question,[18] and as I shall argue from an examination of his correspondence with Hill, the fault often lay on the other side.

It is probably germane to observe that Pope's protestations of sincerity are not entirely the result of personal motivation, but are, in large part, a reaction to the age in which he lived. As we have already seen, and shall see further, sincerity was becoming a significant psychological counter in the dangerous game of sanity. In Pope's protestations we can see him reacting predictably to society's expectations in the language that society had sanctified for that purpose. As his career progressed, Pope became more embittered over the political and religious difficulties that England was experiencing. This led him farther along the road to retirement and the sincere ideal.

At first his hopes for that ideal were expressed in nationalistic ardour. The triumphant strains of *Windsor Forest* call on Britain to extend her rule concurrently with that of "Peace":

> Oh stretch thy Reign, fair Peace! from Shore to Shore,
> Till Conquest cease, and Slav'ry be no more: . . .
>
> (407–8)[19]

This may reflect Pope's ardent hope, but probably not his realistic evaluation of actuality. Early in the year following the publication of *Windsor Forest*, he wrote to Addison thus despondently:

> This miserable age is so sunk between animosities of Party and Religion, that I begin to fear, most men have politicks enough to make (thro' violence) the best Scheme of Government a bad one; and faith enough to hinder their own Salvation. I hope for my own part, never to have more of either than is consistent

18. *New Light on Pope* (London: Methuen, 1949), pp. 298–324.
19. All references to Pope's poetry are to *The Twickenham Edition of the Poems of Alexander Pope.*

with common justice and charity, and always as much as becomes a christian and honest man. (*Corr.*, 1, 209)

Outrage at "this sliding age," as Thomson called it, is common to all
poets who affect the sincere pose. The outrage seems to have come
first, driving the individual poet from the active life to retirement or
semi-retirement, where he then had the leisure to contemplate the
abuses of the times and the wrongs done to himself. This would not
in any particular case seem an extraordinary occurrence. Those who
are rejected by the world often react adversely to those who reject
them. But in the eighteenth century the pattern of rejection and reaction among poets is almost universal. The case is a complex one,
but at least one fact is apparent: poets, who, during the seventeenth
century and earlier, had held positions of the highest responsibility
in the government, are no longer found useful there. The court,
which had provided place and prestige for other poets whose talents
were not administrative, was now closed to them. In reaction to these
adverse circumstances, poetry becomes more personal.

Even though the trend toward retirement was beginning to become more real than mythic, retirement was not sufficient to create
a poetry of sincerity. Poetry remained so closely bound up with
party politics and religious controversy during the later seventeenth
century that the tendency to see it as necessarily political or religious
persisted in the early eighteenth. The strife of factionalism made
sincere self-revelation in poetry all but impossible. Even the most
impassioned personal defences in verse employed strong irony to
shield the poet from the ridicule that his pretence to candour was
sure to bring down upon him.

For these reasons, the familiar letter was gaining a new prominence and utility. During most of the seventeenth century the letter
in English was modelled on the epistles of classical authors such as
Cicero and Pliny the Younger. It was often Ciceronian in style, but
even as a simpler style was coming into being, the impersonality of
Pliny was maintained.

With the rise of Puritanism, the Pauline epistle became the chief
model for the letter and the trend toward self-revelation in correspondence began. But this is not to say that all eighteenth-century

authors developed a sincere, personal voice for their correspondence. Most letter writers maintain a strict correlation between function and tone. If business is to be transacted, formality is required; but where feelings and personal relations are concerned, a new tone of sensibility—even sentimentality—is developed. We have already noted the exorbitant sentimentality of some of Thomson's letters and will see much the same thing in the letters of Aaron Hill and Samuel Richardson. On the other hand, great figures such as Swift and Gray maintain a nice balance between sensibility and classical formalism without ever descending into bathos.

Pope, however, indulges himself, more often than either Swift or Gray, in what may be called a sincere epistolary style. If the public nature of poetry as Pope understood it rendered poetry unsuitable for the revelation of personal feelings, the familiar letter seemed to provide a more natural outlet. The following excerpt from a letter from Pope to Congreve is indicative of a common use to which he put the letter form:

> Methinks when I write to you, I am making a confession, I have got (I can't tell how) such a custom of throwing myself out upon paper without reserve. You were not mistaken in what you judg'd of my temper of mind when I writ last. My faults will not be hid from you, and perhaps it is no dispraise to me that they will not. The cleanness and purity of one's mind is never better prov'd, than in discovering its own faults at first view: as when a Stream shows the dirt at its bottom, it shows also the transparency of the water. (*Corr.*, 1, 274)

Here Pope recognizes both the advantages and dangers of a sincere style. Yet a clear distinction is implied between poetry and letter-writing. Perhaps that distinction obtains as well when in a letter to the Earl of Oxford he realizes the impossibility of expressing his feelings accurately: "It is . . . a most certain truth, that *one can never Express any thing that one really feels*" (*Corr.*, 2, 337). And the italics are Pope's! This is surely the beginning of sincere writing in any author. The first step is to correlate one's feelings with the symbols on the paper.[20] When Pope writes about how he "feels" he means

20. See David Perkins, *Wordsworth and the Poetry of Sincerity*, Chapter 1.

neither large issues of philosophy, politics, and religion nor artistic decisions. Rather the realm of feelings consists almost wholly of human relationships, with some concern reserved for the natural scene.

Pope's clearest commitment to sensibility and sincerity comes in his letters. In writing to Hugh Bethel, Pope, after apologizing for his life and actions in moving terms, concludes with the following affirmation: "I have not chosen my companions for any of the qualities in fashion, but almost intirely for that which is the most out-of-fashion, sincerity" (*Corr.*, 2, 501).

Pope's letters are not perfect examples of sincerity, however. They were carefully written and often studiously rewritten. Pope showed great concern for his reputation and believed that he was a better man than he was credited with being. Thus after attempting to justify himself to his friends in his letters, he connived to publish them in order to reach a wider audience.

This state of affairs is not one that we might expect of a man of candour. Yet the fact that he did have a strong regard for the state of his reputation among his friends is proof that he was no complete moral delinquent. The attempt to see himself as an honest lover of sincerity and good works may be a pose, but we need not believe that a more malignant self existed beneath the mask. If Pope was not a man of impeccable virtue, he nonetheless cherished his aspiration to a moral ideal, and the assumption of the pose was part of the attempt to live up to the ideal. At some point imposture and reality are identical; but since human beings are personalities in flux, there is no single point at which we can say imposture ends and reality begins. We have instead fluctuation through various points of behaviour, some of which reflect developed tendencies and others only latent ones. The developed traits, in terms of personality, may be called real, and the latent or incipient ones imposture. There is such a thing as outright disingenuousness, but that is possible only at the simplest levels of behaviour. As mendacity becomes a trait, it comes closer and closer to reflecting reality. Indeed at various points in a behaviour pattern, it *is* reality. In Pope's case, whatever sincerity he feigned, gradually became part of his personality and directed other of his tendencies accordingly. But Pope's sincerity is no more at issue here than that of any other poet. Whether or not he believed what he was saying, he did use in his letters and in certain of his poems the vocabulary and imagery of the sincere ideal.

In his *Epistle to Dr. Arbuthnot*, Pope explores some of the results of his supposed honesty. At first the problem is stated in rather simple terms: how can he, as famous author, escape those unknown authors who wish to gain recognition through his intercession?

> Seiz'd and ty'd down to judge, how wretched I!
> Who can't be silent, and who will not lye; . . .
>
> (33–34)

In this poem, his apology for poetry, Pope first declares that poetry was for him no abdication of duty, but rather a devotion that helped him bear the difficulties of his life:

> Why did I write? what sin to me unknown
> Dipt me in Ink, my Parents', or my own?
> As yet a Child, nor yet a Fool to Fame,
> I lisp'd in Numbers, for the Numbers came.
> I left no Calling for this idle trade,
> No duty broke, no Father dis-obey'd.
> The Muse but serv'd to ease some Friend, not Wife,
> To help me thro' this long Disease, my Life,
> To second, Arbuthnot! thy Art and Care,
> And teach, the Being you preserv'd to bear.
>
> (125–34)

Encouraged by his friends (135–44) Pope undertook to publish his works, which, though they were poems of "pure Description," suffered the attacks of several critics:

> Yet then did Gildon draw his venal quill;
> I wish'd the man a dinner, and sate still:
> Yet then did Dennis rave in furious fret;
> I never answer'd, I was not in debt: . . .
>
> (151–54)

The Epistle then gains momentum as Pope catalogues those who represented threats to himself and his poetry, among them Atticus

and Bufo. Gay's memory is invoked, his death lamented, and the
familiar myth of retirement expounded. Even in Pope's restrained,
essentially rational verse, an indication of strong emotion breaks
through:

> Oh let me live my own! and die so too!
> ("To live and die is all I have to do:")
> Maintain a Poet's Dignity and Ease,
> And see what friends, and read what books I please.
> Above a Patron, tho' I condescend
> Sometimes to call a Minister my Friend:
> I was not born for Courts or great Affairs,
> I pay my Debts, believe, and say my Pray'rs,
> Can sleep without a Poem in my head,
> Nor know, if Dennis be alive or dead.
>
> (261–70)

This personal defence, ending in the unkind comment on Dennis,
leads Pope, after assurances that

> A Lash like mine no honest man shall dread,
> But all such babling blockheads in his stead . . .
>
> (303–4)

to his most savage portrait—that of Sporus:

> Let *Sporus* tremble—"What? that Thing of silk,
> Sporus, that mere white Curd of Ass's milk?
> Satire or Sense alas! can Sporus feel?
> Who breaks a Butterfly upon a Wheel?"
> Yet let me flap this Bug with gilded wings,
> This painted Child of Dirt that stinks and stings; . . .
> . . . .
> Amphibious Thing! that acting either Part,
> The trifling Head, or the corrupted Heart!
> Fop at the Toilet, Flatt'rer at the Board,
> Now trips a Lady, and now struts a Lord.
> Eve's Tempter thus the Rabbins have exprest,
> A Cherub's face, a Reptile all the rest;

Beauty that shocks you, Parts that none will trust,
Wit that can creep, and Pride that licks the dust.

(305–10, 326–33)

More brilliantly venomous lines would be difficult to find anywhere.
This is first and foremost brilliant satire; but it has another minor
function, to justify and set in relief Pope's own character. This advantage is followed up with a syntactical peculiarity, a catalogue of
innocence, contrasted implicitly with Sporus's unnatural qualities.
At first we do not know the antecedent of all these innocent
states:

Not Fortune's Worshipper, nor Fashion's Fool,
Not Lucre's Madman, nor Ambition's Tool,
Not proud, nor servile, be one Poet's praise
That, if he pleas'd he pleas'd by manly ways; . . .

(334–37)

Then as the positive virtues accumulate, we realize that Pope is
speaking of himself:

That Flatt'ry, ev'n to Kings, he held a shame,
And thought a Lye in Verse or Prose the same:
That not in Fancy's Maze he wander'd long,
But stoop'd to Truth, and moraliz'd his song: . . .

(338–41)

The final lines of the poem, a defence of his mother and father, are
not the less sincere because Pope wrote them separately—apart from
the rest of the poem—and, indeed, sent a version of them to Aaron
Hill in 1731.

The Epistle to Dr. Arbuthnot is a remarkably personal poem; but
of course it is still in Pope's Horatian style, and, although it contains
elements of sensibility, is by and large dazzling satire. It should be
remembered that poets whose works more exactly fit the sincere
ideal criticized Pope for not being sincere enough. Edward Young in
his "Two Epistles to Mr. Pope, Concerning the Authors of the Age"
(1730) explicitly demanded sincerity in poetry:

Yet more, believe a truth, to you severe,
Nor mortal can write well, but who's sincere:
In all that charms or strongly moves, the heart
Must aid the head, and bear the greater part.
Can they, tho' tongu'd as angels sweet, persuade
The soul to day, who yesterday betray'd?
Wit in a knave, my brethren! is no more
Than beauty, in a rank, abandon'd whore.[21]

This passage is addressed to poets at large, as well as to Pope, but there can be little doubt that this is a more than implicit criticism of him. Since Pope must have read this poem, furthermore, it is evident that the question of the relation of a poet's sincerity to his poetry was raised explicitly in his mind.[22]

There is only one remark by Pope that suggests specifically a relationship between sincerity and poetry. This he wrote to Martha Blount in 1724, in a most playful tone, on the occasion of her birthday: "Yet were I to tell you what I wish for you in particular, it would be only to repeat in prose, what I told you last year in rhyme; (so sincere is my poetry:) . . ." (*Corr.*, 2, 235). This is slight evidence, but it does show at least that the question was in Pope's mind as early as 1724—even if it did not seem to him an important question.

Sincerity in human relations continued to be of real importance to him throughout his career. A few days after making the above remarks, he described an admirable old family to Martha, ending his letter with a protestation: "Believe me ever yours with a sincerity as old-fashioned, and as different from Modern Sincerity, as This house, this family, & these ruins, are from the Court, & all its Neighbourhood" (*Corr.*, 2, 240). By "Modern Sincerity" Pope may have meant this cynical view, expressed by Swift nearly five years later: "It is more probable that there may be an equal quantity of virtues always in the world, but sometimes there may be a peck of it in Asia, and hardly a thimble-full in Europe. But if there be no virtue, there is abundance of sincerity; for I will venture all I am

21. Young, *Works* (1755), 1, 128.
22. Young expunged these lines from editions of his works published after 1755. Could Warburton have influenced Young to do so?

worth, that there is not one humane creature in power who will not
be modest enough to confess that he proceeds wholly upon a principle of Corruption. . . ." (*Corr.*, 3, 29).[23] This is characteristic of
Swift. Sincerity was not his concern, at least not in the sentimental
terms that were capturing the imagination of the age. It might even
be said that Swift saw sincerity as a pose, a dodge, and by recognizing
it as such committed himself to a sincerity identified with the highest
truth. That this may be so illustrates what a confused issue the
question of sincerity is.

Pope's other poetic investigation of sincerity is Dialogue II of the
Epilogue to the Satires. The first Dialogue is largely a catalogue of
current abuses in government and society. Pessimistic in the extreme, the poem ends with the following summary:

All, all look up, with reverential Awe,
On Crimes that scape, or triumph o'er the Law:
While Truth, Worth, Wisdom, daily they decry—
"Nothing is Sacred now but Villany."

(167–70)

Then, unexpectedly, a new tone is introduced in the last couplet:
Yet may this Verse (if such a Verse remain)
Show there was one who held it in disdain.

(171–72)

Here the poet, while maintaining his individual identity, becomes the
voice crying in the wilderness. This motif is found consistently in
Pope's late poetry and in the work of other poets as the century wore
on. The opening of Book IV of *The Dunciad* is a case in point:

Yet, yet a moment, one dim Ray of Light
Indulge, dread Chaos, and eternal Night!
Of darkness visible so much be lent,
As half to shew, half veil the deep Intent.
Ye Pow'rs! whose Mysteries restor'd I sing,
To whom Time bears me on his rapid wing,

23. Swift to Pope and Bolingbroke.

Suspend a while your Force inertly strong,
Then take at once the Poet and the Song.

(1–8)

In Dialogue II of the *Epilogue to the Satires*, however, Pope takes
a more optimistic point of view. Here he emphasizes the virtues of
his friends; but through his interlocutor, he examines their right to
his praise:

—What are you thinking? Fr. Faith, the thought's no Sin,
I think your Friends are out, and would be in.

(22–23)

This suggestion that Pope's friends would be rogues if they were in
power cuts to the heart of the sincere ideal, for the basis of Pope's
idealism is the belief that there is at least a small number of good men
who are above factionalism and strife. In questioning this social
aspect of the ideal, Pope shows that he was moving toward the
pessimism of the voice crying in the wilderness. But for a moment
the question is put aside:

P. If merely to come in, Sir, they go out,
The way they take is strangely round about.
Fr. They too may be corrupted, you'll allow?
P. I only call those Knaves who are so now.
Is that too little: Come then, I'll comply—
Spirit of Arnall! aid me while I lye.
Cobham's a Coward, Polwarth is a Slave,
And Lyttleton a dark, designing Knave,
St. John has ever been a wealthy Fool—.

(124–32)

By the end of the poem Pope's bitter pessimism again obtrudes
upon the reader. Here, however, he asserts that ridicule is the only
servant of truth:

Yes, I am proud; I must be proud to see
Men not afraid of God, afraid of me:
Safe from the Bar, the Pulpit, and the Throne,

Yet touch'd and sham'd by Ridicule alone.
O sacred Weapon! left for Truth's defence,
Sole Dread of Folly, Vice, and Insolence!

(208-13)

Pope then goes beyond any profession of sincerity to assert the truth of his position:

Truth guards the Poet, sanctifies the line,
And makes Immortal, Verse as mean as mine.

(246-47)

Despite Pope's defence of many of the "sincere" motifs examined in this study, sincerity did not become for him the pre-eminent ideal that it had been for others. The final test that gives sincerity pre-eminence is that it must be equivalent to truth, and for Pope, as for Swift, sincerity was not truth. As we have seen in the final lines of the *Epilogue to the Satires*, Pope sees truth, perhaps, as a necessary guide to poetic utterance. But he has no smug confidence in the validity of the subjective impulse. In fact his final pessimistic vision in Book IV of the *Dunciad* is an implicit denial of the reliability of the human spirit. The Dunces are Dunces because they reject all the truths external to man which render man human:

See skulking *Truth* to her old Cavern fled,
Mountains of Casuistry heap'd o'er her head!
Philosophy, that lean'd on Heav'n before,
Shrinks to her second cause, and is no more.
Physic of *Metaphysic* begs defence,
And *Metaphysic* calls for aid on *Sense*!
See *Mystery* to *Mathematics* fly!
In vain! they gaze, turn giddy, rave, and die.
Religion blushing veils her sacred fires,
And unawares *Morality* expires.

(641-50)

And without these all human values are destroyed:

Nor *public* Flame, nor *private* dares to shine;
Nor *human* Spark is left, nor Glimpse *divine*!

Lo! thy dread Empire, CHAOS! is restor'd;
Light dies before thy uncreating word:
Thy hand, great Anarch! lets the curtain fall;
And Universal Darkness buries All.

(651–56)

Though he flirted with some radical and popular attitudes, Pope is finally a traditionalist who has enough confidence in the existence of traditional values, such as religion, philosophy, and morality, to call them by their proper names. He could not do as Hoadly had done before him: reduce everything to sincerity and the subjective impulse.

JONATHAN RICHARDSON

Jonathan Richardson (1665–1745) was, according to his own testimony, a lover of painting and poetry, with the former his chief occupational concern: "I have from my infancy lov'd and practic'd painting and poetry; one I possess'd as a wife, the other I kept privately. . . ."[24]

Richardson's youthful studies under the famed portraitist Riley suited him admirably for his profession. Admired subsequently by Sir Joshua Reynolds both for his art and art criticism, Richardson specialized in paintings and sketches of the human head, which are among the best of his time. His attention to the body in painting was, however, not great; and his portraits show the unfortunate results of this unconcern. The direction of Richardson's interest can be seen when he insists that "a portrait-painter must understand mankind, and enter into their characters, and express their minds as well as their faces: . . ."[25] Richardson concentrates all his artistic efforts to capture the mind. But it is not merely the mind of man that interests him. Rather it is the mind in its ideal moral state.

Richardson's theory of art is essentially neoclassical. His

24. *Explanatory Notes and Remarks on Milton's Paradise Lost* (London, 1734), p. clxxviii.
25. *The Works*, p. 13.

pronouncements are often similar to those of Sidney and Ben Jonson, as for example his comments on the central task of art:

> Common nature is no more fit for a picture than plain narration is for a poem: a painter must raise his ideas beyond what he sees, and form a model of perfection in his own mind which is not to be found in reality; but yet such a one as is probable, and rational. Particularly with respect to mankind, he must as it were raise the whole species, and give them all imaginable beauty, and grace, dignity, and perfection; every several character, whether it be good, or bad, amiable, or detestable, must be stronger, and more perfect. (*Works*, p. 73)

Richardson's Aristotelian theory of painting holds good for poetry as well, since poetry "raises and embellishes . . . what is seen in nature."[26]

Richardson's poetry does not deserve attention here on the grounds of its intrinsic merit. But aside from its quality as poetry, it reflects in a remarkable way the individual and personal approach to poetic composition which began to figure importantly in the eighteenth century. This poetry is peculiarly Protestant and Puritan, pre-eminently self-conscious, and reflective of the sincere ideal. It will reach its best expression in the works of such poets as Young and Cowper.

We find such poetry in its infancy in the work of Jonathan Richardson, but Richardson looked to Milton as an example of all that could be achieved. Richardson admired particularly the man Milton as he was revealed in his works, especially in his moving personal comments. This admiration of long-standing finally culminated in the publication of *Explanatory Notes and Remarks on Milton's Paradise Lost* (1734). In the long preface to this volume Richardson, while deploring the extremism of the Puritan revolt, underscores his belief that Milton's adherence to such principles was sincere. Even after the Restoration "he scorn'd to flatter power, as many did; the same openness and honesty was seen in him, his old principles were known to continue, they are seen even in *Paradise Lost*."[27] During the incipient stages of the revolution and there-

---

26. *Explanatory Notes*, p. clvii.   27. Ibid., p. xxi.

after, Milton, according to Richardson, ceased to write poetry and entered the "gloomy ways" of disputation because he felt that was his duty: "I am not justifying his principles," Richardson writes, "but his sincerity."[28] Though Richardson never employs the word sincerity in describing Milton's poetry, he does emphasize Milton's own claim of "unpremeditated verse," insisting upon his spontaneity of genius and individuality of language.

It is not surprising that Richardson should emphasize the personal aspects of Milton's art, since, by his own admission, knowing nothing of Latin and Greek, his understanding of classical imitation must have been severely limited. A curious by-product of Richardson's ignorance of the classics was that in the preparation of his book, he engaged the assistance of his classicist son, whom he described as his telescope through which he could view Milton's classical allusions. This absurdly innocent admission provoked Hogarth to caricature the painter in his own imagery, portraying an elderly gentleman peering through a combination telescope-son at a copy of Ovid.

Richardson's relative ignorance is, however, indicative of the new class of people entering the artistic professions. The commitment of these men and women to the classics was, understandably, not very great, although many of them were prepared to give lip service to the greatness of the Greek and Latin authors. Their taste in literature was bound to be for English authors, or at least for moderns. And later in the century, when a "modern" ancient, Ossian, arrived on the scene, Greek-less ladies preferred his works to those of Homer. These *nouveaux littérateurs* were addicted especially to "original" writing, since their lack of expertise in the classics deprived them of the joys of classical imitation.

But Richardson did not identify his commitment to a new kind of poetry with revolution. The only poetry that he rejected was that which had no moral purpose, and he was able to tolerate a good deal of that in the name of the classics which he did not know. Since the purpose of art was to improve mankind, the highest art demanded the highest morality:

28. Ibid., p. xxii.

It has been the practice of all polite people in all ages, and countries to disguise, or hide those saletés, and defects which though common to all animals are a sort of reproach to our nature; and to endeavour to exalt our species as much as possible to what we conceive of the angelic state: this also is one end of painting and poetry; they are to impregnate our minds with the most sublime, and beautiful images of things; and thus in our imaginations to raise all nature some degrees above what is commonly, or ever seen . . . (*Works*, p. 238).

The emphasis on moral purpose is in accord with the views of most of the writers examined in this study. It was born, in part, of a revulsion from the political excesses and immorality of the Restoration period, and reflected a deep, ineradicable commitment to Puritan ideals. Puritanism took root in England because it was culturally congenial; it lost its political strength because it could not cope effectively with practical affairs. Yet because it was compatible with the English mind, Puritanism remained a source of idealism to many. For most people ideals serve as a means of criticizing the imperfect present system; yet those who hold such ideals could not be made happy by their actualization. Utopias are drab when actual, but, unrealized, they continue to be sources of inspiration. So it was with various Puritan ideals in the Restoration period and eighteenth century. Unsuccessful in practice because of their uncompromising spirituality, they became viable once more when their removal from the public arena made people forget how unsatisfactory they had been. A gradually liberalizing tendency too made these ideals attractive to those who could never have been Puritans and who regarded the new teachings of Wesley and Whitefield as hopelessly dour. These new "Puritans" were moral men who found more satisfaction in social concern than in religious dogma. But as society became increasingly corrupt, these men turned to their inner kingdom in the quest for the sincere ideal.

Jonathan Richardson was very much one of these men. Only one reflection of his "Puritan" orientation is his rejection of authority, specifically in painting:

As in reasoning a man ought not to rest upon authorities, but to have recourse to those principles on which those are, or ought to be founded, so to rely upon what others have done is to be always copying. A painter therefore should have original ideas of grace, and greatness, taken from his own observation of nature, under the conduct, and assistance however of those who with success have trod the same path before him. What he sees excellent in others he must not implicitly follow, but make his own by entering into the reason of the thing, as those must have done who originally produced that excellence; for such things happen not by chance. (*Works*, p. 88)

That independence of taste, reliant on reason, was indeed a plain Protestant virtue, Richardson made clear in 1719 in his *Science of a Connoisseur*. Here the emphasis is on critical, rather than artistic, independence:

It is the glory of the Protestant church, and especially of the church of England, as being indubitably the head of the reformed churches; and so upon that account, as well as the purity and excellency of its doctrines, and the piety, and learning of its clergy (so far as I am able to judge) the best national church in the world: I say it is the glory of the reformation, that thereby men are set at liberty to judge for themselves; we are thus a body of free men; not the major part in subjection to the rest. Here we are all connoisseurs as we are Protestants; though (as it must needs happen) some are abler connoisseurs than others. And we have abundantly experienced the advantages of this, since we have thus resumed our natural rights as rational creatures. May the like reformation be made, in a matter of much less importance indeed, but considerable enough to justify my wishes and endeavours; I mean in relation to connoissance: may every one of us in this case also be able to judge for ourselves without implicitly, and tamely resigning our understandings to those who are naturally our equals, and the advantages will be proportionable. (*Works*, pp. 259–60)

The Church here described is very much that of Benjamin Hoadly, in which sincerity is, to use William Law's phrase, "the great universal atonement for all." Many proponents of sincerity may well be called connoisseurs of religion, as they exercise their intelligence and sensibility in every area of spiritual concern. The Church is not praised for being a Church, but rather for removing all restrictions, in short, for *not* being one. Though conservatives in the English Church would have blanched at Richardson's assumptions, he has put his finger on the newly emerging genius of that Church. With the Revolution of 1688, the days of dogmatic principles and excommunication were numbered. The Church was to open its doors to all who sincerely believed themselves to be members in good standing. No matter what one's beliefs, it was becoming increasingly difficult not to have some quality that would recommend oneself for membership.

Thus Richardson recommends a Church for connoisseurs by analogy with the English Church. Independence of critical judgement functions in much the same way as complete freedom in religious matters, however. Following "our natural rights as rational creatures" leads to the formulation of an independent poetical character, and in Richardson's case this is precisely what happened. Despite a contradictory admiration for classical models and poets like Pope who best exemplified them, Richardson, depending upon his own sincerity, writes verse almost entirely bereft of classical influence. In its own incompetent way, it is poetry of a clearly revolutionary character.

But an age that could appreciate the neoclassical posturing of such curiosities as Stephen Duck and Phyllis Wheatley was not prepared for Richardson's originality. If he made attempts to publish a volume of verse during his lifetime, he was unsuccessful, although he felt free to show his manuscript poems to friends and obtrude those poems from time to time upon his other works. Horace Walpole's comments upon Richardson's poetry probably reflected general opinion: "Richardson . . . was as incapable of reaching the sublime in poetry as he was in painting, though so capable of illustrating both. Some specimens of verse, that he has given us here and there in his works excite no curiosity for more, . . ."[29]

29. George Vertue and Horace Walpole, *Anecdotes of Painting in England* (Strawberry Hill, 1765–71), 4, 18. Walpole's later comments on *Morning Thoughts*, that it was "not much to the honour of his muse, but exceedingly so to that of his piety and

The first collection of Richardson's poems, entitled *Morning Thoughts or Poetical Meditations* and edited by his son, appeared at long last in 1776, thirty-one years after his death and five years after that of his son. According to the publishers, this ample collection of some two-hundred and forty poems, with additional miscellaneous efforts, was only part of a much larger number of poems intended for publication. Unfortunately for our understanding of Richardson no further volume appeared. But the loss for poetry was probably not correspondingly great.

The preface to this collection was written by his son, who quotes from the personal writings of his father some interesting comments about the poetry. In one of these excerpts, Richardson states the rationale behind his verse:

> I pretend . . . to no finished poetry, no nice corrections; they are works of another kind, like sketches in drawing; and which connoisseurs are very far from despising for being so; these having an ease and spirit not to be found often in accuracy and labour. The truth is, new thoughts allow me neither leisure nor inclination to polish the circumstances of their predecessors.
>
> I call these, *Thoughts*, not poems; consider them accordingly; or as in verse what *familiar letters* are in prose, where the natural flow of the soul hath a beauty and force which the most studied orations frequently want.[30]

The comparison of his poems with familiar letters recalls the use Pope makes of his letters and suggests a provenience for at least some sincere poetry.

Richardson's poems are, for the most part, rational expositions of moral problems. In a poem called "Use of My Writing," he considers the function of his "pictures" after his death:

> Some, of the multitudes who still pursue,
> May peradventure these my pictures view;
> (For here, alone examining my breast,

---

amiable heart" are cited by Lionel Cust in his article on Richardson in the *Dictionary of National Biography*.

30. *Morning Thoughts or Poetical Meditations* (1776), pp. 3–4. All references to Richardson's poems are to this text.

Are my soul's lineaments with care exprest,)
What will they say?—I neither know, nor fear,
So they will learn from them to be sincere,
So they will learn (rememb'ring well, that me
They too must follow,) what they ought to be.

(p. 62)

Just as Richardson's own sincerity in his painting will teach others
to emulate him, his poetry in all its unadorned simplicity will teach
to others the art of sincere meditation:

Alone, as oft I am, ('tis my delight)
I think, and think, and what I think, I write.
The naked thought, an unsubstantial shade,
Embody'd thus, a living creature's made;
It else had wander'd in the air; at most
It had to all but to myself been lost;
Perhaps had by myself forgotten been;
Not so, substantial now, 'tis felt, 'tis seen;
A faithful friend, a monitor, a guide,
And always ready to applaud, or chide.
Learn thou of me this necessary art,
To write I not pretend, but mend the heart.

(pp. 62–63)

Richardson had few illusions about his poetical talents; but his admiration of spontaneity and disdain for the art of revision must bear
much responsibility for his poor poetic showing. In another poem,
"Best Poetry," he asserts that what is spontaneous is best: "Rapture
not condescends to speak in prose, / Its nobler language naturally
flows" (p. 119). In "My Manner of Writing" he notes the difference
between his own method of composition and that usually pre-
scribed by the learned:

If I am told what some have done,
How wine dropp'd verses one by one;
How Virgil, and how Horace, taught
The muse to drudge a single thought,

My answer is; if I must sing,
My lyre must use its native string;
And if velocity of sense
I feel, such sounds must come from thence,
As that velocity allows,
In all my swift successive nows.
But greatest masters often fetch
More glory from a rapid sketch,
Than from the most completing toil,
And charge of colours, cloth, and oil.

(pp. 125–26)

This is about as successful as Richardson gets, and this little poem has its moments, if one begins by expecting very little. Richardson seemed to realize that his "swift successive nows" were not very good poetry, as a glance at his wry, if awkward, verses "To Mr. Pope, who said 'I had made more verses than he' " will prove:

I make more rhymes than you, you say.
No doubt I do, and well I may:
You them create; I'd have you know,
With me spontaneously they grow.
Your's ven'son are; but I, a glutton,
Must fill my belly with my mutton.

(p. 275)

One might be tempted to imagine what Pope thought of these verses and the other more serious ones, which he undoubtedly read. He had affection for Richardson and probably regarded him as an honest and sincere man. Indeed, he was a man of talent, if not of poetic talent.[31]

Richardson's more serious verse on religious subjects reflects a singular lack of dogmatism. In his poem "That truth is not for us— to encourage imagination," he expresses a kind of religious obscurantism:

---

31. Richardson's son delighted to point out his father's, as well as his own, sincerity. *Morning Thoughts*, p. 4.

We tumble nature's volume o'er,
Would all her mysteries explore,
With probability a scheme
One forms, another baffles him;
Des Cartes was, Sir Isaac is,
Hereafter neither may be wise.

(p. 190)

Then he turns to a rather peculiar notion of sincerity, reminiscent of
Swift's cynicism cited earlier. But Richardson finds a reason for the
insincerity of the world:

We hide our bodies nakedness;
And are our minds regarded less?
We talk and look as if sincere,
But woe be to us, if we are;
The man who most to truth pretends,
You may be sure, hath selfish ends;
His claim to this sincerity
Is an accumulated lie.
In short, the naked truth and we
Do not in circumstance agree;
We are for earth, for heaven is she.
All is sincere and perfect there,
But we must breathe polluted air. . . .

(pp. 190–91)

This view of the partial quality of sincerity on earth is very much
like that of Young, to be examined later. Here on earth "sincerity"
seems to mean "convinced of truth." But in heaven it takes on its
real meaning, "pure" or "uncorrupt." This may be connected with
Richardson's remarks about poetry's going beyond "mere truth."
Poetry, in effect, embodies to some small degree the perfect sincerity
of eternity. But Richardson is not cognizant of the implications of
his own imaginative effort. He consistently retreats to the obscurantism described above. In all this his one positive ideal remains:
sincerity is all that men on earth need to know:

All useful truth in narrow compass lies;
The man sincere sufficiently is wise.

(p. 118)

Although his theory of poetry is subtler than his practice,
Richardson quite often composed poems in which deep personal
emotion is expressed. In fact his meditations form a diary of sorts in
which personal feelings are set down to be consulted later, much as
Puritans set down their daily progress, in prose. A longer poem,
"Written in the time of my religious scruples," and composed early
in his career, reflects a series of doubts which he seems to have resolved in his later life. Other good examples of "occasional sincerity"
are some short poems on the death of his wife, the first of which
follows:

Adieu, dear life! here am I left alone,
The world is strangely chang'd since thou art gone.
Compose thyself to rest, all will be well;
I'll come to bed "as fast as possible."

(p. 174)[32]

Once again, it is not necessary to insist that Richardson's poems
are "sincere" in any sense of that difficult and elusive word. It is
enough to note that his poetry was written for the purpose of private
meditation, composed "spontaneously," and destined for a didactic
use. It is often religious poetry, but is lacking in dogmatism and even
lacking in religion. Though his poems seem oriented toward rationalism and though he enjoyed numerous and glittering associations
with some of the master-craftsmen of neoclassicism, Richardson
divined a personal and private use for poetry, which was relatively
uncommon during his own lifetime, but one that was to become
important in later years.

32. Richardson's son annotated this poem as follows: " 'As fast as possible' was an
expression so frequent with him, that my dear mother used to make herself and him,
now and then, merry with rallying him on this perpetual proof of the activity of his
spirit; so that it has an affecting propriety here."

AARON HILL

Aaron Hill was one of the most energetic men of his time. A "projector" like Defoe, he conceived schemes for producing beech-nut oil and for procuring Scottish masts for the British Navy. At fifteen years of age he travelled throughout the Near East, visiting, if we can believe him, Cairo, Mecca, and other exotic places, all the time having incredible adventures. His dramatic, poetic, and prose contributions are exceptional in bulk. Yet this abundance of energy is usually converted in his writings to vaporous emotion of very limited literary value. It is this very dedication to literary emotionalism, however, which makes Hill relevant to this study. Both his poetry and his letters reflect a uniquely confused adherence to the sincere ideal.

Hill's basic assumptions in writing poetry can be seen in his preface to *The Creation* (1720), in which he expresses a strong admiration for the lofty plainness of Hebrew scriptural poetry.[33] Ambitious and idealistic, he sought to write on the most sublime religious subjects, thereby rescuing poetry from the triviality in which he believed it was usually lost. His admiration of simplicity coupled with loftiness led him to compose soaring Pindarics in plain, chaste language. Since his imagery, then, is of little interest, we are left with the meagre sustenance of his conventional moralizing. What imagery we do find imitates spiritual aspiration; and since it is in no way concrete, his poems convey only an impression of vagueness. We soar with Hill without being uplifted. Here, for example, is the opening of a poem called "The Transport":

> Mount my freed soul! forsake thy
>   loos'ning clay,
> Broadly, at once, expand thy wingy zeal,
>   Rapture, involv'd in raptures, feel,
> And, thro' yon dazzling regions, cut thy way!
>
>   (3, 232)[34]

33. *The Augustan Reprint Society* (1949), p. 6.
34. All references to Hill's poetry are to *The Works*.

Hill characteristically intensifies the intense ("Rapture, involv'd in raptures") to such a degree, that, far from being transported, we feel the tedium of undefined, unrelieved generality. But this is the way Hill's imagination functions. In the rapturous couplets of his "Advice to the Poets," Hill describes his imaginative experience:

> *She, she,* the muse—Oh! ne'er to be *defin'd*;
> Thou *flame* of *purpose*! and thou flow of mind!
> Thou *path* of *praise*, by heav'n's first fav'rites trod,
> Thou *voice* of *prophets*, and thou *breath* of God!
>   I feel her now—th'invader fires my breast;
> And my soul swells, to suit the heav'nly guest. . . .
>
>   (3, 209)

Though this experience is not unlike that of the Sibyl in the sixth book of the *Aeneid*, the meaning of all this is that poets ought to devote their efforts to religious subjects:

>   O! That all verse would senseless sound expel,
> And the big *subject* bid the numbers swell!
>
>   (3, 218)

Hill's poetic admits of divine inspiration in a rather facile way. Here is no complicated theory of "originality" or spiritual insight, but rather mere enthusiasm:

> Then, when kind heav'n inspires the vast *sublime*,
> And your verse *lives*, and claims the *stamp* of *time*,
> *Hist'ry* shall *die*, and scarce preserve a *name*;
> While *poets* flourish, in immortal fame.
>
>   (3, 222)

The best single example of Hill's imagination in flight is "The Excursion of Fancy," a difficult, somewhat obscure, Pindaric ode of some twenty-seven pages in length. The poem opens with reflections on the evil of the world, and having decided along with the deists that "It is enough for us, that there *must* be / Ends in this, we cannot see!", Hill resolves "in spite of *villany*, to *thrive*" (4, 312). Learning and power are both rejected after imaginative excursions

to their respective realms. With fancy, however, the poet soars into
the spiritual world where all the virtues are victorious in their war
against vice. At last a shore is reached and a Christ-like figure (who
may be George II) comes forth. Thence follows an apocalyptical
view of England and a statement of her mission:

> Inspir'd, at once, I *see*, and *own*, 'twas heaven's
>   *unerring* aim!
> Hail! immortal son of fame!
> Take these *legions*, they are *thine*!
> With, *theirs*, thy *navy* shall, resistless join:
> And virtue's *squadrons*, led by thee, o'er earth's
>   whole surface shine.
> Root out *oppression*, wheresoe'er she grows
> Let stubborn *tyranny* fall dead, beneath thy
>   pond'rous blows!
> And, over all the wide-watch'd *world*, leave
>   *innocence* no *foes*.
>
>   (4, 336)

Thus Hill's poetry reaches out for an earthly utopia seen mainly in
spiritual terms. Although the final stanza of the poem expresses hope
for realization of a thoroughly good world, it must be remembered
that it is only a vision inspired by fancy. Hill's determination "in
spite of *villany*, to *thrive*" reflects a fairly realistic evaluation of the
world's problems. Yet there is a basic optimism in the belief that
fancy does set the world right, if only in our moral eye. Fancy,
then, for Hill, is a faculty which somehow bridges the gap between
the real and ideal, suggesting Coleridge's use of Imagination nearly
a hundred years later. If fancy does not actually improve the real
situation, it does at least sharpen our perspective and give us a clear
understanding of how things ought to be. Spontaneity, trust in the
subjective impulse (sometimes identified with reason), and a vision
of prelapsarian innocence are all characteristic of Hill's "sublime"
verse. And all of these tendencies often find their form in bursts of
nationalistic ardour.

Besides his poetry, Hill made other contributions to a definition
of the sincere ideal. Like so many other men of his time, he was ex-

tremely interested in the reformation of manners and the ethics of personal relationship. It is not surprising, then, that the familiar letter held a high place in his pantheon of literary concern. We have already examined some aspects of Hill's correspondence with James Thomson. The difficult question of sincerity in human relationships was of prime significance as well in Hill's exchanges of letters with Pope and Samuel Richardson. These correspondences reveal aspects of Hill's personality as different as Pope and Richardson are from one another.

The relationship between Pope and Hill was a complex one, and has been treated in great detail.[35] In 1718 Hill published, with his poem *The Northern Star*, a preface in which he excoriated Pope for adverse remarks allegedly made about the poem. For this Hill had only the word of Lintot, and though "honest Bernard" may have been a reliable witness, on the face of it Hill acted rashly and with insufficient evidence. Despite a pusillanimous retraction in the preface to *The Creation*, Pope was unwilling to overlook Hill's original indiscretion. Hill later appeared, not without some justice on the basis of merit, in both *Peri Bathous* and *The Dunciad* of 1728 and 1729.

In *Peri Bathous* Hill, identified as A.H., is numbered among the "Flying Fishes," who

> are writers who now and then rise upon their fins and fly out of the Profund; but their wings are soon dry, and they drop down to the bottom.[36]

In the 1729 *Dunciad* the name "Aaron" is to be supplied:

> Then * * try'd, but hardly snatch'd from sight,
> Instant buoys up, and rises into light;
> He bears no token of the sabler streams,
> And mounts far off, among the swans of Thames.
>
> (2, 283–86)[37]

---

35. See Dorothy Brewster, *Aaron Hill* (New York: Columbia University Press, 1913), pp. 201–38. Although I disagree with some of Miss Brewster's conclusions, this is a fine documentation.

36. Chapter 6, *Literary Criticism of Alexander Pope*, ed. Bertrand A. Goldgar (Lincoln: University of Nebraska Press, 1965), p. 54.

37. *The Dunciad*. The Twickenham Edition.

The passage is annotated with a curiously ironic footnote which refers to another attack on Pope published by Hill in retaliation for the piece in *Peri Bathous*. It should not be impertinent to point out that Pope's satiric attacks have the virtue of being very good literary criticism, characterizing Hill's verse exactly.

After such exchanges it was particularly naive of Hill to attempt a reconciliation less than a year later. He wrote a letter to Pope openly offering forgiveness and friendship, an action for which his biographer praises him.[38] Pope's answer is a mass of contradictions, probably expressing his confusion at Hill's overture. It is in some ways an ironical defence of his own actions toward Hill; but its ending is a clear, if awkward, attempt at conciliation. Pope assumes again the attitude of sincerity:

> —I see, by many Marks, you distinguish'd me from others, as a *Man*, and no ill, or ill-natur'd one. I only wish you knew, as well as I do, how much I prefer Qualities of the Heart to those of the Head: I vow to God, I never thought any great Matters of my poetical Capacity; I only thought it a little better, comparatively, than that of some very mean Writers, who are too proud.—But I do know *certainly*, my moral Life is *superior* to that of most of the *Wits* of these days. This is a silly Letter, but it will shew you my Mind honestly . . . (*Corr.*, 3, 166).[39]

But Hill, by attacking Pope's motives and cavilling over trivial points, chose not to effect a reconciliation. For example, he treats Pope's self-conscious attempt at humility in this unpleasant, irrelevant way:

> I am sorry to hear you say, you never thought any great Matters of your *Poetry*.—It is, in my Opinion, the Characteristic you are to hope your *Distinction* from: To be *Honest* is the Duty of every *plain Man*! Nor, since the *Soul* of Poetry is Sentiment, can a *Great Poet* want *Morality*. But your *Honesty* you possess in common with a *Million*, who will never be *remembered*; whereas your *Poetry* is a Peculiar, that will make it impossible, you should be forgotten. (*Corr.*, 3, 168)

38. Brewster, *Aaron Hill*, p. 211.   39. Pope, *Correspondence*.

Beyond the superficial flattery, this is first a cavil and second an insult. It is a cavil because Pope's attempt at modesty has to be accepted at face value to effect a reconciliation. A contradiction of a man's attempt to be humble is bad manners at the least. Pope is not in need of moral correction at this point in the relationship, and Hill's remarks seem to be an open attempt to gain the upper hand. The point he makes might be a good one between friends, but in trying to effect a reconciliation, it is disastrous. Second, it is an insult partly because it is an outrageous cavil, but more because Pope's honesty is called in question. "Your *Honesty* you possess in common with a *Million*" may be interpreted to suggest that his honesty is limited. "Can a *Great Poet* want *Morality*" may mean that Pope is not great because he does indeed lack morality. Such comment whether innocently meant or not must have seemed severe to the letter's recipient. And in this case where mistrust already existed, a negative interpretation is justified. Even if Pope recognized Hill's sincerity and his own faults, Hill's ineptitude in this letter may have counted heavily against him.

Further, many of Hill's objections are overly serious and moralistic, the caveats of a humourless man. Pope did respect the sincere ideal, but he had other allegiances as well, which is one reason why his work is so wonderfully various.[40] Pope, who was not wont to suffer fools gladly, could not tolerate Hill as an equal largely because the author of *The Creation* was not nearly as complex and gifted as he. Hill insisted upon subjecting Pope's every action and utterance to his own narrow standard of morality, a failure of imagination which made a real friendship between them impossible. Pope was, indeed, consistently the victim of rather narrow-minded moralists. Hill's standards might have comprehended James Thomson, for example, but Alexander Pope was another matter. This is I think the fairest way of looking at the Pope–Hill squabble over sincerity, and one that gains support from Pope's own remarks in answer to Hill's charges: "I told you I thought my Letter a silly one; but the more I thought so, the more in sending it I shew'd my Trust in your good Disposition toward me. I am sorry you took it to have an Air of

40. See Tillotson, *Pope and Human Nature*, chapter 7.

Neglect, or Superiority . . ." (*Corr.,* 3, 169). It is of course possible that Pope consciously engineered this test of Hill's personality, half knowing what the outcome would be. In any case, a test it was, and Hill did not pass.

Samuel Richardson presented for Hill no such problem. Although Richardson was by far the greater artist of the two, they were kindred souls. With the publication of *Pamela,* Hill and his three daughters (Urania, Minerva, and Astraea) came to be as ardent as any of the novel's admirers. In the Hill family there was also a little boy, the son of an impoverished soldier, who, upon overhearing a reading from *Pamela,* became that heroine's youngest convert: "his eyes were quite lost in his tears; which running down from his cheeks in free currents, had formed two sincere little fountains on that part of the carpet he hung over."[41]

This outrageous but sincerely felt sentimentality is in part the result of both Hill's and Richardson's adherence to the sincere ideal. Richardson so relished these tales of little Harry's innocent passion that he sent both compliments and gifts to the boy, which resulted in further effusions, sure to be approved of in the Hill household. It is idle to inquire whether Harry was sincere, but children, like most human beings, desire approbation, and in congenial surroundings will attempt to fulfil expectations. In Hill and his daughters, little Harry evidently had remarkable models for imitation. Utopians, in looking to the younger generation to fulfil their hopes, emphasize education as the means to their ends. In a later letter about the same little child, Hill expresses a Rousseauistic confidence in the natural goodness of man, or rather, of child: "what a tedious long story of childish insignificance were here; but that I know you feel pleasure in observing with how early a tendency nature forms our first passions to virtue! How unhappy is it, that the human degeneracy to evil should be a consequence but of increase in our knowledge" (Richardson, *Corr.,* 1, 65–66). What a fine young pupil Harry proved to be! To Richardson and Hill the sincere ideal must have seemed almost within reach, at least as long as they listened to the prattle of the child.

41.Samuel Richardson, *Correspondence,* 1, 58. Cited in the text as Richardson, *Corr.*

The view of the natural goodness of man has been seen in many forms in the course of this study. The very attack on guile gains its momentum from the assumption that insincerity of any kind is unnatural to man. The images used to describe guile: the mask, the false smile, and courtly dress, are examples of an artificial imposition on man's essentially good character. Here, in Hill's description, the utterly innocent child reacts with benevolence and sentiment to Pamela's tribulations. He is the natural man, completely sincere in his expression. Here is a herald of the Wordsworthian notion of child as best philosopher.

For Hill, Richardson's contribution was one of re-establishing the virtue of the prelapsarian world and of showing it in triumph. Simple, guileless Pamela was not for him the Shamela that Fielding made her out to be. *Pamela* was, Hill wrote, an effort to "unite all mankind in one sentiment" (Richardson, *Corr.*, 1, 70–71). This was, of course, the object which most of our sincere poets had in view. The human common denominator was sentiment or the religion of the heart. The way to unite all men was to eliminate the inessentials which create difference, whether they be wealth, faith, or intelligence. How well this movement has succeeded may be gauged by a comment by Felix in Djuna Barnes's *Nightwood*: "The modern child has nothing left to hold to, or, to put it better, he has nothing to hold with. We are adhering to life now with our last muscle—the heart."[42]

Pamela, for Hill, takes its place as an unadulterated manifestation of "heart" in literature: "The heart of man is said to be inscrutable: but this can scarce be truly said of any writing man. The heart of such still shews, and needs must show itself, beyond all power of concealment; and without the writer's purpose, or even knowledge, will a thousand times, and in a thousand places, start up in its own true native colour, let the subject it is displayed upon bend never so remotely from the un-intended manifestation" (Richardson, *Corr.*, 1, 105). If this is so, then sincerity is an absolute imperative for the creative writer.

In other letters Hill shows his admiration of sincerity in social affairs. In 1731 he wrote to Arthur Onslow, praising him for his

---

42. *The Selected Works of Djuna Barnes* (New York, 1962), p. 263.

conversation regarding Pope's poetry: "it was easy to discern, that you spoke, from a heart, by nature, an enemy to disguise, and noble enough to consider an elevated openness in the sentiments, as the soul that lights up poetry" (Hill, *Works*, 1, 155). In a later missive to Chesterfield, Hill expresses passionately his belief in complete frankness in human relations:

> Indeed, my Lord, however *dear* the blessing we admire, in *liberty*, there would be little in it worth a *frank* heart's wishing for, if that, of *speaking* every honest *truth*, we *think*, were subject to restraint by licenses. Let the wicked, or the narrow-hearted, borrow *cover*, from these cautionary decencies. In their case, I confess them salutary and protective requisites. But, minds, beloved by, and that love mankind, approve no forms of fetters, and would even disdain those most, which bound the spirit of their enemies—if such a mind as I now contemplate, could possibly create an enemy. (Hill, *Works*, 2, 275)

Hill seems to espouse, then, the fantastic ideal which Molière examined with such penetration in *Le Misanthrope*. Yet the difference between Alceste and his own ideal, Hill would argue, is benevolence. Since human nature is essentially benevolent, sincere remarks could never be harmful and would ordinarily be favourable. As Hill wrote to Mallet less than a year and a half before he died, "It is the never failing mark of a true genius, to disdain all reserves, and jealousies, and not *feel* only, but *proclaim* felt transports, with effusion of benevolence . . ." (Hill, *Works*, 2, 317).

Yet, as I noted earlier in this section, much of this optimism was grounded in despair. Hill admired Thomson's *Liberty* enthusiastically, but attributed to it a curious relationship to the times: "I look upon this mighty work, as the last *stretched* blaze of our expiring genius. It is the dying effort of despairing and indignant virtue, and will stand, like one of those immortal *pyramids*, which carry their magnificence thro' times, that wonder, to see nothing round them, but uncomfitable desart" (Hill, *Works*, 1, 248).[43] Far from being the

---

43. Hill to Thomson, 17 Feb. 1735. The date given in this edition is 1734, an impossibility. 17 Feb. 1735 is probably correct in as much as Thomson sent Hill a copy of the poem on 7 Feb. 1735. See A. D. McKillop, *Letters and Documents*, p. 92.

egregious optimists they are often thought to be, Hill and his associates banded together in what they feared was a futile attempt to
keep poetic inspiration and virtue alive in their own time.
Aaron Hill seems to have thrived on a despair which may at times
have been a pleasing melancholy. He was humourless; took religion
seriously (or at least said he did); and found a great alternative to the
world's difficulties in sentimentality and emotional effusion. He is
one of the earliest of the neoclassicists to emphasize spiritual aspiration as a means of escaping the real world. But despite his many
revolutionary and innovative tendencies, Hill is superficial. His
powers of analysis were not great enough to give him adequate control of his ideas or to make him aware of their implications.

EDWARD YOUNG

It is a minor irony to include Young in a study of the development of
sincerity, since he has been specifically accused of insincerity by no
less a literary figure than George Eliot.[44] But later critics of Young
have exonerated him on that score by pointing out that Eliot's
criterion of sincerity is vague and that better artists than he could be
rejected for the same reasons.[45]
    Though Eliot's objections to Young involve a demand for genetic
sincerity, they reflect, more importantly, her own notions of what
poetry should be. The language of *Night Thoughts* disturbs her
particularly. His poetry is, she says, a "disruption of language from
genuine thought and feeling. . . ."[46] And further, "his insincerity is
the more likely to betray him into absurdity, because he habitually
treats of abstractions, and not of concrete objects or specific emotions."[47] But perhaps her most serious objection is to the abstrac-

44. "Worldliness and Other-Worldliness: The Poet Young" in *Essays and Leaves
from a Notebook* (New York, 1884). For background on Eliot's reading of Young's
Night Thoughts see Gordon S. Haight, *George Eliot: A Biography* (New York: Oxford University Press, 1968), especially pp. 216–17.
45. Martin Price, *To the Palace of Wisdom: Studies in Order and Energy from Dryden to Blake* (Garden City: Doubleday & Co., 1964), p. 347.
46. Eliot, "Worldliness and Other-Worldliness," p. 46.   47. Ibid., p. 46.

tions that Young employs: "The adherence to abstractions, is closely allied in Young to the *want of genuine emotion*."[48]

There is a tendency in Eliot to equate the use of abstractions with insincerity and lack of feeling, but many in the eighteenth century thought that the use of abstractions, on the contrary, could denote intensity of emotion.[49] But even conceding Eliot's point, Young's use of abstractions is not extensive, and an equally cogent case can be made for the sincerity of his verse.[50]

As I indicated earlier, genetic sincerity is too vague to be a legitimate criterion of literary judgement. Though George Eliot's chief assumption is that the conventions of "sincere" poetry are in no way artificial and the conventions of more ornate poetry are entirely so, underlying this is the notion that genetic sincerity is not only possible but can be identified by the language it uses.

Edward Young shares some of Eliot's assumptions about sincerity, but he is in sharp disagreement with her about others. In his *Night Thoughts* he sees verse as in itself a free medium, well-suited to the sincere ideal. His own poetry, addressed to men who are willing to be men, will utter plain Protestant truths:

> Ye sons of earth! (nor willing to be more!)
> Since verse you think from priestcraft somewhat free,
> Thus, in an age so gay, the muse plain truths
> (Truths, which, at church, you might have heard in prose)
> Has ventured into light; well-pleased the verse
> Should be forgot, if you the truths retain,
> And crown her with your welfare, not your praise.
>
> (8, 1385–91)[51]

But Young's view of truth is abstracted from the ordinary concerns of human life. It is implicit in the opening address, "Ye sons of

48. Ibid., p. 51.

49. Earl R. Wasserman, "The Inherent Values of Eighteenth-Century Personification," *PMLA*, 65 (1950): 448.

50. Margery Bailey writes of Young's "un-Augustan candor," "Edward Young" in F. W. Hilles, ed., *The Age of Johnson* (New Haven: Yale University Press, 1949), pp. 204–5.

51. All references to *Night Thoughts* are to *The Complete Works, Poetry and Prose, of the Rev. Edward Young, LL.D.*, 2 vols. (London, 1854).

earth! (nor willing to be more!)." Beginning with the unconverted soul, Young will lead it through the diapason of aspiration to eventual completeness and unity with heaven. As Martin Price has put it:

> Young offers eternity as the fulfillment of the latent energy within man rather than as a more traditional death and rebirth; the movement of the poem is the bursting out of constrictions, expansion into infinite space, progress toward unreachable perfection.[52]

The psychology of Young's aspiration is fairly complex. It gains momentum from his despair over the possibilities of earthly existence; yet this despair is not as thoroughgoing as it might appear. Most simply stated, Young rejects the world in favour of eternity: "All, all on earth is shadow, all beyond / Is substance . . ." (1, 120–21). The world, however, is pleasant, and therefore deceiving:

> How, like a worm, was I wrapt round and round
> In silken thought, which reptile Fancy spun,
> Till darken'd Reason lay quite clouded o'er
> With soft conceit of endless comfort here,
>
> . . . .
>
> How richly were my noon-tide trances hung
> With gorgeous tapestries of pictured joys!
> Joy behind joy, in endless perspective.
>
> (1, 158–61, 169–71)

Such joys Young has found to be false and, what is more, an infringement on the "rights of heaven" (1, 201) to be the only possessor of lasting bliss. The lesson has come with the deaths of three of his loved ones: "Thy shaft flew thrice; and thrice my peace was slain; / And thrice, ere thrice yon moon had filled her horn" (1, 213–14). If we read this as an autobiographical passage, it is inaccurate, for many reasons amply treated elsewhere.[53] But George Eliot's indictment of insincerity on this score should be disregarded as well. If Philander is Henry Temple and Narcissa, Elizabeth Temple,

52. *To the Palace of Wisdom*, p. 349.
53. See C. V. Wicker, *Edward Young and the Fear of Death* (Albuquerque: University of New Mexico Publications in Language and Literature, 1952), p. 43.

Young's reversal of the actual order of their deaths later in the poem, putting Philander's death first, serves to emphasize the ideal of male friendship which is made so much of in the debates with Lorenzo. Narcissa's loss is felt all the more acutely because she was Philander's wife. Had the actual order been followed, Young's concern for Narcissa might have been read as having adulterous overtones. Such a possibility should not be ruled out when we remember the outcry over Pomfret's famous assertion in *The Choice* that he "would have no wife." A mistress, it was thought, was the likely substitute, and Pomfret's remonstrations were to no avail. Few of the first readers of *Night Thoughts* would have known the truth of Young's relationship to Narcissa, and he seems unwilling to raise questions which could not be easily answered. Thus for reasons of art and propriety (always closely related in Young), he seems to have reversed the order to good advantage.

The rejection of earthly things contains an implicit attack on some general opinions held by the deists. Young strikes out in Night 5 against the defenders of natural religion:

> Let Indians, and the gay, like Indians, fond
> Of feather'd fopperies, the sun adore:
> Darkness has more divinity for me:
> It strikes thought inward; it drives back the soul
> to settle on herself, our point supreme!
>
> (5, 126–30)

Not only the deists, but other optimistic ideologues are treated to Young's sarcasm. His insistence on darkness is in contradistinction to the deist's love of sunshine (mocked perhaps in the sun image here) and open vistas, notable in the poetry of Thomson and Akenside. Nonetheless Young has no love for the superstitious gloom associated with the Roman Church. Although he admits the possibility of miracles, for example, he prefers the course of nature "rationally seen" in an "un-miraculous survey" (9, 1263, 1266) as proof of God's existence. His darkness is a positive quality representing otherworldliness, to be sure, but also it provides the conditions under which reason can function most effectively. By substituting darkness for light as positive quality and metaphor, Young signals his attempt to find truth in paradox. Indeed, perhaps the chief force of Young's didactic argument lies in his use of paradox to undermine the worldly point of view. His method of argument is to surprise his antagonist at every opportunity and to consolidate that victory by compounding the argument with the force of intense passion.

His verse composed in the sobriety of night, Young excoriates the "basking bards" who are

> Inebriate at fair Fortune's fountain-head,
> And reeling through the wilderness of joy;
> Where Sense runs savage, broke from Reason's chain,
> And sings false peace, till smother'd by the pall.
>
> (3, 20–23)

These are the deist poets and others who fail to find Christian religious themes for their poetry. The deists are specified as "Those pompous sons of Reason idolized / And vilified at once" (4, 771–72). The deists' use of Socrates is attacked in a direct address to God Himself:

> Talk they of morals? O Thou bleeding Love!
> Thou Maker of new morals to mankind!
> The grand morality is love of Thee.
> As wise as Socrates, if such they were,
> (Nor will they 'bate of that sublime renown,)
> "As wise as Socrates," might justly stand
> The definition of a modern fool.
>
> (4, 782–87)

This follows, of course, from the introduction of the Christian dispensation. Young accuses the deists of regression to the philosophy of a more ignorant time:

> A CHRISTIAN is the highest style of man.
> And is there who the blessed cross wipes off,
> As a foul blot, from his dishonour'd brow?
>
> (4, 788–90)

Yet both Young and the deists begin with many of the same suppositions about man's present condition. Employing much the same imagery that Thomson used in *The Seasons*, Young looks out to see men preying upon one another:

I see the circling hunt, of noisy men,
Burst Law's enclosure, leap the mounds of Right,
Pursuing and pursued, each other's prey;
As wolves, for rapine; as the fox, for wiles;
Till Death, that mighty hunter, earths them all.

(4, 92–96)

Young's answer to the problem is also much like that of the deists: man must be renovated and, if possible, returned to a kind of Eden. But Young's spiritual aspiration will lead him to a reinterpretation of the Eden motif, after a brief survey of earthly possibilities. These possibilities are given no real consideration, however, since they are rejected at the outset of *Night Thoughts*. It will be germane to survey Young's uses of the Eden motif, since it is central to his point of view.

Narcissa, like some of Thomson's heroines, lived in an age of innocence:

Sweet harmonist! and beautiful as sweet!
And young as beautiful! and soft as young!
And gay as soft! and innocent as gay!

(3, 81–83)

She is summed up in the following metaphor:

Song, beauty, youth, love, virtue, joy! this group
Of bright ideas, flowers of paradise,
As yet unforfeit. . . .

(3, 94–96)

In Narcissa's case, as with every other good Christian, Death provides ample recompense for the loss of Eden: "Where blooming Eden withers in our sight: / Death gives us more than was in Eden lost" (3, 532–33). This is eternity, of course; and by the end of the poem, heaven will be seen as the only possible Eden.

But Young does not reject human life on earth. He attacks, for example, the cult of suicide that was rampant in England in the eighteenth century. These older relatives of Young Werther, he argues, are not influenced by the English climate, as some were wont to argue:

> Blame not thy clime, nor chide the distant sun;
> The sun is innocent, thy clime absolved:
> Immoral climes kind Nature never made.
> The cause I sing in Eden might prevail,
> And proves it is thy folly, not thy fate.
>
> (5, 450–54)

This is a significant rebuttal to those who argued for environmental influence. Since the original sin was committed in Eden, utopia could never be the panacea for immorality. On the contrary, utopian ideals, if earthly, distract man from his real end which is eternity. Though life is difficult, man should live out the portion given him, while his soul is

> Studious of home, and ardent to return,—
> Of Earth suspicious, Earth's enchanted cup
> With cool reserve light touching, should indulge
> On Immortality her godlike taste;
> There take large draughts; make her chief banquet there.
>
> (5, 461–65)

Later in the poem, Young elaborates on the purpose of life, indicating that its essence is hope for eternity:

> This hope is earth's most estimable prize:
> This is man's portion, while no more than man:
> Hope, of all passions, most befriends us here;
> Passions of prouder name befriend us less.
> Joy has her tears; and Transport has her death:
> Hope, like a cordial, innocent, though strong,
> Man's heart at once inspirits and serenes;
> Nor makes him pay his wisdom for his joys.
>
> (7, 1459–66)

From this life takes on meaning. Suicide fails to recognize the dignified end for which man was created; indeed it fails to recognize even the dignity that man can attain on earth, if his aspirations are properly directed.

On earth there is no innocence without blemish. Narcissa's earthly gifts are as nothing when death claims her. But after that her heavenly attainments are glorified. Even Lorenzo's little son, Florello, is "guiltless, and sad! a wretch before the fall!" who needs his father's example and guidance (8, 261).

Pleasure is another positive quality to which Young devotes much attention. There is, of course, seductive pleasure, which lies in wait for the unsuspecting. But pleasure, nonetheless, had its origin in heaven and has as its purpose "to build / Divine on human" (8, 641–42). Further, "Pleasure first succours Virtue; in return, / Virtue gives Pleasure an eternal reign" (8, 645–46). Pleasure does create an Eden, as Young suggests, but not a lasting one:

Glide, then, for ever, Pleasure's sacred stream!
Through Eden, as Euphrates ran, it runs,
And fosters every growth of happy life;
Makes a new Eden where it flows;—but such
As must be lost, Lorenzo, by thy fall.

(8, 655–59)

By his fall Young means that Lorenzo is bound to violate the principles under which pleasure is virtuous. Then, of course, pleasure becomes the most corrupt of influences, since it makes us lose sight of our eternal end.

In Night 9 Young proceeds to a glorification of pain and death, accepting and echoing Pope's "whatever is, is right": "All, all is right, by God ordain'd or done; . . ." (9, 373). We further learn that "Pain is to save from pain; all punishment, / To make for peace; and Death, to save from death; . . ." (9, 379–80). Thus the same hand "That planted Eden, and high-bloom'd for man / A fairer Eden, endless, in the skies . . ." (9, 385–86) has ordained that "All evils natural are moral goods: / All discipline, indulgence, on the whole" (9, 389–90). Young's great emphasis on individual responsibility is consistent with the optimism which comes out of an initial pessimism:

None are unhappy: all have cause to smile
But such as to themselves that cause deny.
Our faults are at the bottom of our pains: ...

(9, 391–93)

Later in Night 9 the "fairer Eden" is specified as God's abode and identified with the great astronomical world:

Call it "the garden of the DEITY,"
Blossom'd with stars, redundant in the growth
Of fruit ambrosial, moral fruit to man.

(9, 1040–42)

The universal heavens are to Young "An Eden . . . a Paradise un-lost" (9, 1069).

In this way Young replaces the worldly (though merely vision-ary) utopia of the deists with a heavenly Eden that is barely less naturalistic. Young's description of God's "garden" is clearly de-pendent on his readings in contemporary scientific writings. The stars and whirling planets are "the seats majestic" of "angelic dele-gates," a scene which, apart from its absurdity, seems very unlike a garden. But Young gained from his astronomical knowledge an exhilaration similar to that of the deists. His own Christianity put him at odds with the deists, of course, but the conception of God that comes through *Night Thoughts* is not very different from the Deity in the poems of Thomson and Akenside. Further Young and the deists share both pessimism and optimism. All are upset about the present condition of the world but resolve their tensions in a unified view of creation. The deists create an elaborate visionary myth of the sincere society, while Young finds a similar world in the "garden" of God. The deists would have agreed whole-heartedly with these lines from Night 6: "Each man makes his own stature, builds himself: / Virtue alone out builds the pyramids; . . ." (6, 311–12). And just as deists do, Young believes in the essential goodness of the passions:

Think not our passions from Corruption sprung,
Though to Corruption now they lend their wings;

That is their mistress, not their mother. All
(And justly) Reason deem Divine: I see,
I feel a grandeur in the Passions too,
Which speaks their high descent, and glorious end;
Which speaks them rays of an eternal fire.
In Paradise itself they burnt as strong,
Ere Adam fell, though wiser in their aim.

(7, 524–32)

Nature for the deist evidenced God's handiwork. For Young the
astronomical world holds the same fascination:

This prospect vast, what is it?—Weigh'd aright,
'Tis Nature's system of divinity,
And every student of the night inspires.
'Tis elder Scripture, writ by GOD'S own hand;
Scripture authentic, uncorrupt by man.

(9, 641–45)

This is, in its way, an indictment of the very Scripture which he had
recommended, with some irony, to men of mirth: "Retire, and read
thy Bible, to be gay" (8, 771).

Young's rather mild but explicit attack on laughter (it is "half-
immoral" (8, 750) may be thought of as an attack on Shaftesbury's
doctrine of ridicule as a test of truth; but more likely it is a manifestation of Young's own dour sympathies with Puritan attitudes.

Much more important to note is Young's essential agreement with
the deists that Nature is the best proof of God's existence. He rejects
the "metaphysic pinions" and "logic thorns" of scholasticism and
its partisans:

Nature no such hard task enjoins: she gave
A make to man directive of his thought;
A make set upright, pointing to the stars,
As who should say, "Read thy chief lesson there."

(9, 867–70)

Young further accepts the deistic attitude in favour of benevolence,
although his pessimistic turn of mind will not permit him to believe

that the perfection of such attitudes is possible in the world. In the
eternal heavens, however, man finds an unparalleled model for his
own behaviour:

> The planets of each system represent
> Kind neighbours; mutual amity prevails;
> Sweet interchange of rays, received, return'd;
> Enlightening, and enlighten'd! All, at once,
> Attracting, and attracted! Patriot-like,
> None sins against the welfare of the whole;
> But their reciprocal, unselfish aid
> Affords an emblem of millennial love.
> Nothing in Nature, much less conscious being,
> Was e'er created solely for itself:
> Thus man his sovereign duty learns in this
> Material picture of benevolence.

(9, 696–707)

This model gives us some insight into Young's social views, for,
admittedly, his aspirations for infinity leave little room to social
comment. By putting Eden in the heavens, Young expresses his
acute sense of social inadequacy. This sense is, in part, connected
with his Puritan attitudes, some of which recall Pascal. For example,
Lorenzo, moving from one evil action to another, cannot find for
himself the peace he seeks. Young indicates that this restlessness is
wholly at odds with its object:

> Man's greatest strength is shown in standing still.
> The first sure symptom of a mind in health
> Is rest of heart, and pleasure felt at home.

(8, 922–24)

This may recall Pascal's disarming remark in the *Pensées*, "*J'ai
découvert que tout le malheur des hommes vient d'une seule chose, qui est
de ne savoir pas demeurer en repos, dans une chambre.*"[54] When the
capacity to do this is attained, then the basis for spiritual meditation
has been provided.

Another distinctly Puritan aspect of Young's sensibility is his

---

54. *Pensées*, 139, ed. Ch.-M. des Granges (Paris: Garnier, 1961), p. 109.

concern for the good use of time: "We waste, not use, our time; we breathe, not live. / Time *wasted* is existence, *used* is life" (2, 149–50). Also there is his obsession with conscience, which as a "sly informer minutes every fault, / And her dread diary with horror fills" (2, 262–63). This admonition is intended to strike fear in Lorenzo's heart, and as such is suggestive of Puritan spiritual autobiography at its most fanatical. Indeed the terror motif runs throughout most of Young's poem. Though it is difficult to separate influences, this concern for horror and fear seems more directly related to Puritan sensibility than to the more literary graveyard school of poetry.

Once again Young reacts in good Puritan-deist form by discovering that guile and deceit are the chief enemies of man. Death, "the dreadful masquerader," is guileful, and hides behind a mask (5, 860–78), a fact particularly terrifying to those who are not morally prepared to die. Characteristically, men of the world, in public life, are those "that would blush at being thought sincere" (8, 285). In other words, they turn all value upside down. Young laments:

> The world's all title-page, there's no contents:
> The world's all face; the man who shows his heart
> Is hooted for his nudities, and scorn'd.

> (8, 333–35)

Thus the sincere "feeling heart" is accounted of no worth by ordinary society.

If this is the case, few hopes can be held out for a "sincere" society in which all men will show to each other the most feeling of virtues. Friendship, however, the same limited community of brothers in virtue, idealized by the deists, assumes for Young a preeminent place in social affairs. As we have seen, Philander and Lorenzo take the first places in the hierarchy of friendship and Narcissa, as female friend, comes close behind. Young spares no effort to praise friendship:

> Friendship, the means of wisdom, richly gives
> The precious end which makes our wisdom wise.
> Nature, in zeal for human amity,
> Denies or damps an undivided joy.

Joy is an import; joy is an exchange;
Joy flies monopolists; it calls for two;
Rich fruit, heaven-planted, never pluck'd by one!
Needful auxiliars are our friends, to give
To social man true relish of himself.

(2, 503–11)

All this must lead to spiritual well-being, and, once again, the
"immortal man" is open-hearted and innocently sincere (8, 1129–
1133).

But we should look for the true test of virtue in man on the brink
of eternity. *Night Thoughts* reflects Young's concern for the
Christian death-bed, a significant motif later in his *Conjectures on
Original Composition:*

Dost thou demand a test
(A test at once infallible and short)
Of real greatness? That man greatly lives,
Whate'er his fate or fame, who greatly dies;
High-flush'd with hope where heroes shall despair.
If this a true criterion, many courts,
Illustrious, might afford but few grandees.

(8, 468–74)

The mode of death proves the mode of life. Since the object of
man's earthly pursuits is eternity, the practice of virtue has a
spiritual rather than a social orientation. For this task the imagination is a useful intermediary. By means of the imagination Young
was able to transcend the limitations of mundane experience to
evoke the images of eternity presented in Night 9. His identification of these spiritual elements with Eden or Paradise makes clear
the meaning of this important passage from the *Conjectures*: "so
boundless are the bold excursions of the human mind, that, in the
vast void beyond real existence, it can call forth shadowy beings,
and unknown worlds, as numerous, as bright, and, perhaps, as
lasting, as the stars; such quite-original beauties we may call *paradisaical.*"[55] Thus the human mind moves toward the millennium in

55. *Conjectures*, p. 31. My italics.

the process of original composition. It is essentially the object of eternal bliss that gives the moderns the possibility of superiority over the ancients. The very arguments which Young levels against the deists are employed here in supporting his view of genius. Aspiration toward the spiritual ideal provides all the momentum that a poet could wish. It is not surprising then that the religious and spiritual virtues which Young prizes are demanded in the process of poetic composition.

The preface to the *Night Thoughts* contains the basic elements of Young's views on composition and deserves quotation in full:

> As the occasion of this poem was real, not fictitious; so the method pursued in it was rather imposed by what spontaneously arose in the author's mind on that occasion, than meditated or designed: which will appear very probable from the nature of it; for it differs from the common mode of poetry, which is from long narrations to draw short morals. Here, on the contrary, the narrative is short, and the morality arising from it makes the bulk of the poem. The reason of it is, that the facts mentioned did naturally pour these moral reflections on the thought of the writer.[56]

An important implication of this preface is that poetry based on real occasions and which arises spontaneously tends to be meditative and personal. Narrative or descriptive poetry is less likely to be spontaneous and therefore will be less likely to conform to the sincere ideal.

In asserting the importance of spontaneity, Young further distinguishes between his poetry and that which lacks a proper moral orientation:

> Art, cursed Art! wipes off th'indebted blush
> From Nature's cheek, and bronzes every shame.
> Man smiles in ruin, glories in his guilt,
> And Infamy stands candidate for praise.

> (5, 43–45)

56. *The Complete Works*, Preface to Night 1.

But there is another poetry which Young hopes his poem exemplifies:

> Sing sirens only? Do not angels sing?
> There is in Poesy a decent pride,
>
> . . . .
>
>   Think'st thou, Lorenzo, to find pastimes here?
> No guilty passion blown into a flame,
> No foible flatter'd, dignity disgraced,
> No fairy field of fiction, all on flower,
> No rainbow colours here, or silken tale;
> But solemn counsels, images of awe,
> Truths which Eternity lets fall on man, . . .
>
> (5, 63–64, 67–73)

If one sings truth, as Young says he does, one must be sure of that truth first, and, needless to say, one must be sincere in his presentation of that truth:

> Or if you fail me, know, the wise shall taste
> The truths I sing; the truths I sing shall feel;
> And, feeling, give assent; and their assent
> Is ample recompence; is more than praise.
>
> (5, 84–87)

Young finds his spontaneity, poetically, in the "delightful gloom" of night when "the clust'ring thoughts around / Spontaneous rise, and blossom in the shade; . . ." (5, 205–6). In a later passage in Night 5, he describes the source of his inspiration:

> See, from her tomb, as from an humble shrine,
> Truth, radiant goddess, sallies on my soul,
> And puts Delusion's dusky train to flight;
> Dispels the mists our sultry passions raise,
> From objects low, terrestrial, and obscene;
> And shows the real estimate of things,
> Which no man, unafflicted, ever saw: . . .
>
> (5, 327–33)

Truth, in the form of reason, destroys the effects of passion and raises the afflicted soul to perception. Here perhaps the darkness which creates the situation necessary to spiritual insight is equated with, or at least related to, personal affliction. Thus pain cleanses the doors of perception.

Young goes on to clarify the implications of truth in one of his most beautiful passages:

> Truth bids me look on men as autumn leaves,
> And all they bleed for as the summer's dust,
> Driven by the whirlwind. Lighted by her beams,
> I widen my horizon, gain new powers,
> See things invisible, feel things remote,
> Am present with futurities; . . .
>
> (5, 336–41)

All the images of the first three lines coalesce and reinforce one another. The bleeding of men suggests the redness of the leaves; the dust and the leaves are both driven by the whirlwind, as are the men. By switching from autumn leaves to summer's dust, Young shows that the threat of death and decay knows no one season. Finally in visionary rapture suggesting Walt Whitman, the poet collapses all time, permitting insight into eternity, which is, of course, timeless.

Young's quest for spiritual truth, then, is another form of the deists' search for a terrestrial paradise. In *The Centaur Not Fabulous*, Young's moral work in prose, he employs the image of the garden as a model of the well-ordered soul:

> A garden has ever had the praise, and affection of the wise. What is requisite to make a wise, and happy man, but reflection and peace? and both are the natural growth of a garden. Nor is a garden only a promoter of a good man's happiness, but a picture of it: and, in some sort, shews him to himself. Its culture, order, fruitfulness, and seclusion from the world, compared to the weeds, wildness, and exposure of a common field, is no bad emblem of a good man, compared to the multitude. A garden weeds the mind; it weeds it of worldly thoughts; and sows celestial seed in their stead. For what see we there, but

what awakens in us our gratitude to heaven? A garden to the virtuous is a paradise still extant; a paradise unlost.[57]

Although the garden assumes great importance in the Middle Ages and Renaissance, it is safe to say that Milton's Eden exerted the chief impact on the eighteenth century. The eighteenth-century quest for the sincere ideal begins with concern for the social order. But the ideals of sincerity and benevolence were too grand for the real world, it seems, and their proponents often fell into despair. Young begins *Night Thoughts* in something like this despair and illustrates in that poem a view very much like that of the Quaker George Fox: that "the whole world lies in wickedness." If the world is deceit and guile unmitigated, then immortality is the realm of sincerity. Whether Young had a literal belief in his astronomical notions of heaven is of no importance. The imaginative vision of sincerity is what remains. For Young, as for the deists and the latter-day Puritans, retirement from the world to a personal Eden was the only recourse. But while valuing some of the earthly delights the earlier poets held dear, Young rejects from the beginning the possibility of a terrestrial paradise and finds in the Christian conception of immortality the true exemplification of the sincere ideal.

57. *The Works* (London, 1802), 3, 244.

I shall set down the following fragment which, as it is the genuine language of my heart, will enable any body to determine which of the Classes I belong to. . . .

Robert Burns

6

Augustans and Others to 1800

WILLIAM COLLINS

The poetical aspirations of William Collins seem to move in so many directions that it is difficult to know where to have them. A. S. P. Woodhouse has argued that Collins inhabited two literary worlds— the neoclassical and the preromantic—"abutting on each other and sometimes overlapping, but also sometimes seeming far apart."[1] Such a generalization is hardest to maintain when the task of separating the two worlds is set. Even allowing for overlapping, attitudes identified as romantic will often be found to have a firm basis in neoclassical principles.

In Collins's work this difficulty is pre-eminently apparent. In the "Ode to Pity" and "Ode to Fear," the first two poems in his most significant volume, *Odes on Several Descriptive and Allegoric Subjects*, Collins seems to aspire to the discipline of Greek tragedy. The personifications considered are, after all, the emotions involved in catharsis; and both are treated in a positive way. In the two odes that follow, however, "simplicity" is regarded as the chief of poetic virtues and a wild, natural kind of bard is praised as the epitome of the poetical character. These latter attitudes seem to accord better with preromantic notions and are, therefore, in conflict with those that are neoclassical. Thus Collins's work is viewed as the result of a set of established conventions and some encroaching new ones. He is regarded as an interesting "transitional" figure in whose work we cannot reasonably expect to discover a unified outlook.

---

1. "The Poetry of Collins Reconsidered" in Frederick W. Hilles and Harold Bloom, eds. *From Sensibility to Romanticism: Essays Presented to Frederick A. Pottle* (New York: Oxford University Press, 1965), p. 93.

Before taking direct issue with this view, I should hasten to add that it is not entirely mistaken. There are inconsistencies in Collins's poems which arise from the varied materials upon which he drew. But despite these and certain minor difficulties of lack of clarity, Collins's work communicates an essentially unified vision.

All of his mature poetry may be seen in terms of the sincere ideal. More specifically it is usually an examination of the relationship of the poet to that ideal. In this unified perspective many of the superficial distinctions between neoclassicism and romanticism break down. There is a unity of aspiration on Collins's part, no matter what materials he uses to construct his poetic Eden. But construct it he does, working out in the process the poet's relationship to both society and his art. In selecting varied materials, he is very like James Thomson, who, in *Liberty*, praised the virtue of the Druids,[2] since they were the progenitors of the hoped-for ideal Britain, and could as well admire the same simplicity in the Greeks and Romans. It is not so much the society that matters, but rather the virtues and ideals which a society represents. Thomson pinned what hopes he had for Britain on the analogy that could be drawn with ancient Greece and Rome. In using this analogy, the focus on literature was natural, since, like Greece, England had shown irrefragable greatness in literary endeavour. The works of Chaucer, Spenser, and Shakespeare provided evidence that the English past was one to rival and even surpass the greatest civilizations of antiquity. And poets were left to decide whether progress or decline would follow that earlier greatness.

Initially it was possible to take an optimistic view. The examples of Greece and Rome provided an incentive, since it was popular to assume that those civilizations shared a common historical pattern with England. Thus England, more than any other nation, could benefit from the precept and example of the classical achievement. Indeed, classical and indigenous attitudes could unite to produce an England greater than Greece or Rome had ever been. The achievement of Milton seemed at times to have made this hope a reality, but each new generation of poets needed to reinterpret and consolidate

2. *Liberty*, 4, 624–40.

his gains. Thus Collins set as his goal the unity of classical and British culture.

To illustrate Collins's understanding of the analogy between Britain and the classical world, we can turn to his "Verses ... Address'd to Sir Thomas Hanmer" (1743). This poem in couplets is usually seen as one of his most conventional productions.[3] But what seems a tissue of convention to modern critics had an imaginative life of its own in its own time.

Early in the poem Collins argues, albeit with some reservations, for a progressive view of the arts:

> Each rising Art by slow Gradation moves,
> Toil builds on Toil, and Age on Age improves.
>
> (29–30)[4]

The key qualification consists in the use of the word "rising," since at a point of maximum achievement, the art will no longer "rise." He wonders, later in the poem, whether this apogee has already been reached in England, precluding the writing of great poetry in his own time. He next describes the tragedy of Greece, the comedy of Rome, and, to prove his cosmopolitan viewpoint, the lyrical greatness of Florence. These, in the progressive movement, unite in Shakespeare:

> But Heav'n, still rising in its Works, decreed
> The perfect Boast of Time should last succeed.
> The beauteous Union must appear at length,
> Of *Tuscan* Fancy, and Athenian Strength:
> One greater Muse Eliza's Reign adorn,
> And ev'n a Shakespear to her Fame be born!
>
> (57–62)

Collins emphasizes Shakespeare's cultural orientation and understanding of man: "But stronger *Shakespear* felt for *Man* alone: ..." (76) and "He alone to ev'ry Scene could give / Th'Historian's Truth, and bid the Manners live" (89–90). He attributes to Shakespeare a relationship to "Truth," the primary object of the deist poets

3. "The Poetry of Collins Reconsidered," p. 94.
4. All references are to *Poems of William Collins*, ed. Christopher Stone and Austin Lane Poole (Oxford: Oxford Standard Authors, 1936).

and Edward Young. It is not poetry as art, but poetry as truth
which interests Collins.

The analogy between Britain and Athens, drawn earlier in the
poems of Thomson and Akenside, is made explicit at the end of this
poem, when Hanmer is addressed:

> So spread o'er *Greece*, th'harmonious Whole unknown,
> Ev'n Homer's Numbers charm'd by Parts alone.
> Their own Ulysses scarce had wander'd more,
> By Winds and Waters cast on ev'ry Shore:
> When, rais'd by Fate, some former *Hanmer* join'd
> Each beauteous Image of the tuneful Mind:
> And bad, like Thee, his *Athens* ever claim
> A fond Alliance with the Poet's Name.

(153–60)

Thus the poem to Hanmer presents a number of themes that were
to receive more complex treatment in the later poems.

The "Ode to Pity" expresses veneration for the Greek Tragic
Muse, as I have said, but, further, it begins for Collins a theme only
implicit in the Hanmer poem, the concern with what W. J. Bate so
aptly calls "the burden of the past."[5] In perhaps no English poet before Collins is this important concern so centrally located. Other
poets were indeed concerned that the greatness of the past could not
be rivalled and that there was nothing left to do. But Thomson, for
example, felt his greatest concern for society at large, and only a
secondary one for the decline of the arts. Behind the optimism of
Mark Akenside there is an abiding concern lest the imagination sink
into decay; and his poem, *The Pleasures of Imagination,* is an attempt
to produce a formula or program to insure that poetry continue to
flourish. Collins, however, approaches the problem with greater
sensitivity, less as a philosopher than as an artist. Thus no easy
solutions are forthcoming; rather he examines the alternatives with
a full awareness of the problem. It will be helpful to explore some of
these positions in the poems themselves.

5. *The Burden of the Past and the English Poet* (Cambridge: Harvard University
Press, 1970) and the earlier essay "The English Poet and the Burden of the Past,
1660–1820" in Earl R. Wasserman, ed. *Aspects of the Eighteenth Century* (Baltimore:
The Johns Hopkins Press, 1965), pp. 245–64.

"Pity" in the "Ode to Pity" has a number of ironic meanings, which develop as the poem progresses. First and most important, pity is one of the tragic emotions. In addition to this it is a virtue to be valued in society: she is "the Friend of Man assign'd." By using these two meanings Collins characteristically links social and artistic concern. This combination helps lead to a third meaning of pity, which is self-pity, or pity for the contemporary poet.

The poem begins in dependence upon the Greeks, as Euripides is invoked; but the nagging question of that dependence comes quickly to the fore:

> But wherefore need I wander wide
> To old Ilissus' distant Side,—
> Deserted Stream, and mute?

That is, why must Greece provide examples of the greatness of tender passions when England has its Otway? But the recollection of Otway does no more than raise the poet's hopes, for that poet's example is not enough to settle the issue, as we shall see. But further hopes are raised in the following clamour:

> Come, Pity, come by Fancy's Aid,
> Ev'n now my Thoughts, relenting Maid,
>   Thy Temple's Pride design:
> Its Southern Site, its Truth compleat
> Shall raise a wild Enthusiast Heat,
> In all who view the Shrine.

At last the poet calls upon Pity to let him swell with her in "Dreams of Passion", "Till, Virgin, Thou again delight / To hear a *British* Shell." There is perhaps the suggestion that the poet's experience in Pity's cell will prepare him to produce drama worthy of a Euripides or an Otway, but this is not clear. The desire for retirement seems more passive than active—an attempt to escape from the realization of poetic inferiority to the warm, moist womb of the romanticized past.

The "Ode to Fear" is an obeisance to Aeschylus and Sophocles, whom by implication he relates to Shakespeare and other bards of imagination. Collins does reject, in a mildly ironic way, the ghosts

and goblins in which "Cottage-Maids believe," but sees "Fear" as
the tragic emotion common to both Greek and English tragedians.
Here too Collins articulates his conception of the poet as prophet,
suggesting as well the importance of spontaneous emotion to poetic
creation:

> O Thou whose Spirit most possest
> The sacred Seat of Shakespear's Breast!
> By all that from thy Prophet broke,
> In thy Divine Emotions spoke:
> Hither again thy Fury deal,
> Teach me but once like Him to feel:
> His *Cypress Wreath* my Meed decree,
> And I, O Fear, will dwell with *Thee*!

The realization again that he cannot "feel" as Shakespeare does wells
up most prominently in this emotional passage. "Fear" should be
thought of here in a very positive, sublime sense. "Awe" is usually
its synonym in this poem.

The "Ode to Simplicity" invokes a concept in great currency
during the eighteenth century,[6] a concept which is also discovered in
both ancient Greece and Rome, with Sophocles its chief exemplar.
This would suggest that the ode does not contradict the attitudes
expressed in the two examined above. Collins deals with general
poetic inspiration, apart from generic considerations. Simplicity has
an over-riding importance in all literature, so that "Faints the cold
Work till thou inspire the whole; . . ."

In the "Ode on the Poetical Character" we are in the Spenserian
world of magic girdles that bring poetic inspiration. But again, this
world is lost to Collins's contemporaries:

> Where is the Bard, whose Soul can now
> Its high presuming Hopes avow?
> Where He who thinks, with Rapture blind,
> This hallow'd Work for Him design'd?

(51–54)

---

6. See R. D. Havens, "Simplicity, A Changing Concept," *Journal of the History of
Ideas*, 14 (1953): 3–32.

The poet supposes temporarily, however, that the paradise of the imagination exists for his contemporaries:

> High on some Cliff, to Heav'n up-pil'd,
> Of rude Access, of Prospect wild,
> Where, tangled round the jealous Steep,
> Strange Shades o'erbrow the Valleys deep,
> And holy *Genii* guard the Rock,
> Its Gloomes embrown, its Springs unlock,
> While on its rich ambitious Head,
> An *Eden*, like his own, lies spread: . . .
>
> (55–62)

This is the Eden sought by Collins; "like his own" makes reference to the "Bard," who at the beginning of the poem was Spenser, and now, quite specifically, becomes Milton. But the poet cannot follow Milton in the magnitude of his endeavours. The concluding note is one of despair in which Collins blames "Heav'n and Fancy" for his incapacity:

> And Heav'n and *Fancy*, kindred Pow'rs,
> Have now o'erturn'd th'inspiring Bow'rs,
> Or curtain'd close such Scene from ev'ry future View.
>
> (74–76)

Here end the odes that are most concerned with defining the imagination (with the possible exception of the "Ode to Evening"). We may summarize Collins's attitudes studied thus far: (1) Greek poetry, especially that of the great tragedians, is highly regarded as an example to all succeeding ages. Its qualities are simplicity, spontaneity, truth to Nature, and relevance to society. (2) Shakespeare and other English poets have successfully rivalled the ancients, and have succeeded by employing materials indigenous to England. They have been, to a considerable extent, possessed of all the qualities valued in the Greeks. (3) For some uncertain reason modern poets, and Collins in particular, lack this combination of desirable qualities.

In the odes which follow, Collins finds a centre of gravity in the social situation that confronts him. In other words, he defines a reality to which poetry might have relevance, a first step in composing a suitable poetic.

These next poems, the "Ode, Written in the beginning of the Year 1746," the "Ode to Mercy," and the "Ode to Liberty," deal essentially with social concerns. The seventeen-forties were years of remarkable strife and chaos in public affairs. During these years were fought the so-called "War of Jenkins's Ear" with Spain, the War of the Austrian Succession, and the battles of the second Jacobite rebellion. Of the Austrian war Basil Williams has written: "Primarily the war was 'unintelligible' at the time, and is still more so to us to-day, because it was largely fought on sham issues: the dynastic rights of kings and princes, as illustrated by that gigantic fraud, the Pragmatic Sanction—whereas the real issues, to which most of the statesmen were blind, were concerned with the larger interests of the peoples."[7]

In the absence of clear issues in any of these conflicts, it is not surprising that Collins's own grasp of the situation is articulated in the vague generalities of "freedom" and "justice." These, he supposes, are being defended by Englishmen against the Young Pretender and everyone else who is not specifically English. Collins's staunch nationalism, however, was not outrageous by eighteenth-century standards. Agreeing with Pope and Thomson, Collins saw English imperialism as the world's best hope for peace. For him the extension of British rule would mean the realization of freedom and other material and spiritual benefits to all concerned.

Once again it is necessary to point out that behind Collins's jingoism is a true idealism, to be realized in the sincere ideal. Further, Collins's position, whether political or social, exists only as poetic vision. This vision was no more real to its creator than was Thomson's vision in *Liberty*. The ideal as grasped by the imagination is felt to be desirable, but not actual, and perhaps not possible. Generically, such work is apocalyptical. Few critics today scorn the medieval poets who meditate on the joys of the beatific vision; and for many eighteenth-century poets, heaven was a terrestrial paradise, which seemed not to be hurrying into actuality. With so many in-

7. *The Whig Supremacy, 1714–1760*, revised by C. H. Stuart (Oxford: Clarendon Press, 1962), pp. 265–66.

tractables, such as Charles Edward, France and Spain, barring the way to utopia, it is not surprising that many persons of mild temperament clamoured for war, just as, later in the century, the bloodshed of the French Revolution was countenanced for the sake of social progress. Edward Young, for example, not at all a war-like man, could justify various kinds of "moral wars": "As we are at war with the power, it were well if we were at war with the manners, of France. A land of levity is a land of guilt. A serious mind is the native soil of every virtue, and the single character that does true honour to mankind."[8] In the case of Thomson, the approval of militarism as a solution to the insoluble is the result of exasperation and despair. Whether or not such despair was justified is a difficult question. But it should be asserted frankly that few in the eighteenth century regarded war as immoral. People were only beginning to question such institutions as war and slavery. They did not do so because they possessed greater moral sensitivity than their forbears, but rather because a new morality that emphasized new ideals was emerging. In the context of eighteenth-century beliefs, it is difficult to fault Collins for his attitudes toward war. What he and his fellow poets supported were "just" wars; and only strict conscientious objectors object to such wars today. It is unhistorical as well as unwise to insist that highly moral poets of the eighteenth century, of which Collins is one, meet the moral tests of the present time.

The "Ode to Evening" and the "Ode to Peace" clarify some of the ideals of Collins's utopia: "Fancy, Friendship, Science, smiling Peace"[9] summarize well his poetical and social aspirations, which are, to a large degree, fused. They are ideals worth fighting for.

"The Manners, An Ode" is usually seen as a regression from Collins's romantic preoccupations, when he is assumed to have such. In this poem the poet rejects "Truths . . . from Action's Paths retir'd," which he sought in vain (3–4). The positive concern is social. Collins invokes "Observance" (20), which can be identified with the "Observation" of Johnson's *The Vanity of Human Wishes*. "Observance" is the occupation of social concern, from which personification the poet begs the following favours:

8. *Complete Works*, Preface to Night 7.   9. "Ode to Evening," 1, 50.

To me in Converse sweet impart,
To read in Man the native Heart,
To learn, where Science sure is found,
From Nature as she lives around:
And gazing oft her Mirror true,
By turns each shifting Image view!

(25–30)

No matter what claims the enchanted world of imagination may make, heaven itself "has blest this social Science most" (35–36). Further proof of Collins's social orientation is the esteem he has for the social literature of the comic muse, that of Cervantes and Lesage in particular. The importance of the heart in this literary activity is underscored in a concluding address to Nature:

O Nature boon, from whom proceed
Each forceful Thought, each prompted Deed;
If but from Thee I hope to feel,
On all my Heart imprint thy Seal!
Let some retreating Cynic find,
Those oft-turn'd Scrolls I leave behind,
The *Sports* and I this Hour agree,
To rove thy Scene-full World with Thee!

(71–78)

The concluding poem "The Passions, An Ode for Music" is not merely an ode to be sung, but one addressed to a personified Music and thus for her. In the poem, Music, the teacher of the passions, witnesses an allegorical enactment of those passions' unique powers. Of central interest in the poem, however, is the concluding apostrophe to Music herself in which the loss of her power is lamented:

Why, Goddess, why to us deny'd?
Lay'st Thou thy antient Lyre aside?
As in that lov'd *Athenian* Bow'r,
You learn'd an all-commanding Pow'r,
Thy mimic Soul, O Nymph endear'd,
Can well recall what then it heard.
Where is thy native simple Heart,

Devote to Virtue, Fancy, Art?
Arise as in that elder Time,
Warm, Energic, Chaste, Sublime!

(97–106)

The major concern here is poetry, but more specifically it is the social
poetry of "The Manners." Thus "virtue" is necessary to a poetry
which must do more than "charm." Indeed this new poetry ought to
be like that of the Greeks, which "Had more of Strength, diviner
Rage, / Than all which charms this laggard Age, . ." (111–12).
Music is then called upon to

bid our vain Endeavors cease,
Revive the just Designs of Greece,
Return in all thy simple State!
Confirm the Tales Her Sons relate!

(115–18)

To summarize, it may be said that Collins never abandons, in these
odes, the Greek poetic–social ideal. Imagination is of significance to
him, but its most important role is in the service of highly idealized
social needs.

Collins and Keats have been compared before,[10] but the greatest
similarity between them seems to be in the conflict between the
ideals of imagination and society. Both poets had undoubted talent
in endeavours of "faery fancy," but each had such an extraordinary
regard for poetry that he felt it was fit for better things. Each was
aware of the legitimate demands which society can make on art, and
each, in a remarkably similar way (if we allow for Keats's greater
achievement), strove to meet those demands.

The fragmentary "Ode on the Popular Superstitions of the Highlands of Scotland" seems to reverse the social trend in Collins's
poetry noted thus far. But it would be more accurate to say that in
this poem he emphasizes a theme which in some earlier poems he had
relegated to an inferior position.

The poem, however, is not a clear espousal of romantic fancy.
First, it is addressed to John Home, the dramatist, whom Collins

---

10. See Douglas Bush, *John Keats* (New York: Macmillan, 1966), p. 143.

likens to Shakespeare, by implication, and who consciously imitated
Shakespeare. The ample concern in the poem with Scottish myths is
to justify and praise Home's genius, not Collins's own. Indeed the
use of such myths seems to require a justification:

> Nor need'st thou blush, that such false themes engage
> Thy gentle mind, of fairer stores possesst; . . .
>
> (172–73)

The themes are "false" mainly because they are fantastic, but they
are false in a more pejorative sense too. Home's mind is possessed
of "fairer stores," which is both an allusion to the unlovely quality of
ghosts and goblins and the fact that such subjects are not the most
significant for poetry. The poet, however, encourages Home to
"Proceed, nor quit the tales which, simply told, / Could once so
well my answ'ring bosom pierce; . . ." (183–84). At this stage of the
poem such tales have the impact of recollected experience, of boy-
hood perhaps. The poet recognizes their value and encourages their
telling.

In stanza 12, however, the poet undergoes a fresh emotional experience during which thoughts of past fanciful experiences coalesce
with an immediate intimation of Tasso's greatness. Tasso, indeed, is
very much the sincere poet: "Prevailing poet, whose undoubting
mind / Believ'd the magic wonders which he sung!" (198–99).
Tasso is no mere manipulator of conventions; he is the unself-
conscious poet of wild fancy, naive and childlike. The effect on his
listeners is one of intoxication:

> Hence at each sound imagination glows;
> Hence his warm lay with softest sweetness flows;
> Melting it flows, pure, num'rous, strong and clear,
> And fills th'impassion'd heart, and wins th'harmonious ear.
>
> (200–203)

This leads Collins to distinguish between the world of immediate
sense and that of imagination. Returning to those Scottish scenes
"which, daring to depart / From sober truth, are still to nature
true, / And call forth fresh delight to fancy's view, . . ." (188–90),

the poet addresses them: "All hail, ye scenes that o'er my soul pre-
vail" (204) and expresses a desire to become their bard:

> The time shall come when I, perhaps, may tread
> Your lowly glens, o'erhung with spreading broom,
> Or o'er your stretching heaths by fancy led: . . .
>   (208–10)

The "perhaps" seems to qualify everything rather hopelessly, and
the poem ends in a conventional compliment to Home.

Collins, despite the ambiguity of his conclusion, has at least
raised "the perennial problem of poetry and truth."[11] The relationship between truth and poetry is the question which led to the
creation of a poetry of sincerity. But although this relationship is
central even the use of personification allegory may be seen as an
indication of sincerity.[12] As John More pointed out in his *Strictures,
Critical and Sentimental, On Thomson's Seasons* (1777): "We *pause,
personify,* and *apostrophize,* not to enrich our style, but solely to
exhibit the real state of our minds; and, because no common language can do justice to such an impassioned sensibility. All moderation is at an end, whenever the heart breaks loose; and the sallies of
Genius, under that predicament, are certainly intitled to every
allowance, as ordinary minds are not competent judges of its
ardour."[13]

The important point, however, in establishing Collins as a "sincere" poet is his concern for the relationship between poetry and
truth. Praise of Tasso in the poem to Home implies that "false"
themes can be employed only if they are "true," that is, if the poet
sincerely believes them. And if the impassioned heart is moved by
these themes, then they are true to Nature, since the heart is Nature.
Collins's own regard for "wild fancy" may have begun in uncritical
ecstasy, but it came to fruition in careful reflection. Such use of the
imagination can be justified only if its end is truth, and the examples

---

11. Woodhouse, "The Poetry of Collins Reconsidered," p. 125.
12. See Earl R. Wasserman, "The Inherent Values of Eighteenth-Century Personification," *PMLA*, 65 (1950): 435–63.
13. Cited in Wasserman, "The Inherent Values . . .," p. 448.

of Spenser and Shakespeare seemed to indicate that truth was indeed to be found in wild places.

Yet, as "The Manners" proves, and his other poems suggest, Collins was both unable and unwilling to give himself over to the use of the romantic imagination. He could justify such use only if society could be served by it. He knew full well that such had been the case in past ages; but he suspected that his own imagination was not an architect of truth as Shakespeare's had been. Thus suspecting his powers and turning inward to refine them, he demonstrates a formal pattern of sincerity superior to that of most of his contemporaries, and is perhaps the first poet to create a poetry of sincerity that transcends convention. What Collins felt in his heart of hearts remains a mystery, but, like Gray and the later romantics, he presents the poetic mind in the active search for sincerity.

WILLIAM SHENSTONE

The ideal of sincerity as necessary to every aspect of human existence can be seen clearly in the life and work of William Shenstone, whose achievement may seem trivial, if we fail to notice it as part of the cultural movement that we have been tracing in this study. The preoccupation with sincerity and its related virtues is common in Shenstone's letters. In 1747 he wrote to Lady Luxborough: "I was in Hopes your Ladyship wou'd have weigh'd those trifling verses rather in the scale of *Sincerity* than that of *Poetry*. I meant them as a real expression of the satisfaction I found by your Fireside, & as an Intimation of my Thanks. . . ."[14] Here it is assumed that sincerity will atone for bad poetry, but, in making this distinction, Shenstone goes further, suggesting that sincerity is of greater importance than poetry. In addition, he characteristically disparages his own verse, a tendency of which I shall have more to say later.

In another letter, in 1751, Shenstone relates a situation which, he says, "threw me under a Necessity of offending either against the *Rules* of Politeness, or (what are more sacred with me) the *Laws* of

14. *The Letters of William Shenstone*, ed. Marjorie Williams (Oxford: Clarendon Press, 1939), p. 125.

Sincerity."[15] The distinction between rules and laws is worth noting, since for Shenstone the "*Laws* of Sincerity" are very similar to the natural law. There is no doubt in his mind that these laws must be obeyed in preference to the rules of politeness, which, though important, are much less a part of man's nature.

The relationship between friendship and sincerity has been considered earlier in this study, but nowhere is it more specific than in Shenstone's writings. "There is nothing of Importance in this World, beside the *Life* or *Death* of Friends," he wrote to Lady Luxborough in 1751. For a man with no family, friends become increasingly important as years pass; and therefore the unfriendly act of a friend can strike with the force of a thunderbolt. It is likely that the following insight came to Shenstone in this kind of experience: "Every single instance of a friend's insincerity encreases our dependence on the efficacy of money. It makes one covet what produces an external respect, when one is disappointed of that which is internal and sincere. This, perhaps, with decaying passions, contributes to render age covetous."[16] Although this was for Shenstone a distressing fact of life, it was not a disabling one. Indeed, his contempt for money and affluence is to be found constantly in his letters and poetry. Gray's supposed comment, related by Johnson, that he was always wishing for money seems unkind. But Shenstone did not despise wealth when it served good taste; only it too seldom did so. Markets, in addition to courts, represented for him everything that was false and productive of evil.

Shenstone's elegies are not poems which seem to be sincere. Their form is that of the Tibullan elegy and their language often seems a veritable tissue of phrases imitated from the ancients. Questions surrounding the friends to whom the elegies are addressed and the identity of the famous Delia, led G. A. Aitken to comment that "it is difficult to say how far they are sincere."[17] But Aitkin was concerned with sincerity in a genetic sense, as we are not. Shenstone's professional, neoclassical attitudes on poetic composition expressed in his "Prefatory Essay on Elegy" should not make us question his remarks on the sincerity of love poetry: "Love-verses written without real

15. Ibid., p. 322.   16. *Works*, I, 201.
17. "William Shenstone," *Dictionary of National Biography*.

passion, are often the most nauseous of all conceits. Those written
from the heart will ever bring to mind that delightful season of
youth, and poetry, and love."[18] This, of course, is an echo of Horace,
and Shenstone's elegies are primarily imitative; but it is in imitation
that he attempts to articulate his personal ideals. Indeed Shenstone's
vision is two-fold, joining tradition or convention with personal
sentiment. This combination can be summed up in the title of one of
his poems: "Rural Elegance." Rural elegance suggests that the finest
human principles are those of the heart, uncorrupted by guile and
evil intent. But these rural principles at their best are elegant and refined, reflecting the best lessons of civilized society.

Elegy 1 establishes many of the themes found in the remaining
twenty-five poems. The subtitle describes the poetic situation: "He
arrives at his retirement in the country, and takes occasion to expati-
ate in praise of simplicity." The first theme then is the familiar one
of retirement:

> For rural virtues, and for native skies,
> I bade Augusta's venal sons farewel;
> Now, 'mid the trees, I see my smoke arise;
> Now hear the fountains bubbling round my cell.[19]

In the first stanza, in clear imitation of the opening of Juvenal's
"Third Satire," Shenstone chooses rural England in preference to the
city, where the universal struggle for gain saps the energies of men.
This rural place, unlike the discordant city, belongs to him in a very
important sense, and so the possessive pronouns have a special
emphasis.

In the second stanza the poet calls upon the powers that secure his
peace to provide him with "a friend that's dear!":

> Ne'er may my vintage glad the sordid breast;
> Ne'er tinge the lip that dares be unsincere.

The friend will, of course, be a poet, and so the poem moves naturally into an exhortation to write poetry of a certain kind:

18. *Works*, 2, 178.
19. All references to the poetry are to *Works*, 2.

Far from these paths, ye faithless friends, depart!
   Fly my plain board, abhor my hostile name!
Hence! the faint verse that flows not from the heart,
   But mourns in labour'd strains, the price of fame!

Displaying an extreme fear of the guileful "friend," Shenstone exalts sincere verse that flows from the heart. Hammond, whose elegies seem even more artificial than Shenstone's, is cited as an example of the sincere poet:

Soft as the line of love-sick Hammond flows,
   'Twas his fond heart effus'd the melting theme;
Ah! never could Aonia's hill disclose
   So fair a fountain, or so lov'd a stream.

This sincerity, however, is of a specific and conventional kind: romantic love is its concern:

Ye loveless bards! intent with artful pains
   To form a sigh, or to contrive a tear!
Forego your Pindus, and on _____ plains
   Survey Camilla's charms, and grow sincere.

It is love, then, that is to govern sincerity, according to this elegy. Further the elegy echoes Sidney's "look in thy heart and write" from *Astrophel and Stella*, the central theme of which is love:

Write from thy bosom—let not art controul
   The ready pen, that makes his edicts known.

The fact that Shenstone's constant imitation is no deterrent to his claims for sincerity, suggests that sincere poetry need not be identified with "original" poetry. One could, presumably, be imitative and sincere or original and insincere. Later on in the century and in the case of Gray, however, originality and sincerity were to become almost synonymous.

In Elegy 7 Shenstone explores another motif of sincerity. Here the shade of Wolsey appears to the narrator and tempts him to seek the power that he himself sought. But the narrator answers that the dishonesty necessary to succeed in worldly endeavours is antipathetic to his ideals:

Must I not groan beneath a guilty load,
  Praise him I scorn, and him I love betray?
Does not felonious envy bar the road?
  Or falsehood's treach'rous foot beset the way?

Truth, unfortunately, must be discarded when one strives in the world:

Say shou'd I pass thro' favour's crowded gate,
  Must not fair truth inglorious wait behind?

This is particularly difficult for the man of rural principles:

Nurs'd in the shades by freedom's lenient care,
  Shall I the rigid sway of fortune own?
Taught by the voice of pious truth, prepare
  To spurn an altar and adore a throne?

Particularly distressing about the insincere life is that friendship, in any true sense, is impossible:

And when proud fortune's ebbing tide recedes,
  And when it leaves me no unshaken friend,
Shall I not weep that e'er I left the meads,
  Which oaks embosom, and which hills defend?

Sincerity, friendship, and truth itself are associated with the rural scene and their antitheses with the political world of the metropolis. Though these sentiments clearly echo the classical pastoral tradition, they reflect a viable eighteenth-century view of the world which expressed itself in retirement to the inner world of the imagination.

In Elegy 9 the narrator "describes his disinterestedness to his friends." Again the attack is against worldly affairs represented by the court. The delights of pastoral love are of more worth than gold:

I'll fare my peace, but ev'ry idle toy,
  If to my mind my DELIA'S form it brings,
Has truer worth, imparts sincerer joy,
  Than all that bears the radiant stamp of kings.

The word "sincere" in this stanza carries the meaning of "pure" in addition to the more usual meaning of "honest" or "undissembling." As I have been suggesting throughout, the word often carries this double significance. Once again these "sincerer" joys are regarded as natural attributes:

> Scorn'd be the wretch that quits his genial bowl,
>   His loves, his friendships, ev'n his self, resigns;
> Perverts the sacred instinct of his soul,
>   And to a ducate's dirty sphere confines.

Shenstone defines his ideal of sincerity further by insisting upon the natural goodness of man. Such observations were meant to provide an impetus to sincere behaviour, since to act otherwise was to pervert the natural human inclination.

It is this ideal of sincerity which imbues Shenstone with a patriotism similar to that of Thomson, Akenside, Young, and Collins. In Elegy 14, entitled "Declining an invitation to visit foreign countries, he takes occasion to intimate the advantages of his own," England is associated with every sincere and genuine emotion, while France receives the usual castigation for servility and guile:

> No distant clime shall servile airs impart,
> Or form these limbs with pliant ease to play;
> Trembling I view the Gaul's illusive art,
> That steals my lov'd rusticity away.

The "rusticity," of course, is the sincere sensibility, which France knows nothing of. Indeed, France and her allies are military and moral threats to all the virtues which compose the sincere ideal.

Showing less affection for the classical world than some of his contemporaries, Shenstone describes in Elegy 15 the "lov'd rusticity" of early England, where, if manners were rough, hearts were true:

> 'Twas on those downs, by Roman hosts annoy'd,
>   Fought our bold fathers; rustic, unrefin'd!
> Freedom's plain sons, in martial cares employ'd!
>   They ting'd their bodies, but unmask'd their mind.

The elegy continues to outline the virtues which Shenstone feels are most important to a really vital society. First, these rustics were not victims of their own "wild ambition":

No wild ambition fir'd their tranquil breast,
    To swell with empty sounds a spotless name;
If fost'ring skies, the sun, the show'r were blest,
    Their bounty spread; their field's extent the same.

Those fields, profuse of raiment, food, and fire,
    They scorn'd to lessen, careless to extend;
Bade luxury, to lavish courts aspire,
    And avarice, to city-breasts descend.

Shenstone describes with elegant periphrasis the sexual pleasures of this ideal community:

Here youth's free spirit, innocently gay,
    Enjoy'd the most that innocence can give;
Those wholesome sweets that border virtue's way;
    Those cooling fruits, that we may taste and live.

This paradise is implicitly contrasted with the scene of the fall in *Paradise Lost*. Indeed, early England was more paradisaical than Paradise, since its denizens were guilty of only one form of deception:

Their board no strange ambiguous viand bore;
    From their own streams their choicer fare they drew,
To lure the scaly glutton to the shore,
    The sole deceit their artless bosom knew![20]

As if it were necessary, after all this, Shenstone informs us that this early "natural" society lived in perfect sincerity:

Sincere themselves, ah too secure to find
The common bosom, like their own, sincere!

Shenstone, however, shares the pessimism of his contemporaries. Having sketched this early paradise, he must face the unhappy fact that nearly everything about it has passed away:

20. Guile so obsessed eighteenth-century thinkers that fishing in descriptive poetry can be described as "well-dissembled," and the fish can be "indignant of the guile," Thomson's "Spring," l. 436. Unlike Richardson the novelist (see appendix), Shenstone and Thomson seem amused by the analogy, and are not particularly disapproving.

Farewel, pure spirits! vain the praise we give,
   The praise you sought from lips angelic flows;
Farewel! the virtues which deserve to live,
   Deserve an ampler bliss than life bestows.

Here despair at the death of older and better ideals would seem to
eclipse hopes for their renaissance in modern "rural elegance."
   One of Shenstone's best comparisons of the deceitful world with
the utopian rural life occurs in Elegy 23, "Reflections suggested by
his situation," a poem which again makes use of early English history. At the opening of the poem, the poet invokes the memory of
the young Kenelm, who, according to Dodsley's note, was in the
Saxon heptarchy heir to the kingdom of Mercia. But this promising
youth had been slain by his sister and her lover, and the corpse buried
on a hill facing Shenstone's house, where it is marked by a church
called St. Kenelm's. Thus, in looking out from his own property,
Shenstone is directly reminded of an example of deceit and the death
of innocence.
   Kendrida, the sister, by her arts "a brother's youth beguil'd."
She was ambitious, the victim, in her love, of "sultry passions." The
stanza that takes poor Kenelm to his death further emphasizes the
guile of his sister:

See, garnish'd for the chace, the fraudful maid
   To these lone hills direct his devious way;
The youth, all prone, the sister guide obey'd,
   Ill-fated youth! himself the destin'd prey.

But in death Kenelm becomes the patron saint of those who would
escape the guile that he was the victim of. Looking down upon the
Leasowes, he presides over the world of retirement and sincerity to
which such notables as Lyttelton, Thomson, and Pope belong. The
position from which Kenelm fell, the circumstances of his death, and
the idyllic scene surrounding his grave, lead Shenstone to comment
on the corruption of the royal court:

Tremendous pomp! where hate, distrust, and fear,
   In kindred bosoms solve the social tie;

There not the parent's smile is half sincere;
  Nor void of art the consort's melting eye.

There with the friendly wish, the kindly flame,
  No face is brighten'd, and no bosoms beat;
Youth, manhood, age, avow one sordid aim,
  And ev'n the beardless lip essays deceit.

The emphasis on friendship in the second part of the poem makes its absence in the third part seem a particular deprivation. In this poem, as in all of Shenstone's elegies, there is a remarkable sense of order which permits the felicitous balancing or coupling of ideas. In the following stanza, the motif illustrated by Kendrida is repeated with a more general application:

There all are rivals! sister, son, and sire,
  With horrid purpose hug destructive arms;
There soft-ey'd maids in murd'rous plots conspire,
  And scorn the gentler mischief of their charms.

In a milieu of such rampant deceit, those seemingly least likely to deceive ("the beardless lip" and "soft-ey'd maids") are the worst offenders.

Next the poem returns to the poet, with whom it began. There is an affirmation of beauty and freedom, ending in the shepherd–poet's simple statement of his "ambition":

No midnight pangs the shepherd's peace pursue;
  His tongue, his hand, attempts no secret wound;
He sings his Delia, and if she be true,
  His love at once, and his ambition's crown'd.

This desire is, of course, to be contrasted with the criminal ambition of Kendrida and the corrupt practices of the court. Nor is the shepherd motif new to the poem: throughout there have been strands of pastoral imagery, woven into a close texture with the images of nature and deceit. This poem is admirably organized, giving, nonetheless, a sense of ease and simplicity for which Shenstone consciously sought.

Another, but very inferior, poem, "The Ruin'd Abby; or the

Effects of Superstition" shows one more aspect of guile in the modern world. In this poem the Roman Catholic Church is exposed for all good Englishmen to see, in passages such as the following:

Then from its tow'ring height with horrid sound
Rush'd the proud abby. Then the vaulted roofs,
Torn from their walls, disclos'd the wanton scene
Of monkish chastity! Each angry friar
Crawl'd from his bedded strumpet, mutt'ring low
An ineffectual curse.

Never a master of blank verse, Shenstone here is at best uninspired. But aside from the formal ineptness of "The Ruin'd Abby," the poem makes the much-belaboured point, a deistic and Protestant tradition of long standing, that piety is merely a façade for the hypocritical machinations of the Papist clergy. The walls of the cloister burst to reveal not only the immorality of particular friars but the chronic deceit of the entire Church:

                    The pervious nooks
That, ages past, conveyed the guileful priest
To play some image on the gaping crowd,
Imbibe the novel day-light; and expose
Obvious, the fraudful engin'ry of Rome.

Here all that is rural, Protestant, and English is sincere. Cities, Papists, and foreigners are, *ipso facto*, guileful. But if this seems to be a narrow scheme, we must remember that in the process of stressing the good, there is usually a concomitant over-simplification. Thus the development of sincerity as an ideal and the intensification of British nationalism and imperialism were concurrent and complementary. Confidence in their own unexampled sincerity provided the English with the impetus to treat violently those whom they believed more deceitful than sincere. Plain common sense and open behaviour were worn as the badge of a superior culture.

Shenstone's acceptance of such attitudes, which are now discredited, has led to a fairly low critical estimate of his poetry. But criticism based on modern assumptions is not always fair. Though he has little to say to the modern reader, Shenstone may prove worthwhile as an example. He engaged with vigour and poetic skill the significant political and social issues of his day. Intuiting the mood and needs of his own time, he set forth his perceptions according to the sincere ideal. Preference for the rural retreat, simplicity in art and manners, and the sincere expression of the heart are joined in his ethic with the classical ideals of refinement and learning. These, combined with his particular genius for landscape gardening, characterize Shenstone's commitment and achievement.

All too often the modern critic who turns to Shenstone and other minor poets of the eighteenth century carries with him the prejudices of such major figures as Johnson and Gray. In the case of Shenstone, Johnson's influence has proved catastrophic.

The Life of Shenstone, not one of Johnson's best efforts, is more ironic than most of the Lives, and succeeds in being extremely unfair. Since Johnson liked "The School-Mistress" and almost nothing else, that poem and appreciations of it occupy nearly all the space devoted to Shenstone in anthologies and literary histories.[21] "The School-Mistress" is a happy achievement, but the real Shenstone is the poet of the Elegies.

Neither did Thomas Gray have a very high opinion of Shenstone's work; but, like Johnson, Gray was too much in the tradition of the earlier century to allow him requisite sympathy with the more sentimental and optimistic aspects of modern poetry.

On the other hand, Richard Jago, who could express the following moral indignation over the death of a hare, was not inclined to laugh at Shenstone:

Man even there,

Watching, with foul intent, her secret haunts,
Plants instruments of death, and round her neck
The fatal snare entwines. Thus Innocence,
In human things, by wily Fraud ensnar'd,
Oft helpless falls, while the bold Plund'rer 'scapes.[22]

This passage from *Edge-Hill* employs many conventions of the sin-

---

21. These judgements are Johnson's echoed by George Sherburn, *The Restoration and Eighteenth Century* in Albert C. Baugh, ed., *A Literary History of England* (New York: Appleton–Century–Crofts, 1948), p. 1012.
22. Richard Jago, *Poems, Moral and Descriptive* (London, 1784), p. 49.

cere ideal examined in earlier chapters, but more important it represents the norm of English nature poetry in the later eighteenth
century. Of this norm Shenstone's work had become both model
and epitome.

Important as the sincere ideal may be in his poetry, however,
Shenstone's relationship to the ideal in his letters and personal life is
of great interest too. Preferring the virtues of the heart to the artifice
of poetry, he customarily expresses in his letters open disregard for
his own verse.

For Shenstone, that poetry is best which expresses those internal
qualities. But the sincere poet of the eighteenth century had much
the same difficulty as his Puritan predecessor. Believing that his
achievements in sincere poetry fell far short of an imagined ideal, he
began to question himself more than his assumptions. "Am I
saved?" becomes "Am I a poet?"

To this unhappy rule Shenstone was no exception. His disparage-
ment of his own poetry seems to parallel his penchant for denigrating
his way of life. Lack of family, financial difficulties, and an inability
to achieve in poetry or landscape gardening the high ideals he held,
united to make him an unhappy man.

The positive side of Shenstone's life should not be forgotten,
however. His friends made his life possible and sometimes brought it
close to joy. He succeeded in attaining a degree of personal refinement and integrity which would be uncommon at any time or place.
Johnson's almost contemptuous remark that Shenstone's life was
"unstained by any crime" is totally negative, suggesting that he was
a passive recluse—a man to whom nothing ever happened. This is
unfair. Shenstone's capacity for experience is attested to by his dissatisfaction with the life he led, by his poetry, his essays, and his
letters. If he did indeed recoil from the main currents of life, he
retained exceptional moral vigour. Indeed, his morality is not conven-
tionally religious, but rather almost heroic, based on a pagan aesthetic. If the gossip about his nervousness among ladies is true, it is
possible that he was fearful of intimate experience. But I tend to
believe in part what he says in his poems and letters: that his retirement from the world at large came about for moral reasons. In
other words, his aesthetic and hyper-sensitive idealism were largely

responsible for his retreat from the world. When one loves beauty and elegance of person and behaviour best, the vulgarity of real things can sometimes be unbearable. So it may be that Shenstone's retreat from the real came about not so much in fear as in revulsion. Yet that revulsion was tempered by the hope that in a closely knit social circle there would be a shared idealism. Such hopes are seldom realized, however, and quarrels with good friends will result from such disappointments. These quarrels produce even gloomier disappointments, which lead one to regret that another course of action, for example, marriage, was not undertaken. Thus marriage and family may seem for a time to be the right way out of despair—but perhaps an impossible way. Such notions only persist until the supposed cure is seen to be the cause of the original illness. Idealism causes one to flee from what is not ideal in human relationships; but the failure of other relationships often causes one to turn again to what was originally fled—or at least see it as a path out of despair. The repressed desire to marry then unites with a stronger idealism, creating a permanent dilemma and a lingering sense of regret. James Joyce may have been right when he claimed that the hardest thing a man does in his life is to live with a woman. And for most of the poets of sincerity that difficulty violated their sense of the ideal. For Shenstone Delia was exactly right, but there are few Delia's in the real world.

Shenstone seems to have been caught in such a circle of regrets and self-recriminations. His poetry, and particularly his letters, bear witness to this, though, as we might expect, they are not an unambiguous record. The poetry is a fine example of an attempt to put fancy in the way of despair. Thus, though we find a severely melancholy strain in some of the poems, dominant is an assertion of the pre-eminence of dignity, refinement, and sincerity. The poems, as an attempt at self-justification, reflect accurately the primary concerns of the letters, and, indeed, of all Shenstone's efforts, including his gardening at the Leasowes. Of course he calls his poems trivial, but he says this of his life as well. Despite his disappointments and tendencies to self-reproach, he realized, I think, that his life was an attempt to exemplify the sincere ideal. This he did with at least moderate success.

THOMAS GRAY

Gray's relation to the sincere ideal can best be examined by focusing on what was for him a more central issue, that of imitation and originality.

In book 3 of the *Republic* Socrates defines "everything that's said by tellers of tales or poets" as "a narrative of what has come to pass, what is, or what is going to be."[23] Narration (diēgēsis) is then divided into three categories: simple narration, imitation, and a union of the two. Gray's own notes summarize Plato's position: "Poetick eloquence is divided into narration (in the writer's own person), and imitation (in some assumed character). Dithyrambicks usually consist wholly of the former, dramatick poesy of the latter, the epick, &c. of both mixed."[24] As Gray's note indicates, the question as to whether or not a work is imitative depends solely on our analysis of the speaker's voice. If the poet speaks in his own voice, the poem is pure narrative; if he employs a persona, the work is imitative.

Nearly twenty years after the death of Gray, Thomas Twining, the estimable editor of Aristotle's *Poetics*, reluctantly admitted the relevance of imitation as applied to description, fiction, and sound, but preferred to limit its use to a dramatic meaning: "There seems to be but *one* view in which Poetry can be considered as *Imitation*, in the strict and proper sense of the word. If we look for both *immediate* and *obvious* resemblance, we shall find it only in *dramatic*—or to use a more general term—*personative* Poetry; that is, all Poetry in which, whether essentially or occasionally, the Poet personates; for here, *speech* is imitated by speech."[25] Twining mentions only tragedy, comedy, and epic among literary genres as "personative." Gray's odes, presumably, under the Platonic formula, would be pure narrative, with *The Bard* an exception. Although *The Bard* is ostensibly dithyrambic, the main speaker is the "personated" Welsh Bard. But there is, of course, another speaker in the poem, suggesting that it is, like epic, a mixture of imitation and narrative.

23. *The Republic*, p. 71.
24. Thomas Gray, *The Works*, ed. Edmund Gosse (London, 1884), 4, 233.
25. "Poetry as an Imitative Art," in Elder Olson, ed., *Aristotle's Poetics and English Literature* (Chicago: University of Chicago Press, 1965), p. 57.

There is reason to believe that Gray's concept of imitation was more scholarly, closer to the Greek sources, than that of most of his contemporaries. We know that he undertook a careful study of Aristotle, including the *Poetics*, during 1746. His extensive notes on Plato show his knowledge of the Platonic position on imitation and art in general.

This intimate acquaintance with the sources themselves is characteristic of Gray's approach to any subject, whether poetry, philosophy, or botany. Since he trusted his own ability to understand ancient or modern texts without the help of commentary, he read relatively little contemporary criticism, and thus seems to have been uninfluenced by specific critical trends. Though he knew such critics as his friend Hurd, he seems not to have been excited by their work. He did read widely in modern poetry, however, which accounts in part for his contemporaneity of technique and theme in his own poetry.

Indeed this characteristic independence and first-hand acquaintance with the classics gives Gray's poetry and thought a clarity and good sense lacking in most of his contemporaries. His vast knowledge and acute understanding of the classical authors prevented him from underestimating them and from being taken in by the glitter of newfangled ideas. His editor T. J. Mathias, in lavishly praising Gray's classical sensitivity, makes clear that he "revolted from the vapid, vague, and unmeaning effusions of writers who, refusing to submit to the indispensable laws of lyrical poetry, or from ignorance of them, called their own wildness, genius, and their contempt of rules, originality."[26]

Certainly these sentiments are properly applied to Gray, but they do not tell the whole story. Gray was greatly attracted to the concept of originality. For example, when Goldsmith, greatly admiring Gray's Odes, wrote in *The Monthly Review* that "instead of being an imitator," he should venture "to be more original,"[27] Gray could single out that specific advice for praise: "the Review I have

---

26. *Observations of the Writings and on the Character of Mr. Gray* (London, 1815), p. 75.

27. *Collected Works*, ed. Arthur Friedman (Oxford: Clarendon Press, 1966), 1, 113–14.

read, & admire it, particularly that observation, that the *Bard* is taken from *Pastor cum traheret*, & the advice to be more an original, & in order to be so, the way is (he says) to cultivate the native flowers of the soul, & not introduce the exoticks of another climate."[28]

Some comments on poetic inspiration in a letter to Wharton further reflect the complexity of Gray's view of poetry: "I by no means pretend to inspiration, but yet I affirm, that the faculty in question is by no means voluntary. It is the result (I suppose) of a certain disposition of mind, wch does not depend on oneself, & wch I have not felt this long time, you that are a witness, how seldom this spirit has moved me in my life, may easily give credit to what I say" (*Corr.*, p. 571). Here is the dispassionate Gray somewhere between spontaneity and laboured craft. "You apprehend too much from my resolutions about writing . . ." he wrote to Wharton some six months earlier; "they are only made to be broken, & after all it will be just as the maggot bites" (*Corr.*, p. 541). And fairly late in his life, Gray was to criticize the notion that certain thoughts and expressions were suitable to one species of poetry only: "Rules are but chains, good for little, except when one can break through them; and what is fine gives me so much pleasure, that I never regard what place it is in" (*Corr.*, p. 1169).

The problem of choosing between learned imitation and originality was a serious one for Gray. He comments on the latest volumes of the Dodsley Collection: "particularly Dr. Akenside is in a deplorable way. What signifies Learning and the Ancients, (Mason will say triumphantly) why should people read Greek to lose their imagination, their ear, and their mother tongue? But then there is Mr. Shenstone, who trusts to nature and simple sentiment, why does he do no better? he goes hopping along his own gravel-walks, and never deviates from the beaten paths for fear of being lost" (*Corr.*, p. 566). The simple and pretty style of Shenstone will not do; loftiness can be gained, it seems to Gray, only through imitation; and

---

28. *Correspondence*, ed. Paget Toynbee and Leonard Whibley (Oxford: Clarendon Press, 1935), pp. 532–33. Cited in the text as *Corr. Pastor Cum traheret* is, of course, the XVth Ode of Horace's First Book. The Ode takes the form of Nereus's prophecy, "caneret fera Nereus fata," and may in turn be an imitation of Proteus's account to Menelaus, *Odyssey*, 4: 472–537. See J. L. Lincoln, *Works of Horace* (New York, 1866), p. 330.

yet imitation could go far wrong too, as in the poetry of Akenside. Of course Shenstone is an imitator too, whether of Spenser or Tibullus, as Gray must have recognized, and historians of English poetry have placed Akenside closer to "nature and simple sentiment" than Gray seems to have done. But Goldsmith's call for a simpler, characteristically English style, had, it seemed, been heeded by Shenstone, and the results were unsatisfactory.

Yet in recognizing the deficiencies of Shenstone, Gray may have understood the implications of this call to a simple style. It was a call not only to put aside the neoclassical ideas of separate genres, but an exhortation to the poet to reject the mimic art of many voices and begin the search for one, the poet's own individual voice.

To illustrate Gray's attitude toward this search, we should return to Plato's *Republic*. Plato, as will be recalled, distinguishes between narration (*diēgēsis*) and imitation (*mimēsis*) in that the first is in the poet's own voice, while imitation is personation. Thus, according to Plato, narration "involves only small changes, and, if someone assigns the appropriate harmonic mode and rhythm to the style, it turns out that the man who speaks correctly speaks mostly in the same style and in one mode, for the changes are small, and likewise in a similar rhythm."[29] In other words, there is a sameness of voice in style, inflexion, and so on—readily identifiable as belonging to one man; for in Plato's Republic, "there's no double man among us, nor a manifold one, since each man does one thing."[30] But imitation, on the other hand, requires "all modes and all rhythms—if it's going to speak in its own way, because it involves all species of changes...."[31]

Just as a dramatist must have a voice for every character in his play, the classical author must have a voice appropriate to every genre in which he determines to work.

Edward Young, for example, imitates Dryden in his early heroic verse; and in his plays attempts to imitate Shakespeare. *Love of Fame*, as Howard D. Weinbrot has shown, reveals a tension between genteel mask and apocalypse, resulting in serious internal contradictions.[32] *The Night Thoughts* comes closest to being a conscious

29. *The Republic*, p. 75.   30. Ibid., p. 76.   31. *The Republic*, p. 75.
32. Howard D. Weinbrot, *The Formal Strain: Studies in Augustan Imitation and Satire* (Chicago: University of Chicago Press, 1969), pp. 113–28.

attempt on Young's part to find his own voice, but he cannot liberate the blank verse line from imitation of Milton.

Collins, too, may be said to follow this pattern. From his curious *Persian Eclogues*, he progresses through a learned classical style, concluding his career with "An Ode on the Popular Superstitions of the Highlands of Scotland," in which he used native British material, as Goldsmith was to advise Gray in 1757. Perhaps Collins was on his way to finding his own poetic voice.

W. K. Wimsatt has warned against the assumption that imitation inevitably means servility, and that revolution, whether in politics or poetry, leads to freedom.[33] By showing the possible variety within imitative modes, he suggests that the reverse may be true. Indeed, "originality" or uniqueness, for all its positive connotation, suggests singleness and limitation. Many forms of imitation, on the other hand, require a special act of the imagination. Gray seems to have agreed. In his essay on Samuel Daniel, he writes that elegy "requires no other order or invention than those of pure, simple nature, what is (or what ought to appear) the result of a feeling mind strongly possess'd by its subject, and surely he that is so in poetry has done more than half his work, but it is not every imagination that can throw itself into all the situations of a fictitious subject.[34]

The conflict between the claims of originality and imitation in Gray's poetry has been expressed in different terms in two recent studies of Gray. Mr. F. Doherty in his essay "The Two Voices of Gray" distinguishes a public voice and a private voice. For Mr. Doherty "the characteristics of the public poetry are Gray's scholarly regard for accuracy, occurring as the 'translation' of prose fact into verse, and Gray's habitual desire to escape commonness. . . ."[35] This for Doherty represents Gray's imitative side, but more important is the personal, private aspect. Mr. Doherty writes: "What seems quite plain to me is that he was more truly himself in those poems which are most loved and best known, because it is here that we hear the distinctive voice of Gray, depressed and shaded,

33. "Imitation as Freedom—1717–1798," *New Literary History*, 1 (1970): 215–36.
34. *Essays and Criticisms by Thomas Gray*, ed. C. S. Northup (London, 1911), pp. 120–21.
35. *Essays in Criticism*, 13 (1963): 222.

expressing its gentle and gentlemanly sadness in a tone unique and recognisable."[36]

In a perceptive essay Bertrand Bronson also notices in Gray, this time in the Elegy, an "individual and even personal style and diction."[37] Professor Bronson assumes on Gray's part "personal involvement" and "the poem's inescapable egocentricity."[38] "The immediate, crucial difficulty," he writes, "is how to devise a memorial in the form of inscriptional verses for oneself that shall be perfectly serious and emotionally sincere; that shall be neither objectionably self-abasing nor apparently self-satisfied; neither too cold and impersonal to communicate emotion nor too revealing of private emotion or self-commiseration."[39] Bronson goes on ingeniously to show how a "special decorum" achieves a balance between self-revelation and neoclassical restraint.

In doing this Professor Bronson has provided not only a helpful reading of the Elegy, but a truth to be pondered in a consideration of Gray's other poems. Clearly there is a tension in Gray between the personal and the impersonal, whether in motif or diction, form or style: in short, between subjective expression and objective imitation. Let us turn to the poems themselves to see how this tension operates.

In the "Ode on the Spring" the general application of theme is in tension with the poet's self, though here the self is kept in strict subordination to the thematic concern. Thus in the second stanza, where the poet's self is introduced

Beside some water's rushy brink
With me the Muse shall sit, and think
(At ease reclin'd in rustic state),

$$(15-17)^{40}$$

the poetry is shared with the personified Muse and the stanza hurries on to general truths:

36. Ibid., p. 227.
37. "On a Special Decorum in Gray's Elegy," in *From Sensibility to Romanticism*, p. 172.
38. Ibid., p. 172.   39. Ibid., p. 172.
40. All citations to Gray's poems are to *The Complete Poems of Thomas Gray*, ed. H. W. Starr and J. R. Hendrickson (Oxford: Clarendon Press, 1966).

How vain the ardour of the Crowd,
How low, how little are the Proud,
How indigent the Great!

(18–20)

The third and fourth stanzas by recourse to insect imagery appropriate to the season illustrate how truly vain is the ardour of the crowd:

Yet hark, how thro' the peopled air
The busy murmur glows!
The insect youth are on the wing,
Eager to taste the honied spring, . . .

(23–26)

The moralist poet then draws the moral in stanza four. One is tempted to see this obvious moralizing as a blemish—after all the "insect youth" of stanza three are not merely insects, but human beings as well. The application of the images of spring to man's life is already graphically explicit. But this would not be sufficient to Gray's purpose. The somewhat tedious moralizing of stanza four is drawn to characterize the poet, so that the unanticipated irony of stanza five can be brought home with perfect point: "Poor moralist! and what art thou? / A solitary fly!" (43–44). The poet, here also reduced to an insect, has indeed been a moralist and of the worst kind, one without self-knowledge. The "sportive kind" of line 42 do not succeed in turning from their breast the sharp point of the poet's criticism, but they do succeed in implicating him in the general insufficiency of man. His life is by no means a good alternative to theirs; but even though they enjoy their laugh at the poet's expense, enough irony turns against them in their reply to keep us from preferring their sunny and breezy life to the shaded repose of the moralist poet.

Gray here succeeds in balancing perspectives in such a way that the voice of the poet never becomes the final arbiter. The poet's insufficiency renders him an object of scrutiny on the part of the reader, and this does not permit him to assume the role of authority and control which the voice in an ode usually possesses.

This tendency to undercut or at least balance the personal voice by shifting perspectives is characteristic of many of Gray's poems, suggesting that the attempt to speak in his own voice (if that is what it is) is unsuccessful. This lack of success may account for his increasing tendency to turn to more strictly imitative styles in later poems.

In the "Ode on a Distant Prospect of Eton College" much the same pattern is discernible. The speaker notes the passion, poverty, sickness, and death which await the little boys of the college, reaching his high point of moral understanding in the final stanza:

> To each his suff'rings: all are men,
> Condemn'd alike to groan,
> The tender for another's pain;
> Th'unfeeling for his own.
>
> (91–94)

Here the speaker tempers his own wisdom with the full sympathy he seems to claim for himself. But perhaps this tender sympathy leads him to question the value of the "wisdom" which the poem has sought to express; sympathy leads to the desire to withhold the truth of the human condition from the playing children:

> Yet ah! why should they know their fate?
> Since sorrow never comes too late,
> And happiness too swiftly flies.
> Thought would destroy their paradise.
> No more; where ignorance is bliss,
> 'Tis folly to be wise.
>
> (95–100)

Though it is clear that the children will, as men, learn their fate, there is a desire on the speaker's part to withhold it from them— perhaps even in their adulthood—if that were possible. The melancholy view of man articulated earlier in the poem is in these last lines revealed as too painful for contemplation, thereby undercutting the poet-moralist's position, as was done in the "Ode on the Spring." The poet cuts himself off abruptly: "No more; where ignorance is bliss, / 'Tis folly to be wise." The irony in these lines,

directed against those who prefer ignorance and bliss, is not sufficient to make us reject the truth of the poet's insight into his own
blunder and inadequacy. He is the one who consciously destroys
paradise. He it is who has brought anger, fear, and shame before our
eyes, insisting that we accept them as our ineluctable fate.

By questioning the value of his own earlier observations, Gray
once again creates distance between the speaker and the point of
view communicated by the poem, leaving us to wonder which viewpoint to accept, if any. By undercutting the earlier moralistic expo-
sition, the voice of the poet is left curiously wavering.

The question of sincerity implicit in the quest for the poet's distinguishing voice is raised importantly in the "Sonnet on the Death
of Richard West." Geoffrey Tillotson has noted the essentially
dramatic structure of the sonnet. "When Gray begins his poem,"
he writes, "with

> In vain to me the smileing Mornings shine,
>   And redning Phoebus lifts his golden Fire:
> The Birds in vain their amorous Descant joyn;
>   Or cheerful Fields resume their green Attire;
> These Ears, alas! for other Notes repine . . .

he means us to take the 'poetic diction' as dramatic—for though it is
himself who is speaking, he speaks by means of quotations from
others."[41] These lines are juxtaposed with the diction of real grief:
"I fruitless mourn to him, that cannot hear, / And weep the more
because I weep in vain."

This early poem is something of an exemplum of Gray's struggle
to assume his own voice. Though five of the six "personal" lines
received the approbation of Wordsworth for their purer diction, it
is important to note that the personal effects are strictly limited to
the lonely poet: "My lonely Anguish melts no Heart, but mine."
Here as in the "Ode on the Spring" and the Eton College ode, we
discover the lonely poet who has nothing to offer mankind. The
teeming world of the fields producing "their wonted Tribute," the
birds warming "their little loves," and the cheerful existence of
happier men contrast markedly with the barrenness of the speaker's

41. *Augustan Studies* (London: The Athlone Press, 1961), p. 88.

present mood. His sorrow, akin to pure negation, can only take
shape by comparing it with the joy around him. The "other Notes"
and "different Object" repined for and required remain obscure, but
suggest strains of mourning and weeping and the dead Richard
West. Gray goes even farther. His mourning, in contrast to the
"smileing Mornings," is fruitless, and so he weeps the more because
of the emptiness and worthlessness of that grief.

Here Gray tacitly questions the value of the personal voice, of the
sincerely expressed grief. The world as poets have known it,
warmed by "redning Phoebus" and dressed in "green Attire" is the
world which brings pleasure to men. "Lonely Anguish," however, is
subjective, empty, even though it might be true, and, finally, it is
inexpressible. The imitative mode has, on the other hand, a full
vocabulary suited to communication, tried and tested in the world.

Once again, as in the Odes, Gray engages himself in dialogue,
searching for an appropriate diction and questioning its validity
once it is found. Just as the speaker in the Odes came to question the
value of all that he had expounded earlier, here the speaker questions
the value of the sentiments expressed, the language used, and, ultimately, of the experience of sincere grief itself.

Here, as usual, Gray associates melancholy or grief with "real"
experience, since it characterizes his every thought and action. But,
then, he questions the validity of his own understanding of things
and of the value of that understanding and consequent expression.
It is at this point, however, where his own experience diverges from
that of most men, that he seems to waver between confidence in himself and trust in tradition. To put the question another way, he cannot decide whether to be an artistic imitator or a sincere original.

The problem of the poet reaches its most sublime expression in
The Bard. Just before the bard hurls himself from Mt. Snowdon, he
compares his own state with that of King Edward:

'Enough for me: With joy I see
'The different doom our Fates assign.
'Be thine Despair, and scept'red Care,
'To triumph, and to die, are mine.'

(139–42)

But is this "triumph" convincing, as critics have universally taken it to be? I think not. Most obviously the triumph is linked with self-destruction, a fact the final couplet makes extraordinarily vivid: "He spoke, and headlong from the mountain's height / Deep in the roaring tide he plung'd to endless night" (143–44). "Endless night" suggests at best the very antithesis of what is usually associated with triumph. It is the same punishment inflicted on Milton, Teiresias-like, described in *The Progress of Poesy*:

> He saw; but blasted with excess of light,
>   Closed his eyes in endless night.
>
>   (101–2)

Indeed, even during the lengthy cursing of Edward and his line, the reader is painfully aware that the bard is experiencing much of the suffering which he calls down on the hapless king. All of Edward's family and friends are to be taken from him and he is to die alone:

> "Low on his funeral couch he lies!
> "No pitying heart, no eye, afford
> "A tear to grace his obsequies.
>
>   (64–66)

Now the bard, I suspect, like Gray, has no family, and, placing his entire reliance on his fellow poets, who have been slain, he too dies alone:

> 'Dear lost companions of my tuneful art,
> 'Dear, as the light that visits these sad eyes,
> 'Dear, as the ruddy drops that warm my heart,
> 'Ye died amidst your dying country's cries—
>
>   (38–42)

Their ghosts, of course, appear and join the bard in cursing Edward, but when that is done, disappear, leaving him alone:

> 'Stay, oh stay! nor thus forlorn
> 'Leave me unbless'd, unpitied, here to mourn: . . .
>
>   (101–2)

Here again is the theme of lonely anguish so important in the sonnet to West. The wisdom, the poetry, the very triumph of the bard are questioned in the pessimism of absolute destruction.

The triumph of the bard, such as it is, comes not merely in the predicted downfall of Edward and the rise of the House of Tudor, but more specifically in the greatness to be achieved by future poets. But even that vision of the future is short and indeterminate. "Distant," "lessen," "lost," and "expire" set the dismal tone of the conclusion:

> 'And distant warblings lessen on my ear,
> 'That lost in long futurity expire.
>
> (133–34)

This accords with Gray's rather pessimistic view of the poetry of his own age and of the decline of the English language, which, he wrote in 1742, is "too diffuse, & daily grows more & more enervate" (*Corr.*, p. 196).[42]
The point I wish to emphasize here is the extreme ambiguity surrounding the bard's death. Momentary satisfaction can be gained from the prospect of some future greatness for poetry, or for Gray and the reader, the affirmation of Shakespeare and Milton; but the bard's plunge to "endless night" leaves us to wonder if the hopes for the future are not merely a deception, if moments of greatness are not glimmering preludes to the ineluctable descent. As in the poems discussed earlier, the moral values presented are called in question. The fate of the bard and the uncertainty of his visions suggest a triumph which can be gained only in death. From Gray's viewpoint, I believe, that is a very questionable triumph indeed. Death, then, no matter how sublime it may be in this poem, is the melancholy end which calls in question every serious act of intellect and imagination. It is this death, without the grandeur of sublimity, which is the subject of "The Elegy Written in a Country Church-yard."

---

42. If Gray did feel that he was himself the bard, as reported by Norton Nicholls (*Corr.*, p. 1290), my point would seem to be the stronger. Gray's melancholy was not merely a literary device, and it may be found implicit in some of his most triumphant or self-righteous assertions. By dint of this he is very seldom, perhaps never, triumphant or self-righteous.

The Curfew tolls the knell of parting day,
The lowing herd wind slowly o'er the lea,
The plowman homeward plods his weary way,
And leaves the world to darkness and to me.

(1-4)

Here in the opening stanza we have the first and last direct reference by the speaker to himself. Since he is left in the dark, perhaps it is appropriate that the search for himself which follows be conducted in impersonal dialogue. The generalized impersonality begins directly in the next line: "Now fades the glimmering landscape on the sight, . . ." It would have been easy for Gray to write: "Now fades the glimmering landscape on *my* sight," but apparently the movement away from self was important enough to make clear very early in the poem.

As the speaker proceeds to set up his moral polarities, with the dead of power and fortune on the one side and the humble and good on the other, the poet's curiously intermediate position is defined. The humble dead are remembered neither for their power nor their poetry, since all opportunity was denied them:

Perhaps in this neglected spot is laid
Some heart once pregnant with celestial fire;
Hands, that the rod of empire might have sway'd,
Or wak'd to extasy the living lyre.

(45-48)

The possible guilt of poets, though falling short of that assumed by men of power, is made explicit. The humble dead's lot forbad

The struggling pangs of conscious truth to hide,
To quench the blushes of ingenuous shame,
Or heap the shrine of Luxury and Pride
With incense kindled at the Muse's flame.

(69-72)

In short, the poet, in seeking after honour and immortality, may be a collaborator with the forces of tyranny; thus we see why, even at his best, the poet is: "Beneath the Good how far. . . ."[43]

43. "Progress of Poesy," l. 123.

The poet, then, by placing importance in fame and the art of poetry is neglecting the true values of humanity. This is the point of the stanzas on the rustic poetry on the gravestones:

> Yet ev'n these bones from insult to protect
> Some frail memorial still erected nigh,
> With uncouth rhimes and shapeless sculpture deck'd,
> Implores the passing tribute of a sigh.

> Their name, their years, spelt by th'unletter'd muse,
> The place of fame and elegy supply:
> And many a holy text around she strews,
> That teach the rustic moralist to die.
>
> (77–84)

Here is truly sincere poetry, careless in spelling, carelessly strewing holy texts about; but serving one of the highest human functions, that of teaching men how to die. Somehow the elaborate morality of Gray's poems pales before this simplicity and directness, and Gray seems fully conscious of it.

The poet in the poem, no matter how honest his attempt to understand his relationship to poetry and mankind, is never at one with his humble subject, as is made clear when the inward colloquy takes shape:

> For thee, who mindful of th'unhonour'd Dead
> Dost in these lines their artless tale relate; . . .
>
> (93–94)

Though the speaker is mindful of the humble dead, the emphasis on the artlessness of *their* tale implies the artfulness of his relation of it. Further, the answer by the hoary-headed swain to the kindred spirit's question reveals the spiritual distance between poet and rustic. The swain recalls that

> 'Mutt'ring his wayward fancies he would rove,
> 'Now drooping, woeful wan like one forlorn,
> 'Or craz'd with care, or cross'd in hopeless love.
>
> (106–8)

The swain's search for a reason for the poet's behaviour, that he may be forlorn or crazed with care, or last (and perhaps best) a star-crossed lover, betrays an expected incapacity to understand sympathetically the characteristic melancholy of the serious poet.

If the poet is, whether he likes it or not, beyond the comprehension of the good people he seems to value most and if he is the artful poet yearning for artless simplicity, then the epitaph is curiously inappropriate:

> Here rests his head upon the lap of Earth
> A Youth to Fortune and to Fame unknown,
> Fair Science frown'd not on his humble birth,
> And Melancholy mark'd him for her own.
>
> (117–20)

Neither Richard West, Gray, nor, apparently, the poet–speaker in the poem was a youth unknown to *both* fame and fortune. West's birth was certainly not humble; and Gray would not have regarded his own as especially so. The poet–speaker by implication has already denied his right to such honoured names. Only melancholy is a common denominator:

> Large was his bounty, and his soul sincere,
> Heav'n did a recompence as largely send:
> He gave to Mis'ry all he had, a tear,
> He gain'd from Heav'n ('twas all he wish'd) a friend.
>
> (121–24)

Here again the epitaph seems not to agree with our understanding of the poet–speaker as distinct from the humble, guileless people whose memorial he has erected in the poem. The chief tension is precisely that the poet is not sincere and bountiful—at one with heaven. The epitaph, then, is an expressed hope rather than a realized fact. The poet does in the epitaph attain a oneness with those whose lives are most highly valued. "The paths of glory"—even poetic glory, such as it is—"lead but to the grave," the common end. In the epitaph, then, in death, the outsider poet is integrated into the true community of men, remembered not so much for what he was but for what he wished to be. Like the Bard, his triumph comes only in "endless night."

Thus the dialogue between the learned poet of imitation and the sincere voice of the self is concluded, giving the verdict to the latter, but demonstrating in the failure to achieve the single voice of the poet's sole self and the realization of some of that potential only in death, the impossibility of the task assigned. Gray's commitment to imitation and learning is too great to allow a simpler social and personal consciousness. The way for that can be cleared only by his death.

What I propose here is that Gray's best poems present an inward colloquy between the personated or imitative voices of Gray and that single, serious voice which Plato thought everyone should have, the voice we use to speak to God and the person we love. This is the voice of our religious and social being. This voice, however, is sceptical and regardless of tradition. It inquires after a social reality characterized by simplicity and sincerity, a reality quite different from that sanctioned by the imitative mode.

For some of the complex reasons delineated in this study, English poets at mid-century were struggling toward that voice and that reality. The attempts are often grotesque, as if the poets cannot make up their minds which way to go. To throw off the influence of the classical tradition is to leave oneself with an unsatisfactory trust in nature and simple sentiment. On the other hand, to imitate is to lose one's own voice, or to make certain that it could never be found. Gray, unlike many of his contemporaries, is able to capitalize on this tension, to make poetry out of it. Later, in turning away from this struggle toward more strictly imitative modes (though not necessarily classical ones), his poetry begins to fail him. But in his earlier and sometimes great poetry, the subject of this essay, there is a kind of division which results in two diverse intentions. Perhaps it was this confusion between imitation and originality which made poetic composition at mid-century such a precarious occupation.

Thus Gray's relationship to the sincere ideal is a tenuous one. In questioning the possibility of sincerity in poetry, he questions the entire function of the poet. Though he evidently shares some beliefs with Thomson, Akenside, Collins, and Shenstone, he could not give to myth the credence which is required to create it, and is therefore less a mythic poet than the others. Despite his Whig and deist leanings, his final word on poetry and society is classical and conservative. Yet it is the poetry that reflects the struggle between classical imitation and the originality of the sincere ideal which gives Gray his best claim to greatness.

SAMUEL JOHNSON

Since Johnson's critical approach to poetry may be considered a combination of empiricism and conservative neoclassical principles, it is not to be expected that sincerity would be for him an important critical ideal. But his empiricism does lead him to some concessions to the sincere ideal. Truth to life being his constant criterion in the judgement of poetry, he finds fabulous impossibilities extremely distressing. As he writes in "The Life of Cowley": "No man needs to be so burthened with life as to squander it in voluntary dreams of fictitious occurrences."[44]

This concern for life as it is was born of his sense of the importance of right action. Man could not act properly, he believed, without first understanding action itself, its sources and implications. If clarity then was desirable, where so little of it could be hoped for, the conscious attempt to deceive was among the most execrable crimes. In *Rambler* 79 he is quite specific on this point: "Whoever commits a fraud is guilty not only of the particular injury to him whom he deceives, but of the diminution of that confidence which constitutes not only the ease but the existence of society."[45]

This abhorrence of guile, confirmed again in *Rasselas*, did not, however, lead Johnson to espouse the sincere ideal, though he valued sincerity greatly. His brand of sincerity, however, is more the straightforward Augustan "honesty" and plain-dealing than the state of mind common to most of the poets studied here. Johnson understood better than most of his contemporaries the limits of

44. *Lives of the English Poets*, 1, 7.
45. *The Rambler*, ed. W. J. Bate and Albrecht B. Strauss (New Haven: Yale University Press, 1969), 2, 55.

sincerity and refused to attribute to that ideal more than he believed it could be. He understood what was largely ignored by sincere enthusiasts: that sincerity without good practice is worthless.[46] In other words, he could not accept the notion that deep feeling necessarily led to truth; indeed he believed that it very often led to falsehood and vice. Perhaps his own inclinations to self-indulgence showed him how necessary it was to find a source of truth external to man. This source of truth was inevitably the Church. For Johnson sincerity in poetry is mainly an antidote to falsehood. "Fictitious occurrences" ought to be replaced with material of moral value. The analysis of real experience was sufficient to fill up life.

"The Life of Cowley" contains a good deal of evidence concerning Johnson's position. Johnson criticizes Cowley's "amorous ditties" because they reveal no sincere feeling: "the basis of all excellence is truth: he that professes love ought to feel its power" (*Lives*, 1, 6). He goes on to describe the absurdity of writing falsehood:

> The man that sits down to suppose himself charged with treason or peculation, and heats his mind to an elaborate purgation of his character from crimes which he was never within the possibility of committing, differs only by the infrequency of his folly from him who praises beauty which he never saw, complains of jealousy which he never felt; supposes himself sometimes invited, and sometimes forsaken; fatigues his fancy, and ransacks his memory, for images which may exhibit the gaiety of hope, or the gloominess of despair, and dresses his imaginary Chloris or Phyllis sometimes in flowers fading as her beauty, and sometimes in gems lasting as her virtues (*Lives*, 1, 7).

Of course Johnson would not deny the value of "personation" to the dramatist. He is here discussing lyrical poetry written in the first person. Further, that he is not so much making a positive demand as expressing a dislike for a certain species of poetry is made clear in a comparison between real events and courtly poetic ideals

---

46. James Boswell, *The Life of Samuel Johnson*, ed. G. B. Hill, revised by L. F. Powell (Oxford: Clarendon Press, 1934), 4, 396–97.

in "The Life of Cowley": "At Paris, as secretary to Lord Jermin, he was engaged in transacting things of real importance with real men and real women, and at that time did not much employ his thoughts upon phantoms of gallantry" (*Lives*, 1, 8).

Johnson goes on to object to another poem on the grounds of insufficient passion: "In his poem on the death of Hervey, there is much praise but little passion . . . when he wishes to make us weep, he forgets to weep himself . . ." (*Lives*, 1, 36–37).[47] After these comments on Cowley's lack of passion, Johnson comes to the expected conclusion that Cowley's power is "not so much to move the affections, as to exercise the understanding" (*Lives*, 1, 37). This is remarkably similar to his judgement of Dryden, of whom he writes: "The power that predominated in his intellectual operations, was rather strong reason than quick sensibility" (*Lives*, 1, 457).

This constant motif in Johnson's criticism comes to the fore in his criticism of *Eleonora*: "Dryden confesses that he did not know the lady whom he celebrates; the praise being therefore inevitably general, fixes no impression upon the reader, nor excites any tendency to love, nor much desire of imitation. Knowledge of the subject is to the poet what durable materials are to the architect" (*Lives*, 1, 441–42). Here he argues that only a real knowledge of and perhaps emotional attachment to the person praised can result in the passion necessary for outstanding elegy. The need for particular praise is a subject that Johnson raises again in his essay on Pope's epitaphs.[48]

In his "Life of Milton" Johnson objects to *Lycidas* for many of the reasons mentioned above: it has nothing to do with real life; it is insincere. "It is not," he writes, "to be considered as the effusion of real passion; for passion runs not after remote allusions and obscure opinions" (*Lives*, 1, 163). Further, he objects to the mixture of pastoral and religious imagery.[49]

47. Johnson here recalls Horace and perhaps Boileau's imitation: "Pour me tirer des pleurs, il faut que vous pleuriez." *Art Poetique*, iii, 142.

48. It is curious, however, that he lodges no similar objection to Dryden's Anne Killigrew Ode. Rather he singles out the first part of it for special praise, writing that it "flows with a torrent of enthusiasm." *Lives*, 1, 439.

49. Johnson's objections to pastoral, are further clarified in his "Life of Hammond," *Lives*, 2, 314–15.

In this regard Johnson's views of funeral elegy may be considered. As noted earlier, he approved greatly of Tickell's poem on the death of Addison, which obeys the conventions of sincere elegy rather perfectly. It is to be expected then that Johnson's only elegy "On the Death of Dr. Robert Levet," would stand as a positive assertion of what he thought elegy ought to be. Its language is simple and general, with Johnson's particular knowledge of Levet's personality and situation evident everywhere. There is never in Johnson's verse, however, an attempt to create myth or envision ideals, the hallmark of the sincere poet.

At times Johnson's demand for truth in poetry may be identified with his demand for virtue in life. In his "Life of Waller," he makes this clear: "Poets, indeed, profess fiction; but the legitimate end of fiction is the conveyance of truth; and he that has flattery ready for all whom the vicissitudes of the world happen to exalt must be scorned as a prostituted mind, that may retain the glitter of wit, but has lost the dignity of virtue" (Lives, 1, 271). Here he clarifies a position taken in "The Life of Cowley." Fiction is not in itself useless but may be judged by its relation to truth. Again, this truth is not the knowledge of the heart, but the external reality which Johnson kicked in refuting Berkeley.

Johnson's most serious reservations about the sincere ideal and his shrewdest observations on sincerity are to be found in his analysis of Pope's letters. He questions the sincerity of personal letters on the following grounds: "Very few can boast of hearts which they dare lay open to themselves, and of which, by whatever accident exposed, they do not shun a distinct and continued view; and, certainly, what we hide from ourselves we do not shew to our friends" (Lives, 3, 207). These remarks may well imply a belief that a literature of sincerity is impossible, and, as Paul Fussell has pointed out, Johnson comes out against sincerity in his comments on epitaphs.[50]

But this extreme view may be inconsistent with Johnson's demands for sincerity in other elegiac modes. Besides, Johnson's pessimistic view of human depravity may be somewhat over-subtle. His brilliant awareness of the tragedy of human life was not shared by

50. *The Rhetorical World of Augustan Humanism* (Oxford: Clarendon Press, 1965), pp. 81–82.

authors devoted to the sincere ideal, and tragedy is possible only where the quality of human life is great enough to sustain it. When Johnson writes, "Friendship has no tendency to secure veracity; for by whom can a man so much wish to be thought better than he is, as by him whose kindness he desires to gain or keep?" his insight into possible motives is acute. But he forgets that on a more trusting and common-sense level the profession of friendship and good intent can sometimes be identical with those virtues, if no contradictory action is involved. Indeed the struggle toward friendly acquiescence may well lead to an improved state of virtue.

But Johnson combined a neoclassical notion of static character with an Augustinian view of the depravity of human nature.[51] For Johnson, the failure to recognize the implications of "the treachery of the human heart" was self-deluding fancy: "It is easy to awaken generous sentiments in privacy; to despise death when there is no danger; to glow with benevolence when there is nothing to be given. While such ideas are formed they are felt, and self-love does not suspect the gleam of virtue to be the meteor of fancy" (*Lives*, 3, 208). Johnson here insists upon the hard distinction between real sincerity and that which is a delusion. But we should not forget that his subject is the familiar letter. In poetry, actual or genetic sincerity seems less important than it does in personal communication, and Johnson seems to be content to judge elegy, for example, on the basis of the Horatian appearance of grief.

Initially torn by two allegiances, between the love of the human spirit and the need for external rule, Johnson chooses the latter without completely forsaking the former.[52] Despite this rational decision, the question is never fully resolved. In the resulting tension

51. See Donald Greene, "Augustinianism and Empiricism: A Note on Eighteenth-Century English Intellectual History," *Eighteenth-Century Studies*, 1 (1967): 33–68. Vivian de S. Pinto and Donald Greene, "Augustan or Augustinian? More Demythologizing Needed?" *ECS*, 2 (1968): 286–300. An excellent approach to Johnson's orthodoxy is W. J. Bate, *The Achievement of Samuel Johnson* (New York: Oxford University Press, 1955).

52. Critics who recognize a Johnsonian "split personality" are Stuart Gerry Brown, "Dr. Johnson and the Old Order," *Marxist Quarterly*, 1 (1937). Reprinted in Donald J. Greene, ed., *Samuel Johnson: A Collection of Critical Essays* (Englewood Cliffs, N.J.: Prentice-Hall, 1965), p. 171, and Bertrand H. Bronson, *Johnson Agonistes and Other Essays* (Berkeley: University of California Press, 1965).

between reason and passion, objectivity and subjectivity, Johnson attempts to reconcile the traditional with the new.

THE SCOTS

If the impulse to sincerity in social matters and poetry is influenced by certain Puritan principles, one might expect to find in eighteenth-century Scotland a veritable hot-bed of sincerity. But such is not the case. It is true that many tendencies in Scottish writers are in accord with the sincere ideal; but that is true in the main because of the close kinship of those writers to their English brethren.

Puritanism is, at its most conservative, inimical to the arts, and the Scottish Kirk was no exception to this rule. When, for example, John Home's moral tragedy *Douglas* was performed in Edinburgh in 1756, the orthodox protested with such vehemence that Home, a clergyman, felt it necessary to withdraw his membership from the Kirk.[53]

The best-known Scots writers of the century stood in a very odd relationship to their Scottish heritage. They were, almost without exception, proud of being Scotsmen, but their patriotism was limited. Although the spoken language of even educated Scotsmen was Scots, the written language was fast becoming English.[54] Those Scotsmen who wished to succeed in the literary world believed (quite rightly perhaps) that only in England could they find an appropriate audience. It was common for Scotsmen (Boswell for example) to be ashamed of their native tongue, or, as Hume did, to send their manuscripts to English friends for removal of Scotticisms.[55] Johnson mentioned to David Mallet's credit that he had perfectly eliminated his Scots accent;[56] and James Thomson was

53. David Daiches, *The Paradox of Scottish Culture: The Eighteenth-Century Experience* (London and New York: Oxford University Press, 1964), p. 44. I am indebted to this excellent little book for much of my account in this section. See also Professor Daiches's *Robert Burns* (New York: Macmillan, 1966), pp. 11–37.

54. David Daiches, "The Identity of Burns," in Carroll Camden, ed., *Restoration and Eighteenth-Century Literature* (Chicago: University of Chicago Press, 1963), p. 326.

55. Ibid., p. 326.   56. *Life of Johnson*, 2, 469.

more than once embarrassed by the broad accent that he retained.[57] Thus the dilemma of choosing between Scots and English produced in most Scotsmen a kind of schizophrenia, brilliantly diagnosed by Professor Daiches.

The results of this for our study are complex. First, we can explain very little of the literary output of eighteenth-century Scotsmen by reference to Scottish culture. As the blind acceptance of Mac-Pherson's Ossian forgeries readily proves, most Scottish intellectuals bore a tenuous relationship to their Scottish Gaelic tradition.[58] Second, the important literary achievements of Scotsmen between Thomson and Burns were not poetical. Hume and Adam Smith are the great names. The expository and critical work of Beattie, Blair, Kames, Gerard, and Monboddo are of importance in the history of ideas. Smollett and MacKenzie give Scotland some importance in fiction.

The poetry of Ramsay, Mallet, Beattie, Blacklock, and Falconer amounts to very little in the way of quality. The only poet of originality, Robert Fergusson, wrote in Scots, was ignored by the Edinburgh literati, and died at twenty-four in the public bedlam. Ramsay was importantly involved in the Scottish literary revival; but his verse, in uninspired bastard-Scots or English, is imitative of the most conventional English styles.

David Mallet (1705?–65), whose disregard for his native land made him, in Johnson's words, "the only Scot whom Scotchmen did not commend," wrote the famous ballad-like "William and Margaret," which for a while enjoyed a vogue. His more ambitious efforts, however, were rather sterile. *The Excursion* (1728), in moralistic and descriptive blank verse, gives us in one place Mallet's prescription for poetry, while recalling with admiration the qualities of one Thyrsis:

> Pleasing his speech, by nature taught to flow,
> Persuasive sense and strong, sincere and clear.
> His manners greatly plain. . . .[59]

57. G. C. Macaulay, *James Thomson* (London: Macmillan Co., 1908), pp. 81–82.
58. *The Paradox of Scottish Culture*, p. 93.
59. *The Works* (London, 1759), 1, 80.

In another poem *Amyntor and Theodora: or, the Hermit*, Mallet praises, in the sincere, moralistic tradition, the

> antient *Faith* that binds
> The plain community of guileless hearts
> In love and union. . . .[60]

But there is in Mallet's work no thorough-going commitment to the sincere ideal. His preoccupation with the improvement of society is evident, if not profound. He has much in common with his friend James Thomson, but lacks both his skill and depth.

James Beattie (1735–1803) glimpses the sincere ideal, but like so many minor poets deals superficially with the insights of better imaginations. In his best poem *The Minstrel*, Beattie, in the person of the hermit, excoriates society, whose major crime he himself was once guilty of:

> Like them, abandon'd to Ambition's sway,
> I sought for glory in the paths of guile; . . .
> (2, 119–20)[61]

The remedy for society is not imagination, as Edwin, the young minstrel, believes, but rather the very solution that Thomson had recommended many years earlier:

> 'What cannot Art and Industry perform,
> 'When Science plans the progress of their toil!
> (2, 479–80)

Beattie's strongly neoclassical desire is "To curb Imagination's lawless rage" (2, 400) and to substitute a more rational, socially-oriented poetry:

> Fancy now no more
> Wantons on fickle pinion through the skies;
> But, fix'd in aim, and conscious of her power,
> Aloft from cause to cause exults to rise,
> Creation's blended stores arranging as she flies.
> (2, 501–5)

60.Ibid., 1, 120.   61.*Poetical Works* (London, 1894).

Beattie faces some of the problems encountered earlier by Thomson, Akenside, and Collins, but his solutions are imitative and superficial.

In his "Epistle . . . to Blacklock," Beattie attributes to Thomas Blacklock (1721–91) sincerity of intent and spontaneity of inspiration. But Blacklock's poetry seems utterly conventional and uninspired. He perfunctorily obeys some conventions of sincerity when he writes in his poem "On the Death of Mr. Pope":

No more fond wishes in my breast shall roll,
Distend my heart, and kindle all my soul,
To breathe my honest raptures in thy ear,
And feel thy kindness in returns sincere. . . .

(169–72)[62]

Despite their knowledge of late developments in psychology, Blacklock and most of his associates revert to earlier modes of Augustan verse. The prime purpose of this seems to be the self-conscious attempt to win English recognition of Scottish achievement. Since no Englishman of the eighteenth century would have bothered about Robert Fergusson's superb Scots poetry, Scotsmen took the same tack. Scottish poets, they believed, would win acclaim by out-Poping Pope, a hopeless undertaking at best. Thus William Falconer (1732–69) in his general attack on guile, in *The Demagogue*, praises satire as the truly sincere poetry:

How oft my bosom at thy name has glow'd,
And from my beating heart applause bestow'd;
Applause, that, genuine as the blush of youth
Unknown to guile, was sanctified by truth!

(73–76)[63]

These inept verses express the conventional attitude toward satire that Pope held in justifying his satiric stance. In short, Scottish poetry between Thomson and Burns is almost always a weak

62. *Poems on Several Occasions* (Glasgow, 1746), p. 80.
63. *The Poetical Works of Beattie, Blair, and Falconer*, ed. George Gilfillan (Edinburgh, 1854), p. 270.

imitation of Augustan modes, even when it shows some affinities
with the sincere ideal.

In psychology and aesthetics, however, the Scots were making
significant contributions. Adam Smith's "sympathy" had promptly
become an important part of the Scottish critical canon, as Hugh
Blair testifies in the following passage: "He whose heart is indelicate
or hard, he who has no admiration of what is truly noble or praiseworthy, nor the proper sympathetic sense of what is soft and tender,
must have a very imperfect relish of the highest beauties of eloquence and poetry."[64] In a note to his poem "On the Death of Mr.
Pope" Blacklock had expressed similar sentiments: "What we call
poetical genius, depends entirely on the quickness of moral feeling:
he, therefore, who cannot feel poetry, must either have his affections and internal senses depraved by vice, or be naturally insensible
of the pleasures resulting from the exercise of them. But this natural
insensibility is almost never so great in any heart, as entirely to
hinder the impression of well-painted passion, or natural images
connected with it."[65]

But Blair and the blind poet are concerned with the problem of
taste, not that of composition. Though eighteenth-century developments in psychology were applied widely to the act of perceiving a
poem, the Scottish poets described the psychology of creation in the
time-honoured neoclassical formula of imagination controlled by
judgement. Since the poet's sincere attitude toward his materials was
assumed, and so not examined, sincerity did not become an important factor in the Scottish poetic.

Sincerity as a social virtue, however, gained importance among
Scottish intellectuals. Pre-eminent among these was Henry Home,
Lord Kames (1696–1782), in whose philosophical pantheon the
"culture of the heart" sat in the highest place.

For Kames the moral sense and the development of taste in the
arts were closely allied. Thus the "author of nature" had prepared
for the progressive moral development of man: "the author of
nature, by qualifying the human mind for a succession of enjoy-
ments from the lowest to the highest, leads it by gentle steps from

64. *Lectures on Rhetoric and Belles Lettres* in *Works* (London, 1820), 4, 22–23.
65. Blacklock, *Poems*, p. 75.

the most groveling corporeal pleasures, for which only it is fitted in the beginning of life, to those refined and sublime pleasures which are suited to its maturity."[66] But since, as Kames goes on to point out, this development does not occur without our help, we are therefore bound morally to cultivate our taste for the fine arts. Since taste makes us more sensitive human beings, its development is important to the formation of the good society:

> delicacy of taste tends not less to invigorate the social affections, than to moderate those that are selfish. To be convinced of this tendency, we need only reflect, that delicacy of taste necessarily heightens our sensibility of pain and pleasure, and of course our sympathy, which is the capital branch of every social passion. Sympathy in particular invites a communication of joys and sorrows, hopes and fears: such exercise, soothing and satisfactory in itself, is necessarily productive of mutual good-will and affection.[67]

Kame's morality is based on the development of the aesthetic sense, and is entirely divorced from moral law: "To the man who has acquired a taste so acute and accomplished, every action wrong or improper, must be highly disgustful. . . ."[68] The question of an action's being right or wrong is no longer relevant. We must ask instead whether or not it disgusts the man of sensibility and taste. Kames completely ignores the possibility of tastes being developed for activities which society regards as perversion. He is particularly naive in believing that man, who is good by nature, will choose to obey conventional moral codes.[69]

His ebullient confidence in human nature seemed justified, not only by the apparent innate sincerity of mankind, but also by nature's sincerity. He makes the following generalization at the conclusion of his study of emotions and passions:

> The external signs of passion are a strong indication, that man, by his very constitution, is framed to be open and sincere. A

66. *Elements of Criticism* (Edinburgh, 1765), 1, 4.
67. Ibid., 1, 10.   68. Ibid., 1, 10.
69. Kames's belief that conventional moral codes represented the good tendencies in man suggests that his morality was more enthusiastic than reflective.

child, in all things obedient to the impulses of nature, hides
none of its emotions; the savage and clown, who have no guide
but pure nature, expose their hearts to view, by giving way to
all the natural signs. And even when men learn to dissemble
their sentiments, and when behaviour degenerates into art,
there still remain checks, which keep dissimulation within
bounds, and prevent a great part of its mischievous effects: the
total suppression of the voluntary signs during any vivid
passion, begets the utmost uneasiness, which cannot be en-
dured for any considerable time: this operation becomes indeed
less painful by habit; but luckily, the involuntary signs cannot,
by any effort, be suppressed, not even dissembled. An absolute
hypocrisy, by which the character is concealed and a fictitious
one assumed, is made impracticable; and nature has thereby
prevented much harm to society. We may pronounce, therefore, that Nature, herself sincere and candid, intends that mankind should preserve the same character by cultivating simplicity and truth, and banishing every sort of dissimulation
that tends to mischief.[70]

This passage suggests the proportions that the sincere ideal could
attain. The doctrine of sympathy and the cult of sentimentality provided a fertile field for its development. Just as in Puritanism, when
the support of Church authority was swept away, a new authority
was sought in the human heart, so too, as neoclassical authority fell
into disrepute, the subjective impulse was sought out as the criterion
of poetic composition.

The examination of these Scots literary figures in one section has
been merely a convenient procedure. Scottish culture as such seems
to have little to do with the development of any of these writers,
except that being aware of their paradoxical situation, they reacted
against that culture. Yet such reaction did result in a unique manifestation with which the sincere ideal may be connected.

During the eighteenth century, a large group of talented Scottish
writers, labouring under their sense of inferiority to the London
wits, began to establish in Edinburgh what Professor Daiches calls

70. *Elements of Criticism*, 1, 433–34.

"the heavenly city of the Edinburgh philosophers." Here the Scottish literati hoped (not without reason) that literature and all the arts would flourish. Daiches points out: "They called Edinburgh the 'Athens of the North' and consciously practised civilization."[71] And by reason of the implementation of James Craig's prize-winning plan for extending the city "not only was there a heavenly city implied in the thought of the Scottish moralists of the period—particularly those of the 'moral sense' school—but there was an actual attempt to realize that city in stone."[72] The concept had its ideological base in the belief in progress and the natural goodness of man and is a form of the second Eden of the sincere ideal.

Yet that ideal is seldom stated, but rather simply assumed. It is assumed, not as reality, but as an object of aspiration. If man is naturally sincere, as Kames believed, why was he usually so insincere? Poor environment, poor education, and lack of contact with nature (which is sincere) was the answer. So Kames, following the example of Rousseau and Locke, composed his *Loose Hints Upon Education Chiefly Concerning the Culture of the Heart*, a disorganized set of directions to parents for bringing up sincere offspring. Kames's optimism about human nature is reinforced by this study, since it is largely a compendium of anecdotes illustrating the natural virtue of children.

But when so much energy must be enlisted to actualize an ideal, its critics might be forgiven for seeing it as somewhat unnatural to man. Unnaturalness may not be a cogent objection, of course, but the literati would have thought so. They solved their problem by deciding that the ideal unattainable by man was perfectly natural to him.

WILLIAM COWPER

William Cowper's competence in many modes of poetry kept him from fixing on any single one. At first glance his longer poems seem to be all of a piece: all are in conversational idiom. But upon closer investigation serious differences within the poems themselves

71. *Paradox of Scottish Culture*, p. 73.   72. Ibid., pp. 68–70.

emerge. Some parts are so piously moralistic as to be almost sacerdotal; others contain satiric portraits in the tradition of Pope and William Law; still others are pure whimsy. Cowper combines these in his poetry with a host of other modes. In some of his most pious attitudes, for example, will be found an ironic thrust which calls in question the validity of the sentiment. Such variety makes him a particularly complex figure.

Cowper's poetry is often ideological; but since that ideology results from an interaction of Calvinist principles, personal sentiment, and neoclassical standards, it is complex and confused. Cowper's Calvinism leads him to attach great importance to sincerity of intention in every aspect of human endeavour. Sincerity becomes particularly important in his thought because of his thorough-going belief in the innate evil of man. Given that evil as the primary fact of life, sincerity becomes a classical bridle to the passions. In Cowper's imaginative scheme of things, sincerity is the sole virtue left to man after his eviction from Eden, and so man's only means of deterring evil.

As early as 1755 in one of his "Delia" poems, Cowper identifies rural retreat with Eden, a relationship that was to become more significant as his career progressed:

> Were it my fate with Delia to retire;
> With her to wander through the sylvan shade,
> Each morn, or o'er the moss-imbrowned turf,
> Where, blest as the prime parents of mankind
> In their own Eden, we would envy none; . . .[73]

Cowper's early concern for the problem of lost Eden is not surprising when we recall how important this theme was in the poetry of his earlier contemporaries. But it was the direct influence of Milton that was most important. Cowper tells us in *The Task* of the impact that *Paradise Lost* had on him as a boy:

> Then Milton had indeed a poet's charms:
> New to my taste, his Paradise surpass'd
> The struggling efforts of my boyish tongue
> To speak its excellence. I danced for joy.

---

73. *The Poetical Works*, p. 280. All citations to Cowper's poetry are to this edition.

I marvell'd much that, at so ripe an age
As twice sev'n years, his beauties had then first
Engag'd my wonder; and, admiring still,
And still admiring, with regret suppos'd
The joy half lost because not sooner found.

(4, 709–17)

In a short poem, "Love Abused," written before any of his important productions, domestic bliss provides a "second Eden":

The stream of pure and genuine love
Derives its current from above;
And earth a second Eden shows
Where'er the healing water flows.[74]

Similar sentiments were expressed later in *The Task*:

Domestic happiness, thou only bliss
Of Paradise that has surviv'd the fall!

(3, 41–42)

The possibility of this second Eden, short of the heavenly reward, became the most significant problem of Cowper's life. It was made emphatic by his own persistent belief that he was damned by God and beyond any possibility of salvation. Yet in accord with his urbane, aristocratic sensibility, the quest for a second Eden was undertaken without the benefits of apocalypse. No indication of his periodical insanity is present in his poetry. His work is rational, controlled—yet sensitive and exploratory of important issues.

As we shall see the notion of rural retreat brings Cowper closest to the impossible second Eden he sought. Natural scenery is important to man, since it represents God's love and power, originally exemplified in the prelapsarian Paradise:

                    in spite of sin and woe,
Traces of Eden are still seen below,
Where mountain, river, forest, field, and grove,
Remind him of his Maker's power and love.

(*Retirement*, 27–30)

74. Ibid., p. 307.

Poetry too plays a part in recapturing Eden, and for Cowper the corrupt state of contemporary verse is indicative of the evil times:

> In Eden, ere yet innocence of heart
> Had faded, poetry was not an art;
> Language, above all teaching, or, if taught,
> Only by gratitude and glowing thought,
> Elegant as simplicity, and warm
> As ecstasy, unmanacled by form,
> Not prompted, as in our degen'rate days,
> By low ambition and the thirst of praise,
> Was natural as is the flowing stream,
> And yet magnificent—a God the theme!
>
> (*Table Talk*, 584–93)

Naturalness, spontaneity, simplicity are all part of Cowper's poetic and all are related to the ideals of the second Eden.

Cowper's confidence in the idea of the rural retreat's ever approximating Eden was limited. His own retirement did, at times, prey on his mind. In March of 1780, he wrote the following to Mrs. Newton: "If I were in a condition to leave Olney . . . I certainly would not stay in it. It is no attachment to the place that binds me here, but an unfitness for every other. I lived in it once, but now I am buried in it, and have no business with the world on the outside of my sepulchre; my appearance would startle them, and theirs would be shocking to me."[75] Such thoughts, however, enter the poetry in only the most oblique of ways. He admits in *The Task* that retreat is not an adequate substitute for Paradise; yet he finds in it many desirable qualities:

> Retreat
> Cannot indeed to guilty man restore
> Lost innocence, or cancel follies past;
> But it has peace, and much secures the mind
> From all assaults of evil; proving still

---

75. Cowper, *The Correspondence*, 1, 356. Cited in the text as *Corr.*

A faithful barrier, not o'erleap'd with ease
By vicious custom, raging uncontroll'd. . . .

(3, 676–82)

Later in *The Task* the wish is openly for a golden age:

Would I had fall'n upon those happier days
That poets celebrate; those golden times,
And those Arcadian scenes, that Maro sings,
And Sidney, warbler of poetic prose.
Nymphs were Dianas then, and swains had hearts
That felt their virtues: innocence, it seems,
From courts dismiss'd, found shelter in the groves;
The footsteps of simplicity, impress'd
Upon the yielding herbage, (so they sing)
Then were not all effac'd: then speech profane,
And manners profligate, were rarely found;
Observ'd as prodigies, and soon reclaim'd.

(4, 513–24)

This classical, indeed pagan, side of Cowper's mythology is relatively undeveloped, but expresses the double ideal naively stated in his ode "On Reading Mr. Richardson's History of Sir Charles Grandison," the last stanza of which praises Grandison as the ideal of hero and saint.[76] The dominance of Cowper's Christian belief is seen clearly in his rejection of the golden age of myth:

Vain wish! those days were never: airy dreams
Sat for the picture; and the poet's hand,
Imparting substance to an empty shade,
Impos'd a gay delirium for a truth.

(4, 525–28)

But the mere capacity for such a dream is an object of admiration:

Grant it:—I still must envy them an age
That favour'd such a dream; in days like these
Impossible, when virtue is so scarce,

76. *The Poetical Works*, p. 284.

That to suppose a scene where she presides,
Is tramontane, and stumbles all belief.

(4, 529-33)

Cowper came more and more to believe that his age was unregenerate. But envying the dream of the golden age, he strove to emulate those who had enjoyed it. The dream, he found, was necessary, since the vulgarity of fashion was already corrupting rural life:

The fashion runs
Down into scenes still rural; but, alas,
Scenes rarely grac'd with rural manners now!

(4, 555-57)

But the possible Christian elements in the dream of Paradise give it more reality than any pagan conception. Retreat, then, as a substitute for Paradise in the modern world, is superior to the golden age:

So life glides smoothly and by stealth away,
More golden than that age of fabled gold
Renown'd in ancient song; not vex'd with care
Or stain'd with guilt, beneficent, approv'd
Of God and man, and peaceful in its end.

(6, 995-99)

This plays an important part in the resolution of *The Task*, but even more important is Cowper's attitude toward sincerity, the virtue that must govern human activity in his second Eden.

Cowper sees guile as the most abominable of vices, the one at the bottom of what is wrong with the world:

Now basket up the family of plagues
That waste our vitals; peculation, sale
Of honour, perjury, corruption, frauds
By forgery, by subterfuge of law,
By tricks and lies as num'rous and as keen
As the necessities their authors feel; . . .

(2, 667-72)

All of these crimes are aimed at gaining wealth and power; but all involve deceit, none, violence. There were, to be sure, crimes of violence in eighteenth-century England, as the Newgate Calendar will readily attest; but the English seem to regard intellectual crimes of deceit and corruption as a more profound threat against the fabric of society than ever violence could be. This English repugnance and contempt for the use of violence have made it possible for the police to avoid carrying firearms, except in the most extraordinary circumstances. Social pressures against the use of violence have made the great train robbery, the million pound embezzlement, and other forms of deceit, characteristically English, and as such, the most serious danger to English integrity.

Thus, sincerity is the right medicine for the chief ill of English society. In *Conversation* Cowper indicates that sincerity is man's primary virtue, and when observed makes the Second Eden possible. The art of conversation exemplifies this ideal:

> But Conversation, choose what theme we may,
> And chiefly when religion leads the way,
> Should flow, like waters after summer show'rs,
> Not as if rais'd by mere mechanic pow'rs.
> The Christian, in whose soul, though now distress'd,
> Lives the dear thought of joys he once possess'd,
> When all his glowing language issued forth
> With God's deep stamp upon its current worth,
> Will speak without disguise, and must impart,
> Sad as it is, his undissembling heart,
> Abhors constraint, and dares not feign a zeal,
> Or seem to boast a fire, he does not feel.
>
> *(Conversation, 703–14)*

Cowper probably had in mind the long, amiable but intense religious discussions enjoyed with the Unwins. Thus on the basis of his own experience, he rejects the world's opinion (akin to Hobbes's) that all sincerity is really hypocrisy:

> The world grown old, her deep discernment shows,
> Claps spectacles on her sagacious nose,
> Peruses closely the true Christian's face,
> And finds it a mere mask of sly grimace,

Usurps God's office, lays his bosom bare,
And finds hypocrisy close lurking there,
And, serving God herself, through mere constraint,
Concludes his unfeign'd love of him, a feint.

(*Conversation*, 741–48)

This, Cowper cannot accept; on the contrary, sincerity is man's
chief virtue and the basis for virtue:

And yet, God knows, look human nature through,
(And in due time the world shall know it too)
That since the flow'rs of Eden felt the blast,
That after man's defection laid all waste,
Sincerity towards th'heart-searching God
Has made the new-born creature her abode,
Nor shall be found in unregen'rate souls,
Till the last fire burn all between the poles.
Sincerity! Why 'tis his only pride,
Weak and imperfect in all grace beside,
He knows that God demands his heart entire,
And gives him all his just demands require.

(*Conversation*, 749–60)

This is Puritan sincerity, so important in distinguishing the elect
from the damned, as is made clear in *The Progress of Error*:

he, who seeks a mansion in the sky,
Must watch his purpose with a steadfast eye;
That prize belongs to none but the sincere,
The least obliquity is fatal here.

(576–78)

It is not surprising, then, that Saint Paul should be, for Cowper, a
personification of the sincere ideal:

I would express him simple, grave, sincere;
In doctrine uncorrupt; in language plain,
And plain in manner, decent, solemn, chaste,
And natural in gesture; . . .

(*The Task*, 2, 399–402)

This might have been written a hundred and fifty years earlier by some Puritan divine, though probably not in verse. The verse is important here, particularly because of its high quality. Key Puritan ideas, so significant to the intellectual milieu of the nineteenth century, finally found their way into poetry and found a poetry (and a poet) congenial to their representation.

Cowper's concern for sincerity was in large part a reaction against the corruption of his own times. It is for that reason less optimistic in tendency than the attitudes of some of his earlier contemporaries. Yet the optimism of Whig-oriented poets is less real than fanciful, as I have sought to show.

Cowper's approach to politics is liberal but essentially personal. Although he realized that political and social reforms were necessary, the American Revolution outraged him, for he believed that it was the result of an alliance with hated France, concluded to destroy Britain. Like so many of his contemporaries, he was imbued with a nationalistic ardour which portrayed England as the moral superior of every other nation. The brutality of the French Revolution offended Cowper's aristocratic sensibility; but it was brutality for him because it was French. Nonetheless he saw the need of reform and predicted that without such reform, there would be violent revolution in England (*Corr.*, 4, 335).

The complications and violence of politics frightened him. On many occasions in his letters, he protests that he is unable to understand them at all: "Politics," he wrote in 1783, "are my abhorrence, being almost always hypothetical, fluctuating, and impracticable" (*Corr.*, 2, 126–27). Crises in political and social affairs were greatly responsible for Cowper's retreat from society, just as they had influenced the myth of retirement by which he comprehended his situation. But as we have seen, the rural retreat was not enough, since even the countryside was in the process of corruption. What was needed was a commitment to something of significance. For Cowper that meant religion and the advantages of a religious-minded community.

Solitude that meant retreat from social intercourse was not at all in vogue. Indeed James Grainger's "Solitude" and James Beattie's *The Minstrel* are sharp critiques of the life of solitude, and Cowper's

own "Verses Supposed to be Written by Alexander Selkirk . . .,"
beginning "I am monarch of all I survey," is a contribution to this
mode. Cowper chose society as opposed to complete solitude, but it
was not the large corrupt one that he feared; rather he selected a
small circle of friends among whom all virtues were taken for
granted.

Poetry was not as important to Cowper as it might have been if
he had not had such a strong religious orientation. But his primary
concern for religion led him to believe that poetry ought to serve it
in some important way. Modern verse, to his mind, in conforming
to modern taste, was superficial. As he writes ironically in *Table
Talk*:

> modern taste
> Is so refin'd, and delicate, and chaste,
> That verse, whatever fire the fancy warms,
> Without a creamy smoothness has no charms.
> Thus, all success depending on an ear,
> And thinking I might purchase it too dear,
> If sentiment were sacrific'd to sound,
> And truth cut short to make a period round,
> I judg'd a man of sense could scarce do worse
> Than caper in the morris-dance of verse.
>
> (4, 510–19)

Cowper's dissenter view of the Bible's simplicity in translation gives
him an ideal to apply to poetry:

> The sacred book no longer suffers wrong,
> Bound in the fetters of an unknown tongue;
> But speaks with plainness, art could never mend,
> What simplest minds can soonest comprehend.
>
> (*Hope*, 449–52)

In contrast to this simplicity and its wholesomeness are the dangers
of insincere literature:

> Books are not seldom talismans and spells,
> By which the magic art of shrewder wits

Holds an unthinking multitude enthrall'd.
Some to the fascination of a name
Surrender judgment, hood-wink'd. Some the style
Infatuates, and through labyrinths and wilds
Of error leads them by a tune entranc'd.

(6, 98–104)

The poetry that Cowper looks forward to is religious and prophetic,
the true emanation of the sincere heart:

A terrible sagacity informs
The poet's heart; he looks to distant storms;
He hears the thunder ere the tempest low'rs;
And, arm'd with strength surpassing human pow'rs,
Seizes events as yet unknown to man,
And darts his soul into the dawning plan.

(*Table Talk*, 494–99)

In predicting this direction for poetry, however, Cowper modestly
discounts his own contribution:

But no prophetic fires to me belong;
I play with syllables, and sport in song.

(*Table Talk*, 504–5)

The answer to the question of what is left to be done in poetry (the
same question which haunted Collins) is fairly obvious:

Pity religion has so seldom found
A skilful guide into poetic ground!

(*Table Talk*, 716–17)

Cowper's solution, then, to the burden of the past and the challenge
to produce something new is to devote poetry to religion in a way
that has never been done before. Nonetheless, a certain pessimism
hangs over his proposal:

And 'tis the sad complaint, and almost true,
Whate'er we write, we bring forth nothing new.
'Twere new indeed to see a bard all fire,

Touch'd with a coal from heav'n, assume the lyre,
And tell the world, still kindling as he sung,
With more than mortal music on his tongue,
That He, who died below, and reigns above,
Inspires the song, and that his name is love.

(Table Talk, 732–39)

In a 1783 letter to William Unwin, Cowper reiterated this observation, but in more pessimistic terms:

> To aim with success at the spiritual good of mankind, and to
> become popular by writing on scriptural subjects, were an un-
> reasonable ambition, even for a poet to entertain, in days like
> these. Verse may have many charms, but has none powerful
> enough to conquer the aversion of a dissipated age to such
> instruction *(Corr.,* 2, 91).

To summarize, then, Cowper believed that the kind of poetry he
envisioned could not be popular, and without popularity, it would
not perform its intended moral function. Further, he implies that his
own incapacity in this regard is proof of his pessimistic judgement.

But despite his reservations about his own verse, he continues his
serious attempt to develop a poetic. Fiction is to be banned from
poetry:

Happy the bard (if that fair name belong
To him that blends no fable with his song)
Whose lines, uniting, by an honest art,
The faithful monitor's and poet's part,
Seek to delight, that they may mend mankind,
And, while they captivate, inform the mind: . . .

(Hope, 754–59)

The best poetry of all, however, would be plain, true, and spontaneous:

But happier far, who comfort those that wait
To hear plain truth at Judah's hallow'd gate.
Their language simple, as their manners meek,
No shining ornaments have they to seek;

Nor labour they, nor time, nor talents, waste,
In sorting flow'rs to suit a fickle taste;
But, while they speak the wisdom of the skies,
Which art can only darken and disguise,
Th'abundant harvest, recompense divine,
Repays their work—the gleaning only mine.

(*Hope*, 762–71)

Cowper's doubts about his own achievement are apparent in the last line of this passage, but elsewhere he states more positively his attempts to approximate his poetic ideals. In a letter to William Unwin in 1783, he remarks on the sincerity of his own poetry: "You say you felt my verses; I assure you that in this you followed my example, for I felt them first" (*Corr.*, 2, 128). Here once again is an echo of a famous passage in Horace's *Ars Poetica*. But it is not merely a statement of the original admonition, but rather a personal affirmation of Horace's observation. Indeed it is entirely possible that Cowper, for the moment at least, is unaware of the source of his statement. In *The Task* he again affirms this position:

Thou know'st my praise of nature most sincere,
And that my raptures are not conjur'd up
To serve occasions of poetic pomp,
But genuine, and art partner of them all.

(1, 150–53)

Not only is sincerity important to him, but he unites with it a passion for originality. He wrote to Unwin in 1784 of *The Task*: "My descriptions are all from nature: not one of them second-handed. My delineations of the heart are from my own experience: not one of them borrowed from books, or in the least degree conjectural" (*Corr.*, 2, 252). These assertions are doubtful, especially the one regarding his descriptions. Many descriptive passages in *The Task* bear the impress of Thomson's example. Yet we cannot accuse Cowper of insincerity on this score. Though there was no intention to imitate, the poetic language he inherited did the job for him. Further, he was too good a classicist not to have absorbed the lessons of the ancients, as he shows even in his most "sincere" and personal statements.

In a letter to Unwin, however, he protests that he is free from English influence, at least: "I reckon it among my principal advantages, as a composer of verses, that I have not read an English poet, these thirteen years, and but one these twenty years. Imitation, even of the best models, is my aversion; it is servile and mechanical, a trick that has enabled many to usurp the name of author, who could not have written at all, if they had not written upon the pattern of somebody indeed original" (*Corr.*, 1, 386). Cowper, in adopting sincerity as criterion, rejects the mechanical metaphors used by earlier eighteenth-century poets to describe the poetic process. Sincerity implies organic composition, since spontaneity and truth to nature are usually involved.

The Task is the poem which most closely approximates Cowper's poetic goals. At the end of the final book, he muses on the discrepancy between the task imposed upon him by Lady Austen and the one that he finally assumed:

> It shall not grieve me, then, that once, when call'd
> To dress a Sofa with the flow'rs of verse,
> I play'd awhile, obedient to the fair,
> With that light task; but soon, to please her more,
> Whom flow'rs alone I knew would little please, . . .
>
> (6, 1006–10)

The real task is apparent to God, who appears to be looking for sincerity—even in poetry:

> But all is in his hand whose praise I seek.
> In vain the poet sings, and the world hears,
> If he regard not, though divine the theme.
> 'Tis not in artful measures, in the chime
> And idle tinkling of a minstrel's lyre,
> To charm his ear, whose eye is on the heart;
> Whose frown can disappoint the proudest strain,
> Whose approbation—prosper even mine.
>
> (6, 1017–24)

Cowper's poetry is always about experience or the kind of poetry that is experience. But his poetry falls short of being the experience

itself. Although his achievement is not equivalent to that of Wordsworth, he supplies part of the theory without which a Wordsworth
would have been impossible. If sincerity is the governing virtue in
human experience, then, when poetry becomes experience itself, it
will be governed by that virtue. Cowper's high regard for poetry as
a vehicle of truth led him to demand that it express its author's unadulterated sincerity. What moved him to do so was a combination
of high religious and social ideals and a recognition of how far short
the world fell in making them real. Like his fellow poets of the sincere ideal, he expresses grave reservations about the value of his
poetry and his life in approximating that ideal. Thus once again in
the delineation of an optimistic goal, we discover a disabling pessimism. But the really positive assertion of human ideals comes, for
Cowper, in the imaginative world discovered by his poetry. Thus
what he wrote in apostrophe to Cowley in *The Task* can, with only
the place name set aside, be applied to Cowper himself:

> I still revere thee, courtly though retir'd;
> Though stretch'd at ease in Chertsey's silent bow'rs,
> Not unemploy'd; and finding rich amends
> For a lost world in solitude and verse.

(4, 727–30)

Sincerity is not so much a distinct virtue of itself, as a general quality which gives a stamp, a value, and a very being to all the virtues.

George Walker, F.R.S.

7

Sincerity and Romanticism

WILLIAM BLAKE

The study of sincerity in nineteenth-century poetry, if not in Romantic poetry alone, would require several volumes. Blake and Wordsworth remain, in the company of most of the poets considered here, the giants of sincerity. Wordsworth's concern for sincerity has been ably treated by David Perkins and Blake's sincere ideal is so completely connected to other elements of his world view that is it transformed in the process. Yet it may be useful to consider both these poets in a brief attempt to show how their concern for sincerity is related to that of earlier English poets.

Blake's aversion for guile, deceit, and insincerity is manifest in practically all of his writings. Deceit, he believed, was congenital in what passed for religion in eighteenth-century England. In his annotations to Lavater, Blake pens a resounding "bravo" to the comment "The more honesty a man has, the less he affects the air of a saint—the affectation of sanctity is a blotch on the face of piety."[1]

Bacon's essay "Of Simulation and Dissimulation" elicited a significant response from Blake. Though Blake's marginalia to this essay consists of only one angry comment: "This is Folly Itself" (p. 612), some salient points in Blake's system may be answers, specific or implied, to Bacon's position. For this reason it will be helpful to clarify that position.

For Bacon sincerity is indeed a mark of virtue: "Certainly the ablest men that ever were have had all an openness and frankness of dealing, and a name of certainty and veracity; but then they were like horses well managed, for they could tell passing well when to stop or turn; and at such times when they thought the case indeed

1. *The Poetry and Prose of William Blake*, p. 577. Unless otherwise indicated all citations to Blake's poetry and prose are to this edition.

required dissimulation, if then they used it, it came to pass that the former opinion spread abroad of their good faith and clearness of dealing made them almost invisible."[2] These are subtleties based on a kind of worldly wisdom that Blake would reject, even though he might agree with Bacon's irony that Urizenic heroes can indeed make insincerity pass for virtue. But for Bacon habits of dissimulation are only for those who do not possess the highest powers of judgement, namely the ability to "discern what things are to be laid open, and what to be secreted, and what to be showed at half lights, and to whom and when (which indeed are arts of state and arts of life, as Tacitus well calleth them). . . ."[3]

Blake, however, by his comment seems unwilling to allow Bacon either his distinctions between kinds of "hiding and veiling of a man's self" or his ironic conception of the hero. For Blake the great task is to create a heroic conception that will make the arts of a corrupt society obsolete. Thus, the Shakespearean notion of moderation, namely that sincerity is harmful to those who have too little or too much, a concept shared to some degree by Bacon, is antipathetical to Blake's world view.

Blake's famous remark on his own "active physiognomy" as a cause of social disapproval and a general concern about the meaning of his countenance reminds one of Bacon's remonstration: "the discovery of a man's self, by the tracts of his countenance, is a great weakness and betraying; by how much it is many times more marked, and believed, than a man's words." Blake agreed that this was so, but rejected its corollary that it is wise to be reserved or placid. Indeed the persecution he received for his sincerity suggested that he was possessed of a particular kind of sainthood. Thus we find among the Proverbs of Hell: "Always be ready to speak your mind, and a base man will avoid you" (p. 36). "Blake regards himself," John Beer has written, "as the rough honest character now called upon to re-assert the dominion of energy and overcome the smooth rogueries of Jacob-like deceivers."[4]

2. Francis Bacon, *Essays, Advancement of Learning, New Atlantis, and Other Pieces*, ed. Richard Foster Jones (New York: Odyssey Press, 1937), p. 17.
3. Ibid., p. 16.
4. *Blake's Humanism* (Manchester: Manchester University Press, 1968), p. 49.

Blake's early *Poetical Sketches* show only an incidental concern with sincerity. But the concern is there, not as in Gray, a serious question vital to poetic composition, but as Hebraic or Puritan self-righteousness: "My voice hath used deceit, how should I call on Him who is Truth?" laments the dying youth in "The Couch of Death." In "Samson" Dalila, as in *Samson Agonistes*, symbolizes guile. In the manuscript fragment "then She bore Pale desire," Blake takes a position reiterated in many of his later works: "Policy brought forth Guile & fraud. these Gods last namd live in the Smoke of Cities. on Dusky wing breathing forth Clamour & Destruction. alas in Cities whereas the man whose face is not a mask unto his heart Pride made a Goddess. fair or image rather till knowledge animated it. 'twas Calld Selflove" (p. 439). By this self-love all human relationships are blighted: "Go See. the Natural tie of flesh & blood. Go See more strong the ties of marriage love. thou Scarce Shall find but Self love Stands Between" (p. 439). Here Blake suggests the important theme of self-annihilation which animates such works as *Milton* and *Jerusalem*. It is important to note that selfhood and deceit are directly linked. Though self-annihilation is a form of what was more commonly called disinterestedness, and thus, is a form of self-denial, for Blake such denial is a full and affirmative expression of true humanity. Thus selfhood is the real deceit, since anything which prevents full human development is in its nature insincere.

Some of the short poems omitted from the *Songs of Experience* bear directly on the question of sincerity. In "Silent Silent Night" Blake draws a distinction between joys "used with deceit" and those of an honest, open sort. "To Nobodaddy" reflects Blake's contempt for the concept of the hidden God, but another poem reflects more accurately the ethical problems presented by deceit:

Love to faults is always blind
Always is to joy inclind
Lawless wingd & unconfind
And breaks all chains from every mind

Blake's contempt for Jacob is also discussed in J. G. Davies, *The Theology of William Blake* (Oxford: Clarendon Press, 1948), p. 79.

Deceit to secresy confind
Lawful cautious & refind
To every thing but interest blind
And forges fetters for the mind[.][5]

(p. 463)

In this poem and "To Nobodaddy," Blake unites in condemnation a neoclassical ideal of propriety and the Christian religious doctrine of mystery. Both are forms of affectation, being strict denials of human impulse.

Though the *Songs of Innocence* may be an implicit investigation of some aspects of sincerity, it would be labouring to insist that innocence and sincerity are equivalent in those poems. Indeed the irony of the *Songs of Innocence*, communicated by the constant awareness that innocence is victimized, militates against the view that Blake is working to construct a sincere ideal.

More explicit exploration of sincerity comes in the *Songs of Experience*, as Mark Schorer contends: "The hypocritical 'angel' (of 'I asked a thief to steal me a peach') triumphs over the sincere man of open impulse. Sincerity, Godwin's 'perfect sincerity,' is the great neglected virtue in all these poems."[6] In the following poem from the Rossetti MS, sincerity is seen as victim:

Never seek to tell thy love,
Love that never told can be;
For the gentle wind does move
Silently, invisibly.

I told my love, I told my love,
I told her all my heart;
Trembling, cold, in ghastly fears,
Ah! she doth depart.

Soon as she was gone from me,
A traveller came by,

---

5. Mark Schorer has pointed to this poem in connection with the problem of sincerity. See *William Blake: The Politics of Vision* (1946; reprinted New York: Vintage 1959), p. 205.
6. *William Blake: The Politics of Vision*, p. 207.

Silently, invisibly:
He took her with a sigh.[7]

Here once again the sincere man is rejected in favour of hypocrisy.

But nonetheless, as "A Poison Tree" makes clear, sincerity is necessary to the development of one's full humanity:

I was angry with my friend;
I told my wrath, my wrath did end.
I was angry with my foe:
I told it not, my wrath did grow.

And I waterd it in fears,
Night & morning with my tears:
And I sunned it with smiles,
And with soft deceitful wiles.

While true sincerity brings wrath to an end, the smiles and "soft deceitful wiles" of hypocrisy lead to an inevitable murder of enemy and self:

And it grew both day and night.
Till it bore an apple bright.
And my foe beheld it shine.
And he knew that it was mine.

And into my garden stole,
When the night had veild the pole;
In the morning glad I see;
My foe outstretched beneath the tree.

The necessity for "telling" one's love, that is, for the open relationship between all human beings and God, is made clear by the sharp irony of "The Human Abstract":

Pity would be no more,
If we did not make somebody Poor:
And Mercy no more could be,
If all were as happy as we. . . .

7. *The Poems of William Blake*, ed. John Sampson (Oxford: Oxford Standard Authors, 1913), p. 109.

Since the narrator of this poem employs the most specious and hypo-critical of arguments in this opening stanza, we are not surprised when all action in the poem turns to deceit and mystery:

And mutual fear brings peace;
Till the selfish loves increase.
Then Cruelty knits a snare,
And spreads his baits with care.

He sits down with holy fears,
And waters the ground with tears:
Then Humility takes its root
Underneath his foot.

Soon spreads the dismal shade
Of Mystery over his head;
And the Catterpillar and Fly,
Feed on the Mystery.

And it bears the fruit of Deceit,
Ruddy and sweet to eat;
And the Raven his nest has made
In its thickest shade.

This brilliant half-human, half-arboreal image culminates in the ironic naiveté of the concluding stanza, in which the humanness of the image is made manifest:

The Gods of the earth and sea,
Sought thro' Nature to find this Tree
But their search was all in vain:
There grows one in the Human Brain[.]

Here Blake sides with the deists' attack on mysterious religion. As in the deists' world view all that is dark and guileful is opposed to human nature. But Blake's long poems contain his most specific re-jection of sincerity as a self-sufficient ideal. To the extent that it is merely a natural manifestation of the heart, sincerity is inadequate to Blake's full ethical ideal. This we shall see more clearly when we turn to *Milton* and *Jerusalem*.

There is a remarkable juxtaposition of innocent honesty and

hypocritical deceit in *Visions of the Daughters of Albion*. Oothoon
addresses Theotormon, who has rejected her:

> Infancy, fearless, lustful, happy! nestling for delight
> In laps of pleasure; Innocence! honest, open, seeking
> The vigorous joys of morning light; open to virgin bliss,
> Who taught thee modesty, subtil modesty! child of night &
> > sleep
> When thou awakest. wilt thou dissemble all thy secret joys
> Or wert thou not, awake when all this mystery was disclos'd!
> Then com'st thou forth a modest virgin knowing to dissemble
> With nets found under thy night pillow, to catch virgin joy,
> And brand it with the name of whore; & sell it in the night,
> In silence. ev'n without a whisper, and in seeming sleep:
> Religious dreams and holy vespers, light thy smoky fires:
> Once were thy fires lighted by the eyes of honest morn
> And does my Theotormon seek this hypocrite modesty!
> This knowing, artful, secret, fearful, cautious, trembling
> > hypocrite.

> (Plate 6)

Oothoon as representative of open and innocent love laments the
acceptance by Theotormon of the Urizenic limitations on mankind:

> The moment of desire! the moment of desire! The virgin
> That pines for man; shall awaken her womb to enormous joys
> In the secret shadows of her chamber; the youth shut up from
> The lustful joy. shall forget to generate. & create an amorphous
> > image
> In the shadows of his curtains and in the folds of his silent
> > pillow.
> Are not these the places of religion? the rewards of continence?
> The self enjoyings of self denial? Why dost thou seek religion?
> Is it because acts are not lovely, that thou seekest solitude,
> Where the horrible darkness is impressed with reflections of
> > desire.

> (Plate 7)

Thus a kind of ultimate sincerity is full sexual release without guilt. Ultimate sincerity in another realm comes in the scene of resurrection at the end of "The Song of Los" when "all flesh naked stands" and men appear as they really are.

In the later, long poems, as Jean Hagstrum has noted, the vigorous, energy-oriented philosophy of Blake gives way to a milder emphasis.[8] In *Milton*, for example, the colossal conflict between Spectre and Emanation leads to the twin ideals of self-annihilation and forgiveness.

Harold Bloom's incisive definitions of Emanation and Spectre will help to relate those concepts to our larger topic: "An emanation is literally what comes into being from a process of creation in which a series of effluxes flow from a creator. As a created form an emanation can be male or female or both; either way it is opposed to the Spectre or shadow, a baffled creation or residue of self that has failed to emanate, to reach an outer but connected existence."[9] These definitions are important, for we should note that as Emanation is realized, the movement is from the inner being to full outward existence and action. This is the very movement of sincerity as Samuel Richardson understood it (see appendix). The attempt in Richardson is to express real, inner thoughts in outward action. Though much of what Richardson was doing would have seemed affectation to Blake, these very different authors do share some fundamental interests.[10]

Blake's expression of the real self consists in a form of disinterestedness, self-annihilation, as Milton makes clear to Satan:

Satan! my Spectre! I know my power thee to annihilate
And be a greater in thy place, & be thy Tabernacle
A covering for thee to do thy will, till one greater comes
And smites me as I smote thee & becomes my covering.

8. "William Blake Rejects the Enlightenment" in Northrop Frye, ed., *Blake: A Collection of Critical Essays* (Englewood Cliffs, N.J.: Prentice-Hall, 1966), pp. 149–50.

9. *Blake's Apocalypse: A Study in Poetic Argument* (1963; reprinted Garden City, N.Y.: Anchor–Doubleday, 1965), p. 210.

10. *The Letters of William Blake*, ed. Geoffrey Keynes (New York: Macmillan, 1956), p. 133. A sales catalogue entry of a lost letter says Blake "speaks in high praise of Mrs. Klopstock's Letters and says that Richardson has won his heart."

Such are the Laws of thy false Heavns! but Laws of Eternity
Are not such: know thou: I come to Self Annihilation
Such are the Laws of Eternity that each shall mutually
Annihilate himself for others good, as I for thee.
Thy purpose & the purpose of thy Priests & of thy Churches
Is to impress on men the fear of death; to teach
Trembling & fear, terror, constriction; abject selfishness
Mine is to teach Men to despise death & to go on
In fearless majesty annihilating Self, laughing to scorn
Thy Laws & terrors, shaking down thy Synagogues as webs
I come to discover before Heavn & Hell the Self righteousness
In all its Hypocritic turpitude, opening to every eye
These wonders of Satans holiness shewing to the Earth
The Idol Virtues of the Natural Heart, & Satans Seat
Explore in all its Selfish Natural Virtue & put off
In Self annihilation all that is not of God alone:
To put off Self & all I have ever & ever Amen

(Plate 38)

Though it is not within the scope of this essay to elucidate the
complexities of Blake's prophetic vision, it should be pointed out
that it is Imagination and Poetry by which Golgonooza is built.
Plate 41 of *Milton* makes this clear:

To bathe in the Waters of Life; to wash off the Not Human
I come in Self-annihilation & the grandeur of Inspiration
To cast off Rational Demonstration by Faith in the Saviour
To cast off the rotten rags of Memory by Inspiration
To cast off Bacon, Locke & Newton from Albions covering
To take off his filthy garments, & clothe him with Imagination
To cast aside from Poetry, all that is not Inspiration
That it no longer shall dare to mock with the aspersion of
                                                    Madness
Cast on the Inspired, by the tame high finisher of paltry Blots,
Indefinite, or paltry Rhymes; or paltry Harmonies.

These positions are restated in the magnificent plate 91 of *Jerusalem*,
only, it seems, with more vehemence:

I care not whether a Man is Good or Evil; all that I care
Is whether he is a Wise Man or a Fool. Go! put off Holiness
And put on Intellect: or my thundrous Hammer shall drive thee
To wrath which thou condemnest: till thou obey my voice[.]

Since poetry expresses the true humanity of man and that humanity is totally spiritual, in a sense poetry and the poet are first and last sincere. But Blake breaks with the doctrine of sincerity developed by his contemporaries on at least one important issue. He finds in the assumption of natural goodness an insidious self-righteousness or natural morality. Moving toward the doctrine of self-annihilation and forgiveness of sin,[11] Blake found Voltaire and Rousseau, among others, totally mistaken about the facts of human existence: "Rousseau thought Men Good by Nature; he found them Evil & found no friend. Friendship cannot exist without Forgiveness of Sins continually" (p. 199).

To the extent that sincerity is merely a natural manifestation of the heart, then, Blake rejected it as an ethical ideal. His revulsion against the excesses of violent revolution led him to reject war: "the Religion of Jesus, Forgiveness of Sin, can never be the cause of a War nor of a single Martyrdom," but self-righteousness, he understood, could and did cause war. Thus his remarkable statement, "All the Destruction therefore, in Christian Europe has arisen from Deism, which is Natural Religion" (p. 199).

Sincerity, for Blake, is not found in the natural man, but in the man possessed of faith and spiritual gifts, the man of four-fold vision. Ultimately, perhaps, Blake's sincerity is Imagination.

Though sincerity is a serious issue in Blake, his genius transforms that ideal as it transforms everything else. Yet the clear traces remain. Spontaneity, rejection of mysteries and deceit, and visions of a bright terrestrial paradise form the pattern of Blake's imaginative world.

---

11. Blake does not accept the usual notion of sin, as he explains in his description of the Last Judgment: "Forgiveness of Sin is only at the Judgment Seat of Jesus the Saviour where the Accuser is cast out. not because he Sins but because he torments the Just & makes them do what he condemns as Sin & what he knows is opposite to their own Identity" (p. 555).

WILLIAM WORDSWORTH

If we are to believe Professor David Perkins, Wordsworth's poetry may be called a "poetry of sincerity."[12] But if we consider the criteria used throughout this study to recognize poetry of sincerity, Wordsworth's poetry often seems deficient. Sincerity itself, for example, seems almost never to be a specific issue as it is in the poetry of so many others. Yet, qualities of sincere poetry may be deduced from a careful study of Wordsworth's poetry, as Professor Perkins has done. The reader who desires a full examination of Wordsworth's poetry of sincerity is referred to Perkins' study.

It will not, then, be useful to examine the poetry for assertions of sincerity or dramatic representations of the Jacob–Esau confrontation. I shall deal only briefly with the principal implications for sincerity in the poetry, and turn after that for a more detailed discussion to the preface to *Lyrical Ballads* and the *Essay Upon Epitaphs*.

If the problem of sincerity can be seen in terms of the conflict between the formal qualities of poetry and the "real" self of the poet, as it was in Gray, then sincerity is an important question in the rationale of Wordsworth's poetic as presented in some of his poems, particularly in book 1 of *The Prelude*.[13]

Though this is, in part, the conflict in the Puritan mind, Wordsworth's conception of self is very different from that of his Puritan forbears. Whereas liberal Puritans saw the inner light as a free gift of God (grace), Wordsworth sees the soul as only susceptible to the teaching of Nature. In its early years, the human soul reacts naturally, but without a desirable discipline, to the moral movements of the natural scene. Vulgar or animal joys, Wordsworth calls these reactions. This is sincere action to the extent that it is natural and thoughtless.

But as the soul retreats from its earliest association with Nature,

12. *Wordsworth and the Poetry of Sincerity* (Cambridge: Harvard University Press, 1964).
13. The following analysis is based principally on my reading of Book I of *The Prelude*.

the powers of memory, and, finally, imagination take up the slack where contact with Nature has abated.[14] Whereas the original source of vision had been extrinsic, impressing itself on the animal passions of the child, the ultimate source for the adult, far removed from such passion, is intrinsic. The new source of vision, then, is the developed adult soul, attuned by contact with experience to the realities of vision.

Thus, both in the immature, animalistic, state of the child and the properly attuned soul of the adult sincerity is a fact. At both stages man can confidently consult the promptings of his inner being. But the adult or child cut off from the educative process of Nature cannot rely on his inner light. Indeed, as city dweller and worldly man, his nature is so perverted that it is likely to prompt him to unvirtuous and guileful acts.

For Wordsworth, then, sincerity becomes the chief moral challenge to man. The principal function of his poetry, as he makes iteratively clear, is the renovation of the sensibilities of mankind. Men who cannot feel what they ought to feel, whether about Cumberland beggars, leech-gatherers, idiot boys, or asses, are the objects of Wordsworth's most palpable design. Put another way, the intended result of his efforts is to form in man a completely trustworthy, sincere, and virtuous soul.

Though he shows a more direct concern for sincerity in his *Essay Upon Epitaphs*, Wordsworth's most profound and original contribution to that doctrine is found in his 1800 and 1802 prefaces to *Lyrical Ballads*. In these prefaces Wordsworth brings together, as no one had done before him, the disparate elements of sincerity and unites them in a relatively coherent theory.[15]

14. See Lionel Trilling, "The Immortality Ode" in *The Liberal Imagination: Essays on Literature and Society* (New York: Viking, 1950) and James A. W. Heffernan, *Wordsworth's Theory of Poetry* (Ithaca: Cornell University Press, 1969), pp. 259–63. Heffernan seems to accept Trilling's view of the poem, but whether the substitution of maturity for the childish "best philosopher" is satisfactory, particularly in the Immortality Ode, remains, to my mind, an open question.

15. I am aware of the objections of inconsistency brought against the prefaces. Of particular importance recently is the attempt by James A. W. Heffernan to relegate the prefaces to secondary importance in Wordsworth's poetic theory. Though I agree with Mr. Heffernan's argument that Wordsworth works toward a Coleridgean theory of the imagination, I believe that his attempts to develop a poetry of sincerity

In the opening paragraph of the preface, he states the central issue involved in his poetic experimentation: "The first Volume of these Poems has already been submitted to general perusal. It was published, as an experiment, which, I hoped, might be of some use to ascertain how far, by fitting to metrical arrangement a selection of the real language of men in a state of vivid sensation, that sort of pleasure and that quantity of pleasure may be imparted, which a Poet may rationally endeavour to impart."[16] Here is the duality or contradiction implied in Thomas Gray's quest for sincerity: how far is it possible to express in poetic language the true feelings of men in a state of "vivid sensation"? But Wordsworth has accomplished what Gray could never have brought himself to do. He has chosen to use "the real language of men," thereby coming closer to the real feelings of men. The medium of poetry remains a problem, however, but Wordsworth, later in his essay, attempts to overcome this contradiction.

The point to emphasize is that, though Wordsworth has a high regard for poetry rightly understood, his chief concern is for what he calls "reality" and "truth" and the proper apprehension of them. The poet at last realizes "that no words, which his fancy or imagination can suggest, will be to be compared with those which are the emanations of reality and truth" (p. 50).

Thus it is reality, not formal excellence, which Wordsworth's labours bend toward. He, like most other proponents of sincerity, believes that there is a reality or truth to be apprehended. Once the source of that truth is found, whether it be Nature or an inner light, there is a resulting confidence in the sincere responses of human beings. That is, when the human consciousness finds its proper connection with truth, the emanations of that consciousness become eminently trustworthy. The particular human being is not Wordsworth's chief concern, then: rather it is the general truth to which particularity is linked and of which it is an expression. The same is

---

are his most important theoretical contribution. If Wordsworth backs off from the inconsistencies of his original position, in adopting a certain philosophical consistency, he loses much that is original and vital.

16. *The Literary Criticism of William Wordsworth*, p. 38. All succeeding references are to this edition.

true of a poem. The poem's pattern of imagery, its metrical order and other formal qualities are merely the particular expressions of a more significant general truth. "Its object is truth," he writes of poetry, "not individual and local, but general, and operative . . ." (p. 50). The faith that the link between general truth and particular consciousness is possible is as necessary to Wordsworth's theory as it is to all succeeding theories of imagination.

Wordsworth is in agreement with Plato, then, that poetry falls far short of reality in importance. For Wordsworth, however, poetry does what nothing else can do: it approximates the highest form of human experience for the purpose of presenting it to those who may not themselves be capable of such experience. Presumably, men cut off from truth could be guided toward it by constant intercourse with this kind of poetry.

This activist theory lies back of Wordsworth's concern for the "real language of men." Thus he is able to go a full step beyond Thomas Gray by adopting this sort of language. Wordsworth and Gray, we may assume for a moment, both had some vision of truth; but Wordsworth could at least attempt to use a language directly related to that truth. Gray, on the other hand, was kept from a truly sincere poetry by diction and form. Wordsworth very nearly solved the problem of diction and had only to contend with form.

To underscore the relationship between Wordsworth's preface and sincerity, I will show that the ideal presented in the preface bears an unmistakable resemblance to the pattern of motifs making up the sincere ideal:

1. A pastoral ideal, only incidentally neoclassical, but stressing the value of simplicity, is introduced. "Low and rustic life," Wordsworth writes, "was generally chosen, because in that condition, the essential passions of the heart find a better soil in which they can attain their maturity, are less under restraint . . ." (p. 41).

2. Far from viewing this simplicity as a grinding, limiting poverty of perspective, Wordsworth sees it as "less under restraint." Thus the leech-gatherer or the Cumberland beggar is free in a way that their more affluent fellow men are not. Thus in this, as well as in the more revolutionary attitudes of his early poetry, Wordsworth gives strong support to the ideal of liberty.

3. Spontaneity, perhaps the chief criterion of sincere poetry, is well-known in the context of Wordsworth's poetic theory. That "good poetry is the spontaneous overflow of powerful feelings" (p. 42), with or without the qualifications Wordsworth imposes on his remarks, is perhaps the primary commonplace of the sincere ideal in poetry.

4. Friendship, a key concept in the rhetoric of social change (note the revolutionary rhetoric of "citizen," "comrade," "brother") is a positive value in the preface. At the outset Coleridge is the assisting friend (p. 38), and we learn that "Several of my Friends are anxious for the success of these Poems" (p. 39). The friendship of sensibility, whether with Coleridge or Dorothy, is a significant unifying factor in such poems as *The Prelude* and "Tintern Abbey." This form of apostrophe is reminiscent of the eighteenth-century convention examined in earlier chapters.

5. Another aspect in which Wordsworth's poetic theory is analogous to patterns of sensibility is in the psychology of the poems themselves. "I should mention," he writes in the preface, "one other circumstance which distinguishes these Poems from the popular Poetry of the day; it is this, that the feeling therein developed gives importance to the action and situation, and not the action and situation to the feeling" (p. 43). This psychic movement in the poem is similar to the movement of sensibility in the psychology of Samuel Richardson's characters. The feeling begins the process by which action is realized. In other words, action presupposes feeling.[17]

6. Though Wordsworth carries no brief for science, his respect for truth or reality makes him recognize that science may indeed be intimately concerned with truth: "If the labours of Men of Science should ever create any material revolution, direct or indirect, in our condition, and in the impressions which we habitually receive, the Poet will sleep then no more than at present, but he will be ready to

17. It may seem odd, even to the careful reader, that I compare such seemingly different psychic movements as those of the characters' minds in Richardson's novels with Wordsworth's theory of response to a poem. But in the complexities of sensibility investigated here, psychic movement is not divided into categories. For Wordsworth, who moves back and forth between affective and expressive concepts, all would be combined in the unitary mind of nature. For Richardson, human nature would be the unifying factor.

follow the steps of the Man of Science, not only in those general in-direct effects, but he will be at his side, carrying sensation into the midst of the objects of the Science itself" (pp. 52–53). Thus poetry, as communicator of feeling, is the humanizing quality in truth.

7. In Wordsworth's distinction between dramatic poetry and that in which "the Poet speaks to us in his own person and character" (p. 53), the Platonic distinction between personation and pure narrative seems to be strictly observed. Here Wordsworth violates a cardinal rule of the New Criticism when he assumes that it is perfectly possible to speak in poetry in one's own voice. He has some reser-vations about this, of course, which become clear when he discusses the problems of metre. But his primary point that poetry is subservi-ent to an indefectible truth makes him believe that truth is not wholly ineffable.

8. Another point characteristic of sincere poets is to be found in Wordsworth's belief that poet and reader should follow their own lights in the creation and judgement of poetry. Thus corrections should never be made on the authority of "a few individuals or even of certain classes of men; for where the understanding of an Author is not convinced, or his feelings altered, this cannot be done without great injury to himself: for his own feelings are his stay and support, and, if he sets them aside in one instance, he may be induced to repeat this act till his mind loses all confidence in itself, and becomes utterly debilitated" (p. 59). And to this explanation Wordsworth adds the admonition "that the Reader ought never to forget that he is himself exposed to the same errors as the Poet . . ." (p. 59). This leads finally to the injunction to the reader "that in judging these Poems he would decide by his own feelings genuinely, and not by reflection upon what will probably be the judgment of others" (p. 61).

Thus the preface to *Lyrical Ballads* is the first cogent expression of a theory of poetry which had been developing in England since the seventeenth century. Wordsworth, despite Coleridge's asser-tions to the contrary, is the first poet to unite the theory and practice of sincerity in a satisfactory way. If the theory seems unsatisfactory at times, or inconsistent, we should remember that sincerity in its very nature cannot submit to logic. Indeed, when art and sincerity combine, they unite against logic. But under such conditions sensibility developed and flourished.

The *Essay Upon Epitaphs* contains Wordsworth's most explicit statement of sincerity as a poetic criterion. But though sincerity is a direct concern in these essays as it is not in the preface to *Lyrical Ballads*, the *Essay Upon Epitaphs* shows no theoretical advance over the preface.

In Essay 1 Wordsworth regards epitaphs much as Gray did in his Elegy:

> An Epitaph is not a proud Writing shut up for the studious; it is exposed to all, to the wise and the most ignorant; it is condescending, perspicuous, and lovingly solicits regard; it's story and admonitions are brief, that the thoughtless, the busy and indolent, may not be deterred, nor the impatient tired; the stooping Old Man cons the engraven record like a second hornbook;—the Child is proud that he can read it—and the Stranger is introduced by it's mediation to the company of a Friend: it is concerning all, and for all:—in the Church-yard it is open to the day; the sun looks down upon the stone, and the rains of Heaven beat against it. (p. 103)

But far from desiring a primitive expression of passion, Wordsworth asserts that in an epitaph "The passions should be subdued, the emotions controlled . . ." (p. 104), and goes on to advocate personation as a "tender fiction" suitable to elegiac sentiments (p. 104).

In Essay 2 Wordsworth establishes the criterion of sincerity on a moral basis:

> when a man is treating an interesting subject, or one which he ought not to treat at all unless he be interested, no faults have such a killing power as those which prove that he is not in earnest, that he is acting a part, has leisure for affectation, and feels that without it he could do nothing. This is one of the most odious of faults; because it shocks the moral sense, and is worse in a sepulchral inscription, precisely in the same degree as that mode of composition calls for sincerity more urgently than any other. (p. 107)

As he later points out, this involves a strict identification of literature with morals (p. 113). But what lurks behind this moral poetic is Wordsworth's conception of poetry as the handmaid of truth. In momentary despair, he laments the limitations of his contemporaries: "alas! ages must pass away before men will have their eyes open to the beauty and majesty of Truth, and will be taught to venerate Poetry no further than as she is a handmaid pure as her mistress—the noblest handmaid in her train" (p. 119). Since truth, then, is the object of poetry, it follows that a sincere high seriousness is to be maintained in all poetic effort.

To this end the language of poetry takes on an especial importance. What Wordsworth calls poetic diction cannot, by definition, have the direct connection with truth which words ought to have. In the final essay, he gives to the word a special status: "Words are too awful an instrument for good and evil, to be trifled with; they hold above all other external powers a dominion over thoughts. If words be not . . . an incarnation of the thought, but only a clothing for it, then surely will they prove an ill gift; . . " (p. 125). Finally, then, the necessity for sincerity becomes manifest in the power of language: "Language, if it do not uphold, and feed, and leave in quiet, like the power of gravitation or the air we breathe, is a counter-spirit, unremittingly and noiselessly at work, to subvert, to lay waste, to vitiate, and to dissolve" (p. 126).

Thus the language of sincerity, drawing sustenance from truth, leads men to understand truth. Other forms of language only subvert and distort. Language here is intermediate between man and truth and will be replaced in Wordsworth's later theory by a more Coleridgean conception of imagination serving the same function.[18]

Sincerity as a major issue is generally absent from Wordsworth's poetry. It does, however, provide the underlying moral base for the poetry and is a central principle in the theory. Sincerity's being absent as an issue would seem to result from a paradox peculiar to Wordsworth's genius. Since sincerity is taken for granted as a constant in the relationship of the poet to his poem, the question of

18. For examination of the development of Wordsworth's theory, see also W. J. B. Owen, *Wordsworth as Critic* (Toronto: University of Toronto Press, 1969).

sincerity as a possibility never arises. Sincerity is simply accepted as a fact, as it was not by earlier poets. In achieving this relative freedom from the threat of guile, Wordsworth enables himself to write the first truly "sincere" poetry. In this lies the great originality of his achievement.

Conclusion

Poetry, the familiar letter, autobiography and biography, and various religious forms contribute most significantly to the development of the sincere ideal. The novel becomes important largely through the achievement of Samuel Richardson, and the drama seems to have played a minor role.

Yet even the drama's minor role may not be insubstantial. Restoration drama, reacting to Puritan ideals, contains some direct attacks on sincerity. David Vieth makes precisely this point when he writes that "the hilarious comedy of the ending of *The Country Wife* turns upon the idea that civilized usages cannot exist without a certain amount of collective dissembling."[1] *The Plain Dealer* is another attempt by Wycherley to present a comic examination of the implications of sincerity. It is, as well, a conscious imitation of Molière's *Le Misanthrope*, in which the sincerity of Alceste is held up to ridicule.

In reacting against the Puritan sincere ideal, the Restoration drama attempts to restore a set of ideals that is classical, heroic, and sometimes obscenely masculine. The point of the obscenity and irreligion of the stage of this period is to blaspheme against the deposed ideals of the Commonwealth.

A reaction to this bold development came relatively swiftly. With Colley Cibber's *Love's Last Shift* (1696) the drama begins a profound shift to a pro-sincerity ethic and thus to a new version of Puritan morality. In *The Careless Husband* (1704), which considers the problem of sincerity on several levels, Lady Betty explains her modish philosophy to Lady Easy: "The men of sense, my dear, make the best fools in the world; their sincerity and good breeding

---

1. David M. Vieth, "Wycherley's *The Country Wife*: An Anatomy of Masculinity," *Papers On Language and Literature*, 2 (1966): 347. In *The Way of the World* (1700), Congreve questions the uses of deceit, and may be at the threshold of the sincere ideal.

throws 'em so entirely into one's power, and gives one such an agreeable thirst of using 'em ill, to show that power—'tis impossible not to quench it" (2, i, 64–68).[2] In such a society things are upside-down; for, as Pope observed, modern sincerity is the very reverse of what it has traditionally been. For Lady Betty sincerity is entirely out of style: "sincerity in love is as much out of fashion as sweet snuff; nobody takes it now" (3, i, 606–7). But when Sir Charles returns to virtue after "sincere reflection" (5, vii, 331), he is conscious of his need for a "sincere conversion" (5, vii, 337–38).[3] In *The Conscious Lovers*, Richard Steele, perhaps recalling Alceste and Manly, distinguishes between "rough sincerity" and an implied sentimental kind of which he seems to approve.[4]

Much later in the century Sheridan's *The School For Scandal* is a superb examination of the hypocrisy of a man of sentiment who affects sincerity. But this sensitive, sceptical probe into the super-ficiality of contemporary values and the sincere ideal in particular suggests how formidable an idea sincerity had become. The drama, by its very imitative nature, could not assume great influence in the positive development of sincerity. It is much more effective as an antidote, as in Sheridan's play. At best the drama reflects imperfectly some of the personal concerns which could be realized only in non-dramatic poetry.

We have come so far and through so many details that I shall summarize my findings in a brief, necessarily oversimplified, histori-cal sketch.

The Puritans' obsession with the sincerity of their religious con-victions led to an elaboration of thought and writing on the subject. At the same time, persecution led them to form tightly organized groups of fellow believers who shared the desire to return to what they believed was the pure, simple Christianity of the early Church. Since many Puritans during the period of the Commonwealth believed that their religious ideals could be made a reality for all Englishmen, optimism regarding society flourished for a time. With

2. George H. Nettleton and Arthur E. Case, eds., *British Dramatists From Dryden to Sheridan* (Boston: Houghton Mifflin, 1939), p. 408.
3. Ibid., p. 419, p. 435, p. 435.
4. Ibid. (1, i, 57), p. 443.

the failure of their cause, however, Puritans turned to a more private world to realize their ideals. Pre-eminent among these imaginative worlds was *Paradise Lost*. Some dissenters, like Isaac Watts, were willing to accept a return to monarchy and limit their idealism to religion and the improvement of morals.

After the accession of William and Mary and through the reign of Queen Anne, the improving stability of the religious situation resulted in a good deal of optimism among intellectuals for the betterment of society. The Society for the Reformation of Manners and other such groups discovered deficiencies in the social order for the purpose of remedying them. The success of British armed might on the Continent led to extravagantly idealistic hopes that a new and grand age of British freedom was at hand.

But reality never suffers such enthusiasm gladly. Social and political difficulties multiplied to drive many idealist poets to rural retreats, where they might, by means of imagination, set reality right. Poets were encouraged to come together as the Puritans had done. In the modest estates of Pope and Shenstone and the more elaborate ones of Ralph Allen and Lyttelton the best of a rural atmosphere combined with reasonable proximity to an urban area. In their suburban strongholds these poets sought first to clarify and substantiate the sincere ideal in broad social terms, and when they had failed in that, turned to a more limited conception of society. Finally, when even that society of friends failed to gratify, they turned to lonely self-investigation. As the internal ideal of sincerity seems unable to make an impact on external affairs, it becomes, increasingly, an internal force once again, governing personal religion and imagination. In the final extreme, in England and on the Continent, sincere art becomes the greatest and purest source of happiness.[5]

Many of the eighteenth-century authors we have studied were as revolutionary in their idealism as William Blake and the young Wordsworth. Freedom, their constant cry, meant the vague flight into sincerity and retreat from everything that denied man his

5. See, for example, Diderot's aestheticism, in Francis X. J. Coleman, *The Aesthetic Thought of the French Enlightenment* (Pittsburgh: University of Pittsburgh Press, 1971), p. 133.

humanity. There were many sources of such denial, all characterized by an absence of sincerity: the Roman Catholic Church,[6] the affected manners of France, the tyranny of foreign governments, the corruption of regal courts, the oppression by special interest, the injustice of the legal system, the grinding poverty of the lower classes, and slavery in America, to name the most important. Such poets as Thomson, Akenside, and Cowper, as well as Blake and Wordsworth, supported the revolutionary principles which opposed these abuses with a complex self-righteousness similar to that of the Puritans.

When I claim that sincerity and British nationalism were concurrent ideals, I assume that something as pervasive as a strong nationalism must have a coherent set of ideals to sustain it. Sincerity, in various forms, had such a sustaining effect.

The English ideal of plain-dealing common sense can be traced to the age of Elizabeth, if not earlier. Shakespeare, for all his distrust of sincerity, views his ideal Englishman (vide *Henry V*) as bluff and manly, in contradistinction to wheedling, effeminate Frenchmen. Indeed, the myth that plain Englishmen are because of their plainness superior to humanity on the Continent is recurrent in seventeenth-century English thought, and persists in later ages.

Honesty and plain dealing, assisted by the example of the great Roman satirists, rise to positions of eminence in the work of the two greatest neoclassical poets, Dryden and Pope. But sincerity, nourished by Puritan attitudes and a new sensibility, becomes the more dominant virtue in English culture and literature. This virtue (though the older ideals of plain dealing and honesty did not contradict it, and, indeed, were assimilated by it) was significant in creating the literate Englishman's image of himself. His supposed cultural superiority became a rationalization for the use of military power to dominate other nations and continents. Thus, sincerity may be said to have covered a multitude of sins.

If this was the case, however, other nations did not readily penetrate the fallacy. France and the German states during the eighteenth

6. The Kingsley–Newman controversy in the nineteenth century shows how deeply-felt English anti-Catholicism continued to be. See Newman's *Apologia Pro Vita Sua*.

and early nineteenth centuries followed the English excursion into sensibility. During this period most of the significant cultural ideas originated in England and were subsequently translated to the Continent. If sincerity is English in the main lines of its development, no Englishman went so far as Rousseau in proclaiming its pre-eminence.[7]

In England, political ambitions were on the wane by the middle of the eighteenth century. Collins and Gray, though their work retains a social dimension, are largely absorbed in their art. They may be the only eighteenth-century poets to face directly the problem of sincerity. But we must wait for Wordsworth for a full consciousness of all its implications.

There are few explicit statements regarding sincerity in the formal criticism of the eighteenth century. The true *loci* of sincere theory are the poems themselves, religious or quasi-religious writing,[8] and personal statements in letters, apologies, prefaces, and the like. Formal criticism is so tied to classical rhetorical theory, as P. W. K. Stone has demonstrated, that Wordsworth's "Preface to *Lyrical Ballads*" may be regarded as a revolutionary presentation of the first elaborate theory of sincerity.[9]

An interest in psychology, which was given impetus by the Puritans, was sustained by the authors who followed the sincere ideal. Since sincere poetry proves itself sincere by its spontaneity and spontaneity emanates from a consciously perfected, unironic, psychological state, its concerns are partly with the psychology of the mind that produces it.

But the sincere ideal does not end in solipsism. Indeed mythic conceptions of pastoral and prelapsarian worlds contribute greatly to the final vision. The poetic mind favours a free pastoral–spiritual existence for itself. The eighteenth-century imagination grasps these mythic conceptions more as abstracts or states of mind than as objective situations. Milton's lesson that "The mind is its own place" was well-understood by these poets.

7. Henri Peyre, *Literature and Sincerity* (New Haven: Yale University Press, 1963), pp. 79–110.

8. By this I mean in particular deist views of the universe.

9. P. W. K. Stone, *The Art of Poetry, 1750–1820* (New York: Barnes & Noble, 1967), pp. 100–3.

We may hypothesize about the conditions in eighteenth-century England which nourished the growth of sincerity as a moral and literary ideal.

First, a literature of sincerity requires a consciousness of the problem of sincerity. Writers must believe that sincerity is possible, but they must also believe that it is relatively difficult to attain. A survey of mankind from China to Peru will suggest that it is a rare virtue.

Second, every revolutionary idea must find an established ideal against which to assert itself. That ideal must be susceptible to extreme caricature. Thus sincerity paints certain aspects of neo-classicism as artificial and meretricious. But the object of attack, in addition to providing a convenient anti-ideal, usually sustains a revolutionary ideal in more positive ways. Neoclassicism, for example, in many cases provides or substantiates insights usually identified with sensibility.

For all these attempts to clarify the development of sincerity, the concept remains by its very nature shifting and indefinable. George Walker, F.R.S., finds the difficulty of sincerity in that it "is not so much a distinct virtue of itself, as a general quality which gives a stamp, a value, and a very being to all the virtues."[10] Walker then moves beyond the abstract idea of sincerity to its more concrete exemplar, the sincere man:

> The sincere man . . . in both relations [to God and man] is and must be he, and he alone, whose hand is the servant of his heart; whose soul revolts against dissimulation, and whatever prudence or humanity may bid him to conceal, who never assumes or pretends to what does not belong to him, never appears to the world other than what he is; who has a constant sense of what is decent, right and just, and in all the delicate actions of his life scorns on whatever account to turn aside from his upright path. In fine, to comprehend it in a few words, it is humanity in all its extent without guile or sinister view, and piety without respect of man; it is in all our intercourse with God or Man, with plainness and simplicity to do that which

10. *Sermons on Various Subjects* (London, 1808), 3, 76–77.

conscience and the better affections of human nature pre-
scribe.[11]

Perhaps finally the primary difficulty faced by the student of
sincerity is that it refuses to be a static concept. Walker is right when
he turns from the ideal to the man who exemplifies it. For the importance of sincerity lies not only in that it marks a transition from
the fixed moral concepts of neoclassicism to the free aspiration of the
Romantic age, but also that it permits man to assert his superiority
over moral codes. It tends to make man the measure of all things.

The sincere ideal implied a bold assessment of man's ability to
stand against the troubles of life and to prosper in doing so. It
implied as well that the revelation of man's inner being was something worthy of celebration. As George Walker puts it: "In all the
social intercourses of life, in all the endearing ties which bind man to
man, it is the heart which we are in quest of; if we find not this,
neither professions nor services are of any sterling value; they excite
no gratitude, no affection, they touch no fellow string, they disgust,
they offend."[12] Thus in the power of his own sincerity man controls
the moral code which had, in an earlier age, controlled him. "It is
not enough to say of sincerity that it is an honourable character of
man," Walker writes, "it is that quality without which he can have
nothing honourable."[13]

11.Ibid., 3, 77–78.   12.Ibid., 3, 77.   13.Ibid., 3, 95–96.

Sincerity, a generous and intrepid frankness, will still be found to occupy perhaps the first place in the catalogue of human virtues.

William Godwin

The Novel of Sincerity

Sincerity in the novel is a problem which takes second place in difficulty only to sincerity in the drama. With the tradition that the lyric permitted the poet to speak in his own voice exerting ample influence, poetry and sincerity could be reasonably linked. The distinction between narrative and lyric is fairly easy to make, even when both modes function in the same poem.

In the novel, where the narrative is understood to be a fiction, even when a pretence to historical truth is made by the narrator, the question of genetic sincerity is irrelevant. The sincerity of Moll Flanders and Robinson Crusoe is a relevant question only within their respective fictional worlds. The narrator of *Tom Jones* may be Henry Fielding's idealized version of himself as learned, urbane, and witty author; but to ask if he is the "real" Henry Fielding is to beg several questions.

The drama is by its very nature imitative: everything is masks or mime, hardly promising soil for the cultivation of sincerity. If we are deluded into searching out sincerity in the drama, we shall look for characters who are spokesmen for the playwright, or for actors who play their roles "with sincerity."

As in much of the poetry of the eighteenth century, the fiction of sincerity treats the ideal in narrative form. Thus the only sensible perspective from which to discuss sincerity in the novel is whether the characters and / or the narrator promote the ideal in an explicit way. Whereas poetry and the familiar letter might raise the question of genetic sincerity, the novel shares the didactic function of other moralistic forms. It delineates sincerity, shows how it functions in real-life dramatic situations, and, by such example, the reader is encouraged to adopt the ideal.

Though a majority of eighteenth-century novels serve moralistic purposes, those of Samuel Richardson (particularly his first and last, *Pamela* and *Sir Charles Grandison*), are associated with the promotion of the sincere ideal.

Richardson was himself concerned about sincerity, as his correspondence with Aaron Hill reveals.[1] Richardson was not only an expert on the psychology of others; he often reflected on his own behaviour, as in this part of a letter to Lady Bradshaigh: "I am always jealous of suffering in the Opinion of my Readers, when we come into personal Conversation—And why?—Because the Simplicity of my Character (I hope I may say so) and the Frankness of my Communicativeness, lay me open all at once, and must convince the new Acquaintance that they had thought too highly of me, by their Reading. I design not either Affectation or Reserve; and, if I appear to have Shyness, it is owing more to my native Awkwardness, than to Design."[2]

Simplicity of character and "frankness of heart,"[3] Richardson's personal concerns, are transferred to his heroines, Pamela, Clarissa, and Harriet Byron. The virtues of women, as represented in the novels, are not limited to women, but seem appropriate for adoption by men as well. Mr. B., who is converted by Pamela to her ideals, in this respect anticipates Sir Charles Grandison, who unites manly courage and strength with the "feminine" moral ideals of Pamela and Clarissa. These ideals centre around a strict requirement for the cultivation of a feeling heart and the exact representation of that heart in external actions, namely sincerity.

The critical concern with sex in Richardson's novels has been overdone. Particularly beside the point have been the attempts to psychoanalyse Richardson at a distance of two hundred years.[4] But more harmful than the dubious value of such analysis is that it obscures the real issues in his work. Women are his central characters because they represented a particularly oppressed group, whose excellences he knew at first hand and who were oppressed because

1. See Chapter 5, pp. 168–69.
2. *Selected Letters of Samuel Richardson*, ed. John Carroll (Oxford: Clarendon Press, 1964), p. 319.
3. Ibid., p. 319.
4. See Morris Golden, *Richardson's Characters* (Ann Arbor: University of Michigan Press, 1963).

and by means of their sexual difference. Since the object of male concern is sex, sexual virtue is at the dramatic centre of the novels, but the moral design of those novels includes much more.

Indeed, it may be said that sex, portrayed as deceitful and disruptive, is seen by Richardson as antithetical to the coherent ideal of sincere behaviour. Perhaps the most damaging accusation brought against Pamela, from her point of view, is that she is, in Mr. B.'s words, "an artful young Baggage."[5] The accusation of disguise and hypocrisy is made again and again, and it worries Pamela very much, as can be seen from her response to one such imputation: "I was out of Patience, then; Hold, good Sir, said I; don't impute Disguise and Hypocrisy to me, above all things; for I hate them both, mean as I am" (1, 70). Pamela's comment "mean as I am" asserts her right to virtue and a good conscience despite her low social position. It is the beginning of her moral revolution.

Pamela takes external appearance very seriously; indeed so seriously that clothing takes on symbolic significance.[6] Clothing and other externals ought to reflect one's true state. Thus, a person of humble station ought to wear humble clothing; neatness and cleanliness are ample recompense for a lack of elegance and mirror a plain and simple inner state. But men and women of high station, who are thus entitled to wear elegant clothing, ought to have a correspondingly fine inner state. In this context Pamela's reproach to Mr. B., "Let me ask you, Sir, if this becomes your fine Cloaths, and a Master's Station . . .?" (1, 88) assumes special significance. Mr. B. consistently violates the code of sincerity. Pamela's remarkable self-control, considering the pressures she undergoes, reflects her moral balance. On the other hand, Mr. B.'s excesses, both with Pamela and during his earlier life, mirror the chaos of his inner state.

Pamela does, of course, resort to guile herself; but it is in self-defence. In order to leave notes for Mr. Williams, Pamela is forced to distract Mrs. Jewkes: "And so we chatted on about the Town, to deceive her. But my Deceit intended no Hurt to any body" (1, 162).

5. *The Novels*, 1, 26. All citations to Richardson's novels are by volume and page number.
6. See Carey McIntosh, "Pamela's Clothes," *English Literary History*, 35 (1968): 75–83.

It is important to note that Pamela does feel guilt about her "tricks" and so needs to justify them morally. Her sexual virtue is secure; no serious issue is involved there.[7] But the question of deceit is another matter, and in this Pamela is vulnerable. To signify the importance of the issue of guile, Richardson has Pamela and Mrs. Jewkes plan to angle for fish on the following day.

Fishing and deceit were regularly connected in eighteenth-century literature. James Thomson in *Spring* playfully suggests the implications of the fishing metaphor:

> now is the time,
> While yet the dark-brown water aids the guile,
> To tempt the trout . . .
>
> (382–83)[8]

> There throw, nice judging, the delusive fly;
> And, as you lead it round in artful curve,
> With eye attentive mark the springing game.
>
> (408–10)

Richardson shows us, however, that for him the fishing metaphor has most serious implications. Pamela hooks a carp, reeling it in under the direction of Mrs. Jewkes, but having landed it, casts it back into the pond. Then she sees the fish's state as representative of her own:

> O the Pleasure it seem'd to have, to flounce in, when at Liberty!—Why this? says she. O Mrs. *Jewkes*! said I, I was thinking this poor Carp was the unhappy *Pamela*. I was likening you and myself to my naughty Master. As *we* hooked and deceived the poor Carp, so was I betrayed by false Baits; and when you said, Play it, Play it, it went to my Heart, to think I should sport with the Destruction of the poor Fish I had betray'd; and I could not but fling it in again: And did you not

7. Robert A. Donovan, "The Problem of Pamela, or, Virtue Unrewarded," *Studies in English Literature, 1500–1900*, 3 (1963): 382–83. Reprinted in Donovan's *The Shaping Vision: Imagination in the English Novel from Defoe to Dickens* (Ithaca: Cornell University Press, 1966).
8. *The Complete Poetical Works of James Thomson.*

see the Joy with which the happy Carp flounc'd from us? O!
said I, may some good merciful Body procure me my Liberty
in the same manner; for, to be sure, I think my Danger equal!
(1, 175)

Thomson, again in *Spring*, gives us an even more conventional
statement of the use of guile in the male–female relationship:

> Ah then, ye fair!
> Be greatly cautious of your sliding hearts:
> Dare not the infectious sigh; the pleading look,
> Downcast and low, in meek submission dressed,
> But full of guile. Let not the fervent tongue,
> Prompt to deceive with adulation smooth,
> Gain on your purposed will. Nor in the bower
> Where woodbines flaunt and roses shed a couch,
> While evening draws her crimson curtains round,
> Trust your soft minutes with betraying man.
> (973–82)

Opposed to the deceit of Mr. B., betraying man personified, is the
frankness, the openness of Pamela. When her master determines to
read her letters written to her parents, she counters: "Well, Sir, said
I, since you *will*, you *must* read them; and I think I have no Reason
to be afraid of being found insincere, or having, in any respect, told
you a Falshood; because, tho' I don't remember all I wrote, yet I
know I wrote my Heart; and that is not deceitful" (1, 314). Pamela is
confident here that in "writing to the moment" she has revealed her
true internal state.

Richardson is in *Pamela* delineating an ideal of sincerity, involving the strict correspondence of internal state and external action,
stated intention and actual intention, appearance and reality. The
novel presents an ideal of behaviour, complex and coherent, which
transcends social status and lends integrity to every individual who
practises it. In Richardson's imaginative world, this transcendent
virtue calls in question the hierarchy of wealth and position. Miss
Darnford of *Pamela*, Part 2, is quite specific on this point:

What an Example does this dear Lady [Pamela] set to all who

see her, to all who know her, and to all who hear of her! and
how happy are they who have the Grace to follow it!—What a
publick Blessing would such a Mind as hers be, could it be
vested with the Robes of Royalty, and adorn the Sovereign
Dignity! But what are the Princes of the Earth, look at them in
every Nation, and what have they been for Ages past, compar'd
to this Lady? *who acts from the Impulses of her own Heart, un-
aided, in most Cases, by any human Example.* In short, when I
contemplate her innumerable Excellencies, and that Sweetness
of Temper, and universal Benevolence, which shine in every
thing she says and does, I cannot sometimes help looking upon
her in the Light of an Angel, dropp'd down from Heaven, and
receiv'd into bodily Organs, to live among Men and Women,
in order to shew what the first of the Species was design'd to
be. (4, 53-54)

From this we can gain credence for Aaron Hill's remark that
Richardson's work represented an effort to "unite all mankind in
one sentiment!"[9] This sentiment is formed, of course, where
all the streams of sensibility converge; and that is the sincere
heart.

In *Sir Charles Grandison* most of the action, at least early in the
book, is subordinated to the delineation of the sincere ideal. Much
of the novel before Sir Charles is free to propose marriage to Harriet
concerns itself with the sincerity or lack of it in the chief characters.
True sincerity is distinguished from false when we see Greville's
attempt "to build up a merit for sincerity or plaindealing, by saying
free things . . ." (13, 29) contrasted with Sir Charles's combination
of unreserve and politeness (13, 222). Greville is hypocritical, but
Sir Charles's spontaneity is a virtue.

It is no coincidence that a masquerade is the occasion for Harriet's
abduction by Sir Hargrave Pollexfen. Though Richardson shared
Fielding's disapproval of masquerades as occasions of licentious
behaviour and assignations, the disguise motif seems equally significant. In a world in which the internal state should be mirrored in the
external, costumes, disguises, and masquerades are symbolic of

9. Samuel Richardson, *Correspondence*, I, 70-71.

false seeming. Thus Harriet's bad judgement in consenting to attend a masquerade is made clear by the fact that she is almost undone by it. Her shame at making such a bad moral choice is intensified by her heroic rescue by Sir Charles:

> Do you wonder, Lucy, that I cannot hold up my head, when I recollect the figure I must make in that odious Masquerade-habit, hanging by my clasping arms about the neck of such a young gentleman? Can I be more effectually humbled than by such a recollection? And yet is not this an instance of that *false shame* in me, to which Sir Charles Grandison is so greatly superior?
> Surely, surely, I have *had* my punishment for *my* compliances with this foolish world. False glory, and false shame, the poor Harriet has never been totally above. Why was I so much indulged? . . . But surely, I was past all *shame*, when I gave my consent to make such an appearance as I made, among a thousand strangers, at a Masquerade. (13, 279–80)

The masquerade, as the world in microcosm, is the very antithesis of the frank, sincere ethic represented by Sir Charles and aspired to by Harriet.

During her account of her own disgrace at the masquerade, Harriet begins to show regard for Sir Charles and his sister, Charlotte Grandison. The issue of Sir Charles's possible reserve in failing to confide completely in his sister is raised; and Harriet sees this reserve as a flaw in an otherwise perfect character: "Now this reserve to such a sister, and in points that she thinks it imports her to know, is what I do not like in Sir Charles. A *friend* as well as a sister! ought there to be a secret on one side, when there is none on the other? Very likely, he would be as reserved to a wife: And is not marriage the highest state of friendship that mortals can know? And can friendship and reserve be compatible? Surely, No" (13, 281). Here Harriet shows that even this early she has her eye on Sir Charles as a possible husband. But this question of reserve, which may seem a punctilio to the modern reader, is a serious moral problem in this book. Part of the difficulty for Harriet at this stage is that Sir Charles represents a new and not fully understood ideal. As Harriet learns from Charlotte, Sir Charles "lives to himself, and to his own heart, rather than to the opinion of the world" (13, 278).[10]

A few pages later, Harriet begins to put things in proper perspective, once again reflecting on the probable superiority of Sir Charles's moral state to her own: "But I fansy I am acting the world, in its malevolence, as well as impertinence: That world, which thinks itself affronted by great and superior merit; and takes delight to bring down exalted worth to its own level. But, at least, you will collect from what I have written, an instance of my *impartiality*; and see, that, tho' bound to Sir Charles by a tie of gratitude which never can be dissolved, I cannot excuse him, if he be guilty of a diffidence and reserve to his generous sister, which she is above shewing to him" (13, 283). By seeing herself at one with the malevolent world, a deficiency of character revealed by participation in the masquerade, Harriet is on the way to full conversion to a new ethic. Though her vital concern for Sir Charles's moral state is motivated by her incipient affection for him, that growing love proves her desire to attain the better moral state which he represents and which, also, is natural to her. Harriet must, however, face and overcome a further irony. Although a goodness characterized by sincerity is the object of her feelings, convention dictates that she express those feelings with delicacy:

> Nothing, surely, can be delicate, that is not true, or that gives birth to equivocation. . . .
>
> And are there some situations, in which a woman must conceal her true sentiments? In which it would be thought immodesty to speak out?—Why was I born with a heart so open and sincere? But why, indeed, as Sir Charles has said . . . should women be blamed, for owning modestly a passion for a worthy and suitable object? Is it, that they will not speak out, lest, if their wishes should not be crowned with success by *one* man, they should deprive themselves of a chance to succeed with *another*? Do they not propose to make the man they love, happy?—And is it a crime to acknowledge, that they are so well

10. See also Sir Charles to Dr. Bartlett: "I live to my own heart; and I know (I think I do) that it is not a bad one. . . ." (14, 286).

disposed to a *worthy* object? A *worthy* object, I repeat; for that is what will warrant the open heart. What a littleness is there in the custom that compels us to be insincere! (14, 275–76)

But throughout the long and drawn-out difficulty over Sir Charles's obligation to Clementina, it is Harriet's sincerity that is valued. Charlotte makes this clear early in volume five: "But, Harriet, I write to charge you not to increase your own difficulties by too much parade: Your frankness of heart is a prime considera- tion with him [Sir Charles]. He expects not to meet with the *girl*, but the *sensible woman*, in his address to you" (17, 124). This key phrase, "frankness of heart," is repeated by Sir Charles in one of his freer moments with Harriet: "My *noble* Harriet! said the generous man—Frankness of heart . . . is *her* characteristic. She means all she says; and will perform more than she promises" (18, 154).

The exact correspondence between internal and external states is revealed in several other important metaphors, which provide an insight into the rationale of sensibility. Though natural endowment may be of some importance, one's inner state of mind must be a cultivated one, susceptible of education and taste. Such cultivation is often determined by Richardson's own bourgeois neo-Platonism: the human face expresses inner virtue. When Sir Charles introduces Harriet to Dr. Bartlett, he makes it clear that "Were there fifty Ladies here, my good Dr. Bartlett, whom you had never seen before, you would, I am sure, from the character you have had of Miss Byron, be under no difficulty of reading that character in this young Lady's face." Harriet's response is equally gratulatory: "I reverence . . . good Dr. Bartlett. I borrow Sir Charles's thought: The character he has given you, Sir, is stamped in your countenance. I should have venerated you where-ever I had seen you" (13, 349).

The most ingratiating appearance is of little worth unless it cor- respond to the mind within. Sir Hargrave is wonderfully handsome, but his evil inner state renders him a hypocrite. Sweet-natured Emily Jervois, on the other hand, is "pretty" though her face is pitted with the smallpox. Ugliness is really a concomitant of evil: so Mrs. Jewkes and Colbrand in *Pamela* are excessively ugly to Pamela's mind until they merit by their deeds more sympathetic appraisal.

There is a progression in Richardson's novels toward a more fully realized sincere ideal. Richardson's change from use of the lower-class heroine Pamela to one of the middle class, Clarissa, and thence to Harriet Byron, who is relatively unaffected by social status, seems to point to his wanting to play down the question of class, which had plagued *Pamela* since its first appearance. Though his primary concern was moral issues and the sincere ideal, the problem of maids marrying their masters, a social question, became the object of controversy.

In *Clarissa*, on the other hand, since the issue of class is less important, the sincere virtue of the heroine is permitted to contrast with Lovelace's worldly guile and the hypocrisy of the Harlowe family. Richardson specifically points to the moral shallowness of society as it attempts to cover Clarissa's rape under the blessing of marriage. But neither she nor Richardson will allow their respective societies such an outrage. A social issue cannot be a substitute for a moral one. However, even under these circumstances, Lovelace's superior social position raises some difficult social questions.

In *Grandison*, although it is clear that Harriet's marriage to Sir Charles will bring her up the social ladder, her inferior social position is amply compensated for. Though Sir Charles makes it clear that her fortune means nothing to him, the generous contribution of Harriet's benefactor makes her financially independent.[11] Thus, in an atmosphere where social issues are almost non-existent, the moral ideal is able to develop fully.

If we feel prone to laugh at sentimental effusions in the novels of Richardson, we should know at least what we laugh at. When a heroine expresses herself on bended knee, she signifies her attempt to represent the intensity of her sincere inner feelings; in short, to establish a correlation between external behaviour and internal state. And so far are these "conventions" of sensibility from being insincere,[12] that their impetus comes from the purity of the sincere heart.

Though I do not believe I am claiming too much in calling

11. See 14, 26 and 18, 80 *ff*.

12. Brian W. Downs insists upon the insincerity of sensibility. *Richardson* (London: G. Routledge, 1928), especially pp. 150–92.

Richardson's fictional work "novels of sincerity," it is difficult to find novels by other authors, before or after, that qualify for the same title. Sincerity, in so far as it is an issue in other eighteenth-century novels, tends to merge with other aspects of sensibility more completely than in Richardson. Thus, though we might treat sincerity in Sterne's fiction, we would do so only at the risk of ignoring themes of greater significance.

Jean-Jacques Rousseau, who brings sincerity forthrightly into French literature, admired Richardson greatly and imitated his epistolary technique in *La Nouvelle Héloïse*. But that novel, assuming the existence of the virtue of sincerity, seldom makes it a specific issue. Rousseau, who shares Puritan objections to classical literature, approves only of useful moral literature and obeys his own injunction to sincerity in his *Confessions*.

To the extent that epistolary fiction survived, the novel of sincerity may be said to have survived. But as political issues replaced moral ones in the public eye, notions of sincerity, which had gradually become assimilated, were no longer objects of specific interest. By the end of the eighteenth century, sincerity in personal relationships was accepted as mere convention, and it was the Wordsworthian sincerity in literary composition that had a revolutionary flair.

Something of Richardson's zeal for sincerity reappears as theory in William Godwin's *Enquiry Concerning Political Justice*. Godwin resurrects the Puritan utopianism that kept faith with sincerity: "If a just and impartial character were awarded to all human actions, vice would be universally deserted, and virtue everywhere practised. Sincerity therefore, once introduced into the manners of mankind, would necessarily bring every other virtue in its train."[13]

Godwin's *Fleetwood: or, the New Man of Feeling* comes close to the Richardsonian novel of sincerity. The chief issue of the novel is how the evil Gifford is able to make the hero believe that the best of human beings are really guileful hypocrites. Thus when Fleetwood, as Gifford's victim, contemplates the imagined deceit of Mary, he indicts the entire world of Nature:

13. *Enquiry Concerning Political Justice and its Influence on Morals and Happiness*, ed. F. E. L. Priestley (Toronto: University of Toronto Press, 1946), I, 331.

Yes, said I, this is the very character of the world in which I
live. Storms, and tempests, and volcanoes are all beautiful or
majestic. Destruction smiles on us from every side. Nature herself is the great parent-hypocrite, deluding us onward from the
cradle to the grave. Her daughters do but inherit the same
treacherous smiles, and tempt us to damnation![14]

Suspecting Mary of loving Kenrick, Fleetwood searches her trinket
casket:

I no sooner opened this, than the first thing which met my eye
was the miniature of Kenrick. I looked stedfastly at it: I burst
into an idiot laugh. I examined it again. What lovely features;
what an air of integrity! said I.—No, it is not so! Do not you
see those lines of dissimulation and craft? Now I consider it
more attentively, I mark the devil peeping out from behind the
beauteous mask, and laughing in my face![15]

This is reminiscent of Edward Young's lines on Death the masquerader:

Death leads the dance, or stamps the deadly die,
Nor ever fails the midnight bowl to crown.
Gaily carousing to his gay compeers,
Inly he laughs to see them laugh at him,
As absent far; and when the revel burns,
When Fear is banish'd, and triumphant Thought,
Calling for all the joys beneath the moon,
Against him turns the key, and bids him sup
With their progenitors—he drops his mask,
Frowns out at full: they start, despair, expire.[16]

When at last Fleetwood discovers what a Iago Gifford has been to
him, he employs once again the image of the mask: "Gifford,
Gifford, if in reality you have been playing a traitor's part, it is time
you should drop the mask!"[17] A later observation introduces the

14. *Fleetwood: or, the New Man of Feeling* (1805), 3, 159–60.
15. Ibid., 3, 204–5.   16. *Night Thoughts*, 5, 869–78.   17. *Fleetwood*, 3, 322.

devil once again: "The devil himself sometimes grows tired of the character of a deceiver, and appears in his true colours."[18]

But even knowing Godwin's high estimate of sincerity, it is difficult to see that virtue as the central issue in *Fleetwood*. As in Richardson's novels, complex questions of class, morality, and sensibility arise to defy the oversimplification of reduction to a single ideal. But I do not mean to oversimplify by stressing sincerity. Rather I hope to show that the concept enjoyed some prominence even before it took its important place in Romantic poetics.

18. Ibid., 3, 324.

Bibliography

This list provides full bibliographical information for works identified in the text or notes by short-title only.

AKENSIDE, MARK. *The Poetical Works*, ed. Alexander Dyce. Boston: Aldine Edition, 1854.

ANONYMOUS. *Retirement: A Divine Soliloquy*. London, 1722.

BLAKE, WILLIAM. *The Poetry and Prose*, ed. David V. Erdman. Garden City, N.Y.: Doubleday, 1965.

BROOKE, HENRY. *Universal Beauty, A Philosophical Poem in Six Books*. 1735.

COWPER, WILLIAM. *The Poetical Works*, ed. H. S. Milford. Oxford: Oxford Standard Authors, 1934.

————. *The Correspondence*, ed. Thomas Wright. 4 vols. London, 1904.

CRANE, RONALD S., ed. *A Collection of English Poems, 1660–1800*. New York and London: Harper & Brothers, 1932.

DANTE ALIGHIERI. *La Divina Commedia*, ed. Natalino Sapegno. 3 vols. Firenze: La Nuova Italia Editrice, 1968.

GRAY, THOMAS. *Correspondence*, ed. Paget Toynbee and Leonard Whibley. Oxford: Clarendon Press, 1935.

HILL, AARON. *The Works*. 4 vols. London, 1754.

HOADLY, BENJAMIN. *The Works*. 3 vols. London, 1773.

JOHNSON, SAMUEL. *Lives of the English Poets*, ed. George Birkbeck Hill. 3 vols. Oxford: Clarendon Press, 1905.

MILTON, JOHN. *Paradise Lost*, ed. Merritt Y. Hughes. New York: Odyssey Press, 1962.

PLATO. *The Republic*, trans. Allan Bloom. New York and London: Basic Books, 1968.

POPE, ALEXANDER. *The Twickenham Edition of the Poems*, ed. John Butt et al. 11 vols. London: Methuen, 1939–69. Volumes cited in this book are: John Butt, ed. *Imitations of Horace*. London: Methuen, 1953 and James Sutherland, ed. *The Dunciad*. London: Methuen, 1963.

———. *The Correspondence*, ed. George Sherburn. 5 vols. Oxford: Clarendon Press, 1956.

RICHARDSON, JONATHAN. *Morning Thoughts or Poetical Meditations*. London, 1776.

———. *The Works*. London, 1792. This is vol. 6 (Supplement) to George Vertue and Horace Walpole, *Anecdotes of Painting in England*. Strawberry Hill, 1765–71.

RICHARDSON, SAMUEL. *The Novels*. 18 vols. Oxford: Shakespeare Head Edition, 1929–31.

———. *Correspondence*, ed. Anna Laetitia Barbauld. 6 vols. London, 1804.

SHAFTESBURY, ANTHONY ASHLEY COOPER, The Third Earl of. *Characteristics of Men, Manners, Opinions, Times*, ed. John M. Robertson. 2 vols. 1900; reprinted Indianapolis and New York, 1964.

SHENSTONE, WILLIAM. *The Works in Verse and Prose*. 2 vols. London, 1773.

THOMSON, JAMES. *The Complete Poetical Works*, ed. J. Logie Robertson. Oxford: Oxford Standard Authors, 1908.

WATTS, ISAAC. *Works*. 6 vols. London, 1753.

WORDSWORTH, WILLIAM. *The Literary Criticism*, ed. Paul M. Zall. Lincoln, Neb.: University of Nebraska Press, 1966.

YOUNG, EDWARD. *The Complete Works, Poetry and Prose of the Rev. Edward Young, LL.D.* 2 vols. London, 1854.

———. *Conjectures on Original Composition*, ed. Edith J. Morley. Manchester: Manchester University Press, 1918.

Index

Abney, Sir Thomas, 56
Abrams, M.H., 5n, 76
Addison, Joseph, 101, 127–30
Aeschylus, 193
Aitken, George A., 50n, 136n, 203
Akenside, Mark, 12, 61, 71, 101–18, 120, 121, 122, 123, 124, 128, 179, 207, 217, 218, 230, 239, 282; "Hymn to Science," 104, 117; Odes, 116–18; *The Pleasures of Imagination*, 101–16, 192
Allen, Ralph, 281
American Revolution, 251
Andrewes, Lancelot, 62
Anne, Queen, 281
Aristotle, *Poetics*, 215, 216
Arnold, Matthew, 3
Atterbury, Francis, 65
Ault, Norman, 140
Austen, Lady, 256

Bacon, Francis, 259–60, *The New Atlantis*, 18
Bailey, Margery, 172n
Bangorian Controversy, 65–66
Barnes, Djuna, *Nightwood*, 169
Bate, W.J., 1, 7n, 192, 231n, 235n
Baugh, Albert C., 212n
Baxter, Richard, 26, 39, 40, *Poetical Fragments*, 28–31; *Reliquiae Baxterianae*, 36; *The Saints' Everlasting Rest*, 31
Beattie, James, 237, 238–39, "Epistle to Blacklock," 239; *The Minstrel*, 238, 251
Beer, John, 260
Berkeley, Bishop George, 4, 234
Bethel, Hugh, 143
Blacklock, Thomas, 237, "On the Death of Mr. Pope," 239, 240
Blackmore, Richard, 53, 81

Blackwell, Thomas, *An Enquiry into the Life and Writings of Homer*, 96–97
Blair, Hugh, 237, 240
Blake, William, 40, 73, 259–68, 281, "The Couch of Death," 261; "The Human Abstract," 263; *Jersualem*, 261, 264, 267–68; *Milton*, 59, 261, 264, 266–67; "To Nobodaddy," 261, 262; *Poetical Sketches*, 261; "A Poison Tree," 263; "Proverbs of Hell," 260; "Samson," 261; "then She bore Pale desire," 261; "Silent Silent Night," 261; *Songs of Experience*, 261, 262; *Songs of Innocence*, 262; "The Song of Los," 266; *Visions of the Daughters of Albion*, 265
Blount, Charles, 70
Blount, Martha, 147
Bloom, Harold, 137n, 189n, 266
Boileau, Nicolas Despréaux, 233n
Bond, Donald F., 127
Book of Common Prayer, 44
Boswell, James, 232n, 236
Bradshaigh, Lady, 288
Brewster, Dorothy, 165n
Bronson, Bertrand, 220, 235n
Brooke, Henry, 119–24, *The Fool of Quality*, 120; *Universal Beauty*, 120–24, 135
Brown, Stuart Gerry, 235n
Bunyan, John, 36, *Grace Abounding*, 33, 37, 38; *Pilgrim's Progress*, 37
Burns, Robert, 188, 237, 239
Burton, Henry, 33, 37, 40, 49, "Autobiography," 34–35
Bush, Douglas, 199n
Butt, John, 137

Camden, Carroll, 137n, 138n, 236n
Candour, 104

Carroll, John, 288n

Case, Arthur E., 280n

Catharsis, 189

Cato, 91, 132

Cervantes, Miguel de, 198

Charles II, 13

Chaucer, Geoffrey, 1, 190

Chesterfield, Philip Dormer Stanhope, Earl of, 170

"Chevy-Chase," ballad of, 127

Cheynel, Francis, 65

Chillingworth, William, *The Religion of Protestants a Safe Way to Salvation*, 64–65

Church of England, 66, 113, 155–56, 232

Cibber, Colley, 140, *The Careless Husband*, 279; *Love's Last Shift*, 279

Cicero, 14, 17, 141

Cincinnatus, 91

Clap, Roger, 32

Classical republicans, 16, 93

Clifford, James L., 137n

Cohen, Ralph, 83, 85n, 93, 133

Coleman, Francis X.J., 281n

Coleridge, S.T., 116, 164, 273, 274, "Dejection: An Ode," 131

Collins, William, 189–202, 207, 230, 239, 253, 283, *Odes on Several Descriptive and Allegoric Subjects*, 189–99; "The Manners, An Ode," 197, 199, 202; "Ode to Evening," 195, 197; "Ode to Fear," 189, 193–94; "Ode to Liberty," 196; "Ode to Mercy," 196; "Ode to Peace," 197; "Ode to Pity," 189, 192–93; "Ode on the Poetical Character," 194–95; "Ode on the Popular Superstitions," 128, 199, 219; "Ode to Simplicity," 194; "Ode, Written in the beginning of the Year 1746," 196; "The Passions, An Ode for Music," 198; *Persian Eclogues*, 219; "Verses Address'd to Sir Thomas Hanmer," 191–92

Congreve, William, 142, *The Way of the World*, 279n

Comenius, 17

Contarini, Cardinal Gasparo, 17

Cowley, Abraham, 54, 232, 257

Cowper, William, 86, 152, 243–57, 282, *Conversation*, 249; "Delia poems," 244; "Love Abused," 245; *The Progress of Error*, 250; "On Reading . . . Charles Grandison," 247; *Table Talk*, 252; *The Task*, 244, 245, 246, 247, 255, 256, 257; "Verses Supposed to be Written by Alexander Selkirk," 252

Craig, James, 243

Crane, R.S., 130n

Cromwell, Henry, 137, 139

Cromwell, Oliver, 65

Cust, Lionel, 157n

Daiches, David, 236n, 237, 242, 243

Daniel, Samuel, 219

Dante: *Inferno*, 13, 43–44

Davie, Donald, 2n

Davies, Godfrey, 33n

Davies, J.G., 261n

Dearnley, Moira, 51n

Defoe, Daniel, 162, *Robinson Crusoe*, 16n

Deism, 69–124, 174–76, 179, 180

Delany, Paul, 31n

D'Emillianne, Gabriel, 20

De La Pillonniere, Francis, 64n

Dennis, John, 53, 81, 145

Descartes, René, 70

Dickens, Charles, 52

Diderot, Denis, 281n

Doddridge, Philip, 29, 52, 134

Dodington, George Bubb, 95

Dodsley, Robert, 24, 209

Dodsley Collection, 217

Doherty, F., 219–20

Donne, John, 27, 105

Donovan, Robert A., 290n

Downs, Brian, 296n

Dryden, John, 218, 282, Anne Killigrew Ode, 233n; *Eleonora*, 233

Duck, Stephen, 156

Dury, John, 17

Dyce, Alexander, 101n

Dyche, Thomas, 104

Edwards, Thomas R., 137n, 138

Ehrenpreis, Irvin, 138

Elioseff, Lee Andrew, 128n

Eliot, George, 171–73
Elton, G.R., 4n
Empiricism, 119–20
Enthusiasm, 60
Epicureanism, 14
Erastian ideal, 61
Esau, 14
Euripides, 193, *Suppliant Women*, 10
Ewing, George W., 69

Fairclough, H. Rushton, 10n, 13n
Falconer, William, 237, *The Demagogue*, 239
False surmise, 131
Familiar letter, the, 141–43, 234
Fergusson, Robert, 237, 239
Fielding, Henry, 292, *Shamela*, 169; *Tom Jones*, 287
Fink, Zera, 16n
Fox, George, 20, 63, 187, *Journal*, 38–39
Frank, Joseph, 19n, 20
Fraser, Russell, 40n
French Revolution, 251
Friedman, Arthur, 216n
Frye, Northrop, 110, 266n
Funeral elegy, 233–34
Fussell, Paul, 234

Gay, John, 5, 13n, 145, *Rural Sports*, 23
Gay, Peter, 12n
Gentleman's Magazine, The, 66
George I, 61
George II, 60, 66, 164
Gerard, Alexander, 237
Gilfillan, George, 239n
Glossographia Anglicana Nova, 104
Godwin, William, 262, 286, *Enquiry Concerning Political Justice*, 297; *Fleetwood*, 297–99
Golden, Morris, 288n
Goldgar, Bertrand A., 165n
Goldsmith, Oliver, 218, 219, *The Monthly Review*, 216
"Good old cause," 21
Goodwin, Thomas, 32–33
Goodwin, Thomas, Jr., 33n
Gordon riots, 21
Gosse, Edmund, 215n

Grainger, James, "Solitude," 251
Grave-yard school of poetry, 131, 182
Gray, Thomas, 12, 131, 142, 202, 203, 205, 212, 215–31, 269, 271, 272, 275, 283, *The Bard*, 215, 224, 230; "Elegy . . . in a Country Church-yard," 226–30; "Ode on a Distant Prospect of Eton College," 222–23; "Ode on the Spring," 220–21, 223; *The Progress of Poesy*, 225; "Sonnet on the Death of West," 223–24
Greene, Donald, J., 235n
Grene, David, 10n

Hagstrum, Jean, 266
Haight, Gordon S., 171n
Haller, William, 17n, 19n, 31n, 33n, 34n
Hammond, James, 205
Harrington, James, 17
Hartford, Countess of, 95
Hartley, David, *Observations on Man*, 24
Hartlib, Samuel, 17, *A Description of . . . Macaria*, 18–19
Hartman, Geoffrey H., 131n
Havens, R.D., 194n
Hazard, Paul, 73
Heffernan, James A.W., 270n
Herbert, George, 27, 29–30, 105
Hendrickson, J.R., 220n
Hickes, George, 61
Hill, Aaron, 78–80, 87, 140, 142, 146, 162–71, 288, 292, Pope–Hill Controversy, 165–68; Hill family, 168–69, "Advice to the Poets," 163; preface to *The Creation*, 162, 165; *The Creation*, 167; "The Excursion of Fancy," 163; *The Northern Star*, 165; "The Transport," 162
Hill, G.B., 232n
Hilles, F.W., 137n, 172n, 189n
Hobbes, Thomas, 80, 249
Hoadly, Archbishop John, 60
Hoadly, Benjamin (Jr.), 60
Hoadly, Bishop Benjamin, 60–67, 113, 115, 117, 151, 155, "Preservative Against the Principles and Practices of the Non-jurors," 61, 63; "Sermon Preached Before the King," 63;

"Sermon on St. Paul's Behaviour towards the Civil Magistrate," 62
Hoadly, John, 60
Hogarth, William, 153
Home, John, 199, 200, 201, *Douglas*, 236
Homer, 11, 76, 96–97, 98, 153, *Iliad*, 9–10; *Odyssey*, 10
Hooke, Robert, 119
Horace, 14, 204, 217n, 233n, *Ars Poetica*, 10, 57, 255
Howe, John, 31
Hume, David, 236, 237
Hurd, Bishop Richard, 216

Imagination, 270, 272, Coleridgean conception of, 276
Imitation, 11, 230

Jacob, 14, 15
Jago, Richard, *Edge-Hill*, 212–13
James II, 61
Jesus, 15, 38, 42
Job, Book of, 82
Johnson, Samuel, 4, 13n, 52, 130, 203, 213, 231–36, 237, "On the Death of Dr. Robert Levet," 234; "Life of Cowley," 231, 232–33, 234; "Life of Hammond," 233n; "Life of Milton," 233; "Life of Shenstone," 212; "Life of Waller," 234; *Rambler*, 231; *Rasselas*, 231; *Vanity of Human Wishes*, 197
Jones, Frank William, 10n
Jones, R.F., 119, 260n
Jones, William P., 133n
Jonson, Ben, 152
Jordan, W.K., 17n
Joyce, James, 214
Juvenal, 14, "Third Satire," 204

Kames, Henry Home, Lord, 240–43, *Loose Hints Upon Education*, 243
Keats, John, 107, 199
Ken, Bishop Thomas, 12
Keynes, Geoffrey, 266
Kingsley, Charles, 282n
Kit-Kat Club, 80
Klopstock, Mrs., 266n
Korshin, Paul J., 12n, 50n

La Rochefoucauld, François, 6th Duc de, 8
Lattimore, Richmond, 9n, 10n
Laud, Archbishop William, 33, 62
Lavater, Johann Caspar, 259
Law, William, 65, 155, 244
Leasowes, 214
Lesage, Alain René, 198
Levellers, the, 19–20
Lilburne, John, 19, 20, 33, 36, 37, 49, "Autobiography," 34
Lincoln, J.L., 217n
Lintot, Bernard, 165
Locke, John, 64, 69–70, 72, 243, *Letter Concerning Toleration*, 70; *The Reasonableness of Christianity*, 63–64, 69
Longinus, 128
Lovejoy, Arthur O., 5
Lowth, Robert, *Lectures on the Sacred Poetry of the Hebrews*, 81, 136
Lucretius, 14
Luxborough, Henrietta Knight, Lady, 202, 203
Lyttelton, George, 209, 281

Macaulay, G. C., 237n
Machiavelli, Niccolo, 17
McIntosh, Carey, 289n
Mack, Maynard, 16n, 137
MacKenzie, Henry, 237
McKillop, A.D., 78, 170n
MacPherson, James, 237
Mallet, David, 78–80, 170, 236, 237–38, *Amyntor and Theodora*, 238; *The Excursion*, 237; "William and Margaret," 237
Marsh, Robert, 101n
Mathias, T.J., 216
May, J. Lewis, 73n
Melmoth, William, "Of Active and Retired Life," 23
Miller, Perry, 31n
Milton, John, 1, 17, 19, 28, 30, 39, 54–55, 86, 88, 90, 101, 114, 128, 153, 187, 190, 195, 219, 225, 226, 283, "Apology for Smectymnuus," 58; "Lycidas," 130, 233; *Paradise Lost*, 17, 40–46, 58, 59, 74, 87, 105, 129, 152, 208, 244, 281; *Samson Agonistes*, 261

Molière, *Le Misanthrope*, 170, 279
Monboddo, James Burnett, Lord, 237
Moore, C.A., 83
More, John, *Strictures, Critical and Sentimental, on Thomson's Seasons*, 201
More, Thomas, *Utopia*, 18
Morley, Edith J., 129n

Narrative, 11
Natural Religion, 13, 71
Nature, 269–70, 271
Neoplatonism, 12
Nettleton, G.H., 280n
New Criticism, The, 274
Newgate Calendar, 249
Newman, John Henry, *Apologia Pro Vita Sua*, 282n
New Science, 113
Newton, Isaac, 23
Newton, Mrs. John, 246
Newtonian physics, 22, 23
Nicholls, Norton, 226n
Nicolson, M.H., 121
Norris, John, 40, 53
Northup, C.S., 219n

Odysseus, 14
Olson, Elder, 215n
Onslow, Arthur, 95, 169
Originality, 7, 230
Ossian, 153, 237
Otway, Thomas, 193
Ovid, 153
Owen, W.J.B., 276n
Oxford, Edward Harley, Second Earl of, 142

Pardon, William, 104
Parker, Samuel, 119
Parnell, Thomas, 135, "A Hymn to Contentment," 136n
Pascal, Blaise, 181
Paul, St., 14–15, 32–34, 73, 141, 250
Penn, William, 48
Perkins, David, 3, 59, 142n, 259, 269
Peyre, Henri, 3, 9n, 28, 283n
Philips, Ambrose, 127
Pinto, Vivian de S., 235n

Pitt, William, 95
Plain style, the, 30
Plato, 230, 272, *The Republic*, 10–12, 215, 218
Pliny the Younger, 141
Polybius, 17
Pomfret, John: "The Choice," 21–22, 133, 174
Poole, Austin Lane, 191n
Pope, Alexander, 4, 13n, 57, 92, 129, 130, 134, 136–51, 156, 157, 159, 170, 178, 196, 209, 239, 244, 280, 281, 282, controversy with Hill, 165–68; *The Dunciad*, 148, 150–51, 165; *Epilogue to the Satires*, 148, 149, 150; *Epistle to Dr. Arbuthnot*, 58, 144–46; "Epitaphs," 233; Horatian persona, 138–39; letters, 234; *Peri Bathous*, 165; *Windsor Forest*, 109, 140
Powell, L.F., 232n
Price, Martin, 171n, 173
Priestley, F.E.L., 297n
Prior, Matthew, 126
Prynne, William, 19

Quakers, 38

Radcliffe, Ann, 128
Ramist rhetoric, 30, 54
Ramsay, Allan, 237
Rand, Benjamin, 72n
Read, Herbert, 2n
Reason, 115–16
"Retirement: A Divine Soliloquy," 133–36
Revolution of 1688, 60, 156
Reynolds, Sir Joshua, 151
Richards, I.A., 2n
Richardson, Jonathan, 151–61, *Explanatory Notes and Remarks on Milton's Paradise Lost*, 152; *Morning Thoughts or Poetical Meditations*, 157–61; *Science of a Connoisseur*, 155
Richardson, Jonathan, Jr., 153, 159n, 161n
Richardson, Samuel, 79, 142, 208n, 266, 273, 279, 287–99, Hill–Richardson correspondence, 168–69; *Clarissa*, 296;

Pamela, 168–69, 288, 289, 290, 291–92, 295; *Sir Charles Grandison*, 288, 292–96
Riley, John, 151
Robinson, Henry, 17
Roman Catholic Church, 13, 44, 109, 174, 211, 282
Roston, Murray, 15n
Röstvig, Maren-Sofie, 16
Rousseau, Jean-Jacques, 1, 243, 268, 283, *Confessions*, 297; *La Nouvelle Héloïse*, 297

Sampson, John, 263n
Sasek, Lawrence A., 40
Savage, Richard, 80
Schorer, Mark, 262
Second Eden, 17, 135, 246
Second Jacobite Rebellion, 196
Seneca, 14, 29
Shakespeare, William, 1, 14, 58, 76, 190, 191, 193–94, 195, 200, 202, 218, 226, 260, *Henry V*, 282
Shaftesbury, The Third Earl of, 12, 23, 61, 71, 72–77, 79, 93, 101, 107, 112, 123, 128, 180, *Askémata*, 76–77; *Characteristics*, 73–76
Shenstone, William, 202–14, 217, 218, 230, 281; character of, 213–14; *Essays on Men and Manners*, 28; "Prefatory Essay on Elegy," 203; "Rural Elegance," 204; *The Elegies*, 204–10; "The Ruin'd Abby," 210–11; "The School-Mistress," 212
Sherburn, George, 137, 212n
Sheridan, Richard Brinsley, 13n, *The School for Scandal*, 280
Sherlock, Thomas, 65
Sidney, Algernon, 17
Sidney, Sir Philip, 152, *Astrophel and Stella*, 205
Simplicity, 7, 127–28
Sinclair, John D., 43n
Smith, Adam, 237, 240
Smollett, Tobias, 237
Snape, Andrew, 64n
Society for the Reformation of Manners, 281

Socrates, 11, 73, 93, 175, 215
Sophocles, 193, 194
South, Bishop Robert, 30
Spacks, Patricia M., 2n, 58, 90n
Spectator, The, 127
Spence, Joseph, *Anecdotes*, 137
Spenser, Edmund, 1, 190, 195, 202, 218
Spinoza, Benedict de, 50
Spontaneity, 28, 59, 82–83, 184–85, 273
Starr, H.W., 220n
Steele, Richard, 129, *The Conscious Lovers*, 280; *The Tatler*, 50
Stephen, Leslie, 69
Sterne, Laurence, 297
Stoicism, 14, 73
Stone, Christopher, 191n
Stone, P.W.K., 283
Stoughton, John, *Felicitas Ultimi Saeculi*, 17–18
Stowe, 95
Strauss, Albrecht B., 231n
Stuart, Charles Edward, the Young Pretender, 197
Stuart, C.H., 196n
Suicide, 177–78
Swift, Jonathan, 5, 13n, 30, 92, 138, 142, 147, 148, 150, 160
Sylvester, Matthew, 36n
Sympathy, 7, 77, 240

Tasso, Torquato, 200, 201
Taste, 112
Tatler, The, 50
Taylor, Edward, 29
Temple, Elizabeth, 173
Temple, Henry, 173
Thomson, James, 40, 71, 77–101, 107, 108, 120, 121, 122, 123, 124, 128, 134, 136, 141, 142, 165, 167, 179, 192, 197, 207, 208n, 209, 230, 236, 237n, 238, 239, 255, 282, *The Seasons*, 92, 95, 109, 176, "Autumn," 86, 88–90; "Spring," 83–86, 89, 90, 91–92, 290, 291; "Summer," 86–88, 89; "Winter," 78–80, 97–100; *The Castle of Indolence*, 90, 92; *Liberty*, 87, 91, 95, 96, 98, 170, 190, 196
Tibullan elegy, 203

Tibullus, 218
Tickell, Thomas, "To the Earl of Warwick on the Death of Mr. Addison," 130–33, 234
Tillotson, Geoffrey, 137, 167n, 223
Tillotson, Archbishop John, 15–16, 20, 30, 60
Tillyard, E.M.W., 16n
Toland, John, 50, 68, "Clito: A Poem on the Force of Eloquence," 71
Toynbee, Paget, 217n
Trevor-Roper, H.R., 17n
Trickett, Rachel, 12n
Trilling, Lionel, 3, 9n, 270n
Tucker, Susie I., 6n, 104
Twining, Thomas, 215
"Two Children in the Wood," ballad of, 127
Typology, 50

Underhill, John, 23n
Unwin, William, 249, 254, 255, 256

Vertue, George, 156n
Vieth, David, 279
Virgil, 92, 98, Aeneid, 13, 163; Georgics, 82
Voltaire, 268

Walker, George, F.R.S., 258, 284–85
Walpole, Horace, 156
Walwyn, William, 20, The Power of Love, 19–20
War of the Austrian Succession, 196
War of Jenkins' Ear, 196
Warren, Austin, 2n
Wasserman, Earl R., 2n, 172n, 192n, 201n
Watson, Bishop Richard, 113
Watts, Isaac, 29, 49–60, 81, 134n, 281, "The Adventurous Muse," 55; Divine Songs for Children, 52; Hymns and Spiritual Songs, 51; "Funeral Poem on the Death of Thomas Gunston," 55–56; Preface to the Horae Lyricae, 52–54; Horae Lyricae, 81; Preface to

Hymns and Spiritual Songs, 51; "An Elegiac Ode on the Death of Sir Thomas Abney," 56–57
Weinbrot, Howard D., 218
Wellek, René, 2
Werther, 177
Wesley, John, 12, 154
West, Richard, 229
Wharton, Thomas, 217
Wheatley, Phyllis, 156
Whibley, Leonard, 217n
Whitefield, George, 154
Whitman, Walt, 186
Wicker, C.V., 173n
William and Mary, 281
Williams, Basil, 196
Williams, Marjorie, 202n
Wilmington, Spencer Compton, Earl of, 95
Wimsatt, W.K., 219
Woodhouse, A.S.P., 189, 201n
Wordsworth, Dorothy, 273
Wordsworth, William, 3–4, 5, 169, 223, 257, 259, 269–77, 281, Essay Upon Epitaphs, 269, 270, 275; Immortality Ode, 131, 270n; Lyrical Ballads, 58–59, 269, 275; Preface to Lyrical Ballads, 270, 274, 283; The Prelude, 94, 269, 273; "Tintern Abbey," 273
Wycherley, William, 137, 139, The Country Wife, 279; The Plain Dealer, 279

Young, Edward, 132, 133, 147n, 152, 160, 171–87, 192, 197, 207, The Centaur Not Fabulous, 186; Conjectures on Original Composition, 128–29, 183; Love of Fame, 218; Night Thoughts, 171, 172–87, 218–19, 298; "Two Epistles to Mr. Pope . . .," 146–47; Preface to Night Thoughts, 184
Young, Elizabeth, 100

Zall, Paul M., 59n
Zippel, Otto, 90n